God, Country, Golf

Reflections of an Army Widow

In His Service,

Wesley Bauguess

Wesley Hobbs Bauguess

WESTBOW
PRESS®
A DIVISION OF THOMAS NELSON
& ZONDERVAN

This book is a work of non-fiction. Unless otherwise noted, the author and the publisher make no explicit guarantees as to the accuracy of the information contained in this book and in some cases, names of people and places have been altered to protect their privacy.

WestBow Press books may be ordered through booksellers or by contacting:

WestBow Press
A Division of Thomas Nelson & Zondervan
1663 Liberty Drive
Bloomington, IN 47403
www.westbowpress.com
1 (866) 928-1240

ISBN: 978-1-5127-7139-8 (sc)
ISBN: 978-1-5127-7140-4 (hc)
ISBN: 978-1-5127-7138-1 (e)
Library of Congress Control Number: 2017900315

Print information available on the last page.

WestBow Press rev. date: 4/11/2017

For the boys who don't come home
and the families and friends who love them

We are living the history our children will study.

—Major Larry J. Bauguess Jr.

Contents

Foreword...xi

Chapter 1   Happy Camel, Sad Camel.................................. 1

Part 1: A Girl Named Wesley................................... 15
Chapter 2   The Cart Path Less Traveled 17
Chapter 3   Train a Child.. 28
Chapter 4   Good-bye, Golf Girl; Hello, Commando 36
Chapter 5   Dog Tags and a Camera............................... 48

Part 2: Home Is Where the Army Sends Us....................... 57
Chapter 6   Rendezvous with Destiny 59
Chapter 7   The Land of the Not-Quite-Right 75
Chapter 8   Bayous, Babies, and Broken Hearts 88
Chapter 9   Fortress Bragg, Finally.............................104
Chapter 10 Living the All-American Dream 116
Chapter 11 Afghanistan...135

Part 3: Freedom Isn't Free 155
Chapter 12 Breathless..159
Chapter 13 Critical Decision Point.............................168
Chapter 14 Steps of Faith......................................175
Chapter 15 Somewhere I Belong 187

Part 4: Making a Difference...................................197
Chapter 16 82nd Airborne Division Wounded Warrior
            Committee 199

Chapter 17 Return to Golf 209
Chapter 18 Tattoos and T-shirts 224
Chapter 19 W 235
Chapter 20 The Story Unfolds 244
Chapter 21 Finding Zero 266
Chapter 22 Educate the Legacy 279
Chapter 23 God, Country, Golf 292

Acknowledgments 303
Glossary of Acronyms and Abbreviations 307
Endnotes 309
Works Cited 313

Foreword

by Major Dan Rooney
(Founder and CEO of the Folds of Honor Foundation)

God, country, golf. These are three words that represent the greatest influences in the life of Wesley Bauguess, a Christian, a veteran, and a lifelong golfer. When her husband, Army Major Larry Bauguess, was killed after a peace meeting in Pakistan, those influences came alongside her to give her strength in the midst of her pain and grief. God's grace and love provided comfort, hope, and wisdom. Her love for our country and her army service gave her strength and inspiration to help others. Her passion for golf reminded her to visualize a path forward and to keep her eye on the ball.

I first met Wesley in 2010 at Lipscomb University in Nashville, Tennessee, while attending a Yellow Ribbon Symposium. She was invited to attend because of her work in leading the 82nd Airborne Division Wounded Warrior Committee. I was there as the founder and chief executive officer of the Folds of Honor Foundation. At the event, I had the distinct pleasure of presenting "future use" college scholarships to Ryann and Ellie, who were then only nine and seven years old. It was an honor to meet all three of the Bauguess ladies. My only regret is never having had the chance to meet Larry, but I have gotten to know him through the legacy of his beautiful girls.

I have had the privilege of getting to know Wesley over the past seven years. She is a great American, an iron lady. With respect and admiration, I will tell you that Wesley inspires and haunts me on a daily basis. When she joined the Speakers' Bureau for the Folds of Honor Foundation in 2012, she challenged all of us to live in the moment (be here now), to make a difference (one starfish at a time), and always strive to do the right thing. When I am faced with a tough decision, I often hear her voice in my head and have to ask myself, "Am I choosing the easy wrong or the hard right?" And, though I see Wesley only a few times a year, she always inspires me to do more and be better.

I encourage you to take this journey with her. Wesley's stories are captivating, with heartbreak and joy. If you are a Christian, you will love the fellowship. If you are a veteran, a patriot, or both, you will love the inspirational stories. Great American pride and military values resonate through the book. If you are a golfer, you'll relate to the passion Wesley has for that beloved game. Through this book, Wesley hopes to glorify God, honor our country, and grow the game of golf. *God, Country, Golf* is a book that will change your life in positive ways. Wesley Bauguess is a true blessing in my life and so many others!

Chapter 1

Happy Camel, Sad Camel

As long as there's air to breathe, you'll always be loved by me.
—Ronnie Dunn and Terry McBride (Brooks and
Dunn), "You'll Always Be Loved by Me"

The sky was Carolina blue, and the rugged Afghanistan mountains stood proudly in the background. My husband, Larry, was in army fatigues, waving at us while riding on a camel. The photo captured the irony of the situation and Larry's sense of humor perfectly. He was riding a camel in the middle of a war zone. His crooked little grin and the wave of his hand told me he was thinking of Ryann and Ellie as his buddy snapped the picture. Clearly, he knew his six- and four-year-old daughters would get a kick out of it. The sight of Larry made me giggle, but it made me miss him even more. In an attempt to maintain some sort of connection, we army wives tend to lose ourselves in pictures when our husbands are deployed.

I sat at our computer desk surrounded by the early morning darkness. The only trace of light in the room came from the computer monitor. It was quiet in the house, peaceful. Just as I had done every morning since he left, I was checking my e-mail in the hope of finding a note from Larry. That morning, I found no new e-mails so I had opened the one he sent to the girls the night before. He had surprised us with the camel picture. I stared at the photo a few moments more and basked in the love I had for my husband of nearly fourteen years.

Glancing to the left of the computer, my eyes zeroed in on a framed picture of Larry and our sweet daughters: Ryann, a cute little blonde, and Ellie, a precious brunette. Larry was sitting cross-legged on the floor with both girls seated in his lap, cradled by his strong arms. A beautiful blend of warrior and gentleman, he was our protector, our leader, our hero, a good daddy, and a wonderful husband. We were so blessed. A quick look at the clock showed me it was nearly half past six. My little "Larry daydream" had to end. It was time to get the girls up and ready for school.

Our morning routine was casual. The girls shared a bedroom upstairs. One at a time, I'd sit on the side of their beds and wake them by gently rubbing their backs.

"There you are!" I would say when their big, blue eyes finally opened to welcome a new day.

"Good morning, beautiful girls," I'd sing as I kissed their faces and scooped them up to carry them downstairs.

I usually took Ryann down first and then Ellie. I loved those few extra moments to snuggle with them as we descended the stairs, so thankful to be able to hold them in my arms and whisper sweet *good mornings* to them as they struggled to wake up for the day.

Nibbling on muffins and dry cereal, Ryann and Ellie would sit on opposite ends of the couch and gaze at a morning TV show on the *Disney Channel*. As they ate and continued to wake, I'd slip upstairs to pick out their clothes. Once their bellies were full and they were dressed, we'd brush teeth and hair, gather backpacks, and head for the door.

Our mornings were joyful and easy. May 14, 2007, began like any other day—so simple, so ordinary, and so blissfully normal.

By lunchtime, the construction drill began to roar. Living on Fort Bragg, we were accustomed to the boom of artillery, the overhead thunder of fixed-wing aircraft, and the *thump-thump* of helicopter rotors. These are the elements of the army life soundtrack. The drill, however, was new.

A few weeks earlier, families in our neighborhood had started noticing sinkholes in their lawns. One morning after a thunderstorm, my mom (who was living with us while Larry was deployed) told me she spotted a hole in our backyard. I figured one of the kids had dug a hole, so I told her we'd deal with it later. Amused by my lack of concern, she told me I should go take a look.

After opening the sliding glass door that led to the backyard, I found a miniature replica of the Grand Canyon. It was much more than just a hole; it had great potential as an army fighting position. We just needed a shovel, a few dozen sandbags, and some lumber for overhead cover. But we weren't in a combat zone, and we weren't setting up a fortified perimeter. This was our home. Alarmed by what I saw, I reported it to our neighborhood center, and they added us to the growing list.

Our homes, on a quiet street named Virginia Place, were not even a year old. Apparently, a contractor used debris from demolished Fort Bragg houses as landfill to build up what would become the foundations of our houses. Naturally, we were concerned. Teams of contractors traveled from house to house searching for debris. On May 14, it was our turn. They had to find out exactly where the debris was buried so they could figure out what to do about it.

The drilling bothered all of my neighborhood friends. Everyone had an opinion and reason to worry, but in typical army-wife fashion, we countered the frustration with comedy and sarcasm. Walking to school that afternoon to collect our children, we enjoyed making predictions about what they would actually find under our houses. Letting our imaginations run, we came up with everything from ammunition to old refrigerators. A cool breeze, our own laughter, and the noise of the drill accompanied us as we walked down our street and through the neighborhood toward the school.

We reached the school just as the bell rang. Standing under the North Carolina pines, we watched as our kids began to file out one by one. Ryann grinned when she saw me waiting for her. As I welcomed her with a loving embrace, she reported that she had fallen out of her chair and hurt her hip earlier in the day. I rubbed it, hugged her gently, and told her I'd look at it at home. She tried to be brave and walk with the other kids but started complaining when we were about halfway home, so I scooped her up and carried her the rest of the way. As we approached our houses, over the noise of the drill, we made plans for play dates after homework was done. We waved good-bye and disappeared into the house.

Bothered by her hip and annoyed by the drilling, Ryann wanted to do her homework in her bedroom. She told me it would be quieter and she would be more comfortable on her bed. I kissed her forehead and sent her upstairs.

I found Ellie sitting at the computer desk in the living room. Enrolled in half-day pre-k, I had already picked her up from school at lunchtime. That afternoon, she wanted to stay home with my mom while I collected Ryann from school. Oblivious to the drilling, Ellie was consumed by her task. Taking a few steps closer, I realized she was typing a letter to her daddy. There were very few actual words on there, but she was having fun tapping the keys. I kissed the top of her head, left her to her work, and made my way to the kitchen to fix Ryann an after-school snack.

The doorbell stopped me in my tracks.

Instantly, I assumed it was one of the neighborhood kids wanting to play. I walked to the front door expecting to find an eager little one on our front porch. When I looked through the peephole, I saw something completely different.

Through the tiny glass tunnel, I saw a man dressed in army greens. As I pushed away from the door, blood rushed to my face and a cold chill raced up my spine. When you've been in and around the Army for as long as we have, you know what it means when a man dressed in an army green suit with a chest full of ribbons comes to your house during a time of war.

I lowered my head and leaned against the door.

This isn't happening. I just talked to Larry yesterday. They have the wrong house.

My head was spinning. I tried so hard to come up with a reasonable explanation.

They just need my help. I'm the battalion family readiness group leader. Something has happened. They just need me to help.

I became short of breath, lightheaded, and dizzy.

I just talked to him yesterday. I just got that picture of him riding on a camel. Yesterday was Mother's Day. It can't be Larry. This isn't happening.

Then, I heard myself say, "Open the door, Wesley. You have to open the door."

"Are you Wesley Bauguess?" the army major asked.

I wanted to say no, but instead I obediently answered with a stunned and confused, "Yes?"

He didn't have to say anything else. I knew why he was there.

The army major was a casualty notification officer. He said something. I'm sure it was the official notification statement, but I honestly don't know what he said. His voice faded out as I noticed a gentleman standing to his left. He was a chaplain, also in army greens. He was larger and older but pleasant looking. He had a gentle soul and looked like a teddy bear with a full head of white hair. Then, I saw Major Tim Greenhaw, our brigade rear-detachment commander. He came into view as he slid to the left of the chaplain.

None of it seemed real. I felt like I wasn't even in my body. Everything happened in slow motion. Just moments before, the sound from the drill roared through the house, but at that moment, all I could hear was the ringing in my ears. I looked back at the casualty notification officer and saw that he was speaking to me. His lips were moving, but I couldn't hear him. I couldn't hear anything.

I held onto the thought that it was a mistake until I saw the look on Major Greenhaw's face. He looked like he was going to be sick. He looked the way I felt.

I regained my composure and invited the notification team into our house. As I stepped out of the doorway to let the men in, I realized Ellie wasn't at the computer anymore. She must have gone upstairs to find Ryann.

The casualty notification officer, the chaplain, and I were standing in the entryway when I saw a red streak rush into our house. I don't recall actually looking at her, but I heard the familiar voice of my neighbor, Keli Lowman.

"Where are the girls?" she said in a panic.

I didn't answer her. There was no time to speak.

As if on cue, Ryann and Ellie came bounding down the stairs. Keli put on her happy face, scooped them up, one in each arm, and joyfully said, "You're coming to play at my house!"

"Yay! Bye, Mommy!" they sang as Keli rushed out the door with them. They weren't even wearing shoes.

Keli, a fiery redhead, was one of my closest friends on Virginia Place. She did the best possible thing for me that day, and I would be forever grateful for it. I knew the girls were safe and lovingly distracted. I was able to deal with the initial wave of this tragedy on my own. Keli offered me a precious gift, the gift of time.

By the time the men entered the house and sat down, my mom had come downstairs. She knew something was wrong, though she didn't know exactly what. We stared at each other in disbelief as she walked across the room and joined me on the couch. We had just purchased a sectional sofa from a local furniture store in Fayetteville. Larry had always wanted one. We got it to have plenty of sitting space for company. This was not what I had in mind.

"What is going on?" my mom asked.

Turning my attention to the casualty notification officer, I asked him if he could tell us what had happened. He took a long, slow breath and told me that Larry was in Pakistan for a meeting. After the meeting, there was gunfire. The officer paused, took another breath, and then told me that Larry was shot in the head by small-arms fire as he was boarding a helicopter.

I had a hard time accepting this scenario. The Larry Bauguess I knew wouldn't go down like that. In the cold mist of shock and confusion, I felt the heat of rage. There had to be more to the story. At that moment, I remembered from my army days to meet the first report from the field with caution. That first report is often wrong. The fog of battle can be mighty thick. So I let my anger go for the moment and let shock and confusion return.

Before he left our house, the casualty notification officer had me sign a piece of paper. To this day, I have no idea what I signed. Then, as swiftly as he had arrived, the officer departed. The chaplain stayed with us.

6

"Do you belong to a local church? Is there anyone you would like me to call?" the kind-hearted chaplain asked.

"Lafayette Baptist Church in Fayetteville," I said quietly. "The pastor is Brian Lee."

He knew him well and said he would call him right away. Stepping outside, the chaplain made two phone calls. First, he called back to division headquarters to let them know the notification was complete. Then, he called his friend Brian Lee.

While he was outside closing the loop, I began to fall apart. My legs were shaking uncontrollably. My mind was reeling.

I just talked to Larry, I thought.

The picture of him riding that camel and waving to us was etched in my brain.

Was he waving good-bye? How could he have known? This isn't real. Not my Larry. This just can't be true.

The news of Larry's death permeated through our normally jovial neighborhood. Our neighbors gathered on our beloved street in disbelief. Several Virginia Place ladies froze in place, unsure what to do. Should they enter the house or keep their distance? Following in Keli's footsteps, one brave soul waved off the uncertainty and tested the waters for the others. She wasn't going to wait for an invitation. She was going in to be helpful and offer her loving arms to her friend in need.

Stacy Nix entered our house, slid right next to me on the couch, and wrapped me securely in her arms. We cried and cried. Without even saying a word, Stacy was a wonderful source of comfort. Her husband, Andy, was an army chaplain serving in the 82nd Airborne Division. Her faith in God and her existence as a chaplain's wife brought me peace. I was so grateful for her presence.

Shanna Ratashak, our family readiness group coleader, arrived next. I could see the pain and disbelief in her face as she entered our home. Weak and trembling, my legs nearly betrayed me as I stood to greet her. I stumbled around the couch and met Shanna's embrace.

"I can't believe this," she whispered.

"I know," I replied, choking on my words.

She told me she had rallied the unit care team. Members of

our family readiness group were standing ready to come to our house and help us in any way. I hadn't even thought about the care team. Shanna and I had trained nearly two dozen of our unit ladies to provide assistance for an event just like this. Care teams help keep the house running in a time of crisis. They answer the phone, prepare meals, and protect the grieving family. Imagine the irony—I had spent months training those ladies to take care of *me*. But my head was still spinning, and we had plenty of people in our house already. I told Shanna the care team could wait until the next morning.

Our pastor, Brian Lee, arrived to provide his support and wise counsel. I recall sitting on the couch with Pastor Lee and the army chaplain, soaking up the strength and comfort they provided. Looking at both of them for several long moments with a heavy heart and swollen eyelids, deep in thought, I finally spoke.

"How do I tell these girls?" I asked. "What do I say to them? How do I tell them their daddy isn't coming home?"

After a thoughtful moment, Pastor Lee replied, "You're their mother. You'll find the words. But don't be surprised if they cry and cry and then ask to go play."

I had to chew on that for a moment. His advice caught me off guard, but then it made sense. Kids know how to play. The girls were way too young to process news like this.

Over the next two hours, our front door remained in perpetual motion. Our house was full of loving neighbors and unit friends. Eventually, Keli brought the girls back home to me. Seeing their beautiful, innocent little faces brought me to tears. I kneeled, hugged them tenderly, and asked if they had had fun at Ms. Keli's. Of course they did.

As I rose to my feet, I caught a glimpse of Keli slipping out the front door. I turned to find the once-crowded room completely empty. I looked down at Ryann and Ellie and realized the time had come. I took their hands and asked them to sit with me on the couch.

Nestled on the couch with Ryann on my right and Ellie on my left, I could barely breathe. Not knowing what to say or how to say it, I paused and silently asked God to help me find the words.

My mom joined us in the room but kept her distance. I looked at Ryann and then at Ellie. Their faces were full of wonder. They had no idea what I was about to say. They couldn't possibly understand how their world would soon change. I held their hands and slowly began to speak.

I told them their daddy and some other soldiers went to a meeting that day in Pakistan. I paused for a moment to explain that Pakistan was the country right next to Afghanistan. I told them something bad happened that day and ...

"Daddy ..."

I just couldn't get the words out.

My eyes welled up with tears. My nose started running and my throat tightened. My body was radiating so much heat that I honestly thought I was going to pass out. Stuck on the word *Daddy*, I struggled to find a way to go on. I looked up at the ceiling and tried to blink the tears from my eyes. I fought to control my breathing and finally found the courage to speak again.

"Daddy died today. He is in heaven with Jesus," I said softly. "Oh, my babies, he's not coming home. Daddy's not coming home."

I don't know if they fully understood the words, but they certainly understood my emotion. Ryann and Ellie cried with me, and it was pure agony. As we cried and cried, they buried their faces into my chest, and I could only imagine they were trying to disappear. I know I wanted to. I felt so sick. I felt so badly for Larry and for me, but I felt so much worse for them. Our two beautiful little girls would spend the rest of their lives without their daddy. It wasn't fair. It was wrong—horribly, horribly wrong.

As our wailing cries and tears subsided, Ryann wiped her face with her tiny hands and looked up at me. Her big blue eyes still had tears in them. Her eyelids were puffy, and her nose was red.

"Mommy," she said in the sweetest little voice, "can I go back to Ms. Keli's?"

I looked at her with all the love in my heart and thought about the guidance Pastor Lee had given me just an hour or so before.

"Yes, of course you can, but just for a little while," I said.

She got up from the couch and went into the bathroom. After

washing her face, Ryann met me at the front door. Keli was still on her front porch, talking to a neighbor. Without saying a word, she smiled and waved Ryann over.

Ellie was still on the couch. I sat down with her, and we curled up together. Ellie has always been, and I hope will always be, my snuggle buddy. Pulling her onto my lap, I wrapped my arms around her; brushed my fingers through her wavy, brown hair; and rocked her gently. I kissed the top of her head and hugged her. A few moments later, just like her big sister, she asked if she could go back to Ms. Keli's, too. I didn't want to let go of her, but I realized she needed a break. My mom walked her across the street.

When Ellie disappeared inside our sweet neighbor's house, I finally exhaled. Those girls are the light of my world. I knew they would only be able to process this news in small doses. I was grateful to have a friend like Keli take them in and offer them a safe place to play. Keli gave them a snack and put out some art supplies. They munched and colored but stayed for less than an hour. They wanted to be home, and I was so glad. I knew they needed time to be normal, but I needed them to be in my sight. I needed them home with me.

By the time the sun completely left us, I was mentally, physically, and emotionally exhausted. After thanking the last of our visitors and wishing them a good night, I closed and locked the front door. We needed alone time.

I joined the girls and my mom who were seated at the dinner table eating the pizza that one of our neighbors had delivered. The aroma was inviting. I knew I should have been hungry, but I couldn't bring myself to eat. I would feel that way for many days to come. Looking at us, seated around the dinner table, it appeared to be a very ordinary evening. Trying to reestablish a sense of normal for the girls, we let them eat their fill of pizza and offered them dessert before heading upstairs for bath time.

Just as I began to clear the table, the telephone rang. I didn't want to answer it, so Mom volunteered. To my surprise, it was Lieutenant Colonel Steve Baker calling from Afghanistan. I love and respect him and was thirsting for information, so I took a deep breath and accepted the phone from my mother. Leaving the dishes on the table, she took the girls upstairs to start the bath water and left me to talk with Larry's battalion commander.

I was eager yet nervous to hear what he had to say. I was also impressed that he took the time to call me, especially so soon.

"Hello?"

His familiar voice on the other end of the phone provided instant comfort. The call was so clear, as if he was calling from just down the road.

"Wesley, this is Steve Baker."

Right away I asked him if he was okay.

"I'm fine," he replied. "I am so sorry about Larry."

He told me they had gone into Pakistan for a meeting to negotiate peace along the border. Lieutenant Colonel Baker said that, by all accounts, the meeting was successful. When the meeting ended, the attendees shook hands, took pictures, and exchanged coins.

Then, his speech became labored. I could hear the anger in his voice when he told me that they had been ambushed after the meeting when they were boarding vehicles to head back to the helicopter-landing zone. He didn't give me many details. He just told me that Larry was hit while they were still at the schoolhouse and they tried to get him out of there quickly.

"I don't understand," I said. "The notification officer told me he was shot in the head getting on the helicopter."

Just as I had suspected, Lieutenant Colonel Baker advised me to meet the early reports with caution. He told me not to believe what I heard on the news. Then, he proceeded to tell me what he could.

Fully knowing I wouldn't be able to retain what he had told me, I tried to write down as much as I could while he was still on the line. Having always been a detail girl, I knew I would want to refer to it later and, eventually, investigate further. For that night, though, I had heard enough.

Just as I said a tearful good-bye to Lieutenant Colonel Baker, my mom came into the kitchen with two little girls, freshly bathed and snug in their jammies. I had to compartmentalize the newest information about Larry and put my mommy face back on for the girls. As I squatted down to hug and kiss them, the sweet scent of strawberry bubble bath surrounded us. We sat on the kitchen floor and lost ourselves in a loving embrace.

A half hour later, I took the girls up to bed. In an effort to reclaim some resemblance of a routine, I read them a story and guided them through their nighttime prayers. I kissed them both and told them that we would be okay.

Ryann asked me if I would stay with them until they fell asleep. That wasn't an uncommon request, and, on that night, I was more than willing to oblige. I didn't want to leave them, and I really didn't want to go into my empty bedroom. I kissed them once more, straightened their blankets, turned off the light, and settled into the rocking chair at the foot of their beds.

By the glow of their nightlight, I rocked and stared at each of them. Like cherubs, they looked so peaceful and so beautiful as they drifted off to sleep. My heart ached for them. They were only four and six years old, and now they would face a lifetime without their daddy. When my silent tears turned into sobs, I had to make myself leave their room in fear of waking them.

Reluctantly, I wandered into my bedroom. It had been without Larry's warmth since early February, but at that moment it was especially cold. Passing through our bedroom, I walked into the master bathroom and took a long look at myself in the mirror. Recognizing the disbelief in my own face, I started sobbing again.

Stumbling back into our bedroom, I collapsed on the bed. Drained, cold, and motionless, I had no energy to do anything but stare at the wall. I didn't even have the strength to get under the covers.

How could a day that started so incredibly normal end with such unthinkable sadness?

I thought about the picture of Larry riding that stupid camel. Sixteen hours earlier, that picture made me laugh and filled me with joy. It connected me to my beloved husband. Now, it is the last picture we will ever have of him smiling at a camera.

I'm publishing this book ten years later, but I remember it all as clearly as if it were yesterday. I remember asking myself, "How will I ever get through this?" I had no idea in those early days, weeks, and months. I felt weak, helpless, spent. In the beginning, I could only focus for five minutes at a time. Eventually, I would discover that I already had all the tools I needed. The lessons I had learned at church, in the Army, and on the golf course had already shaped my character. They had already taught me patience and resilience. They would serve me well and give me the strength to carry on. My saving grace came as a remarkable triumvirate of God, country, and golf.

Part I

A Girl Named Wesley

Today you are you! That is truer than true!
There is no one alive who is you-er than you!
—*Dr. Seuss*

I am a girl with a boy's name. I hated it when I was younger, but I love it now. It's different. People remember me, usually because I catch them off guard. One day, I went to the bank to get an official check for a business transaction. After handing the teller my check and making my request for the funds, she looked at me with alarm.

"You're not on this account," she said. "I'm so sorry. I can't give you these funds."

"It's my account. I promise," I replied as I handed her my driver's license.

She blushed and said, "I'm so sorry. I've never met a woman named Wesley."

I smiled and told her, "It's okay. It happens all the time."

It's happened all my life. Growing up and playing golf in southwest Florida, tournament organizers constantly put me in the boys division. My brother thought it was funny.

I can't tell you how many times I was assigned to the male barracks while I was in the Army. When I reported to the US Army

15

Airborne School at Fort Benning, Georgia, in 1992, an instructor scowled at me and told me I was supposed to be a man.

"Not a man, Sergeant Airborne," I answered right before he dropped me for fifty push-ups for talking back to him.

He told me to recover only to drop me again because now he had to reassign me to the female barracks. More work for him meant more push-ups for me. The Airborne School instructors never needed a reason to drop Airborne students, but I thought it was funny that this one made me do push-ups because *they* had assigned me to the wrong barracks.

Clearly, it's not my fault I'm a girl with a boy's name. That credit goes to Grandma Burton. Apparently, when my mom was expecting me, our family sat around the table thinking of names for the new little bundle of joy.

Grandma Burton said, "I like Wesley."

"What if it's a girl?"

"Wesley Ann!" she said.

The name stuck.

Growing up as a girl named Wesley, I was predestined to take the road less traveled. In my youth, I played golf while the other girls did gymnastics, took ballet, or hung out at the beach. In high school, I was a cheerleader and played on the golf team, an unlikely combination. I let the winds of faith take me from a Jewish temple to Presbyterian and Methodist churches before they ultimately delivered me to a sweet Southern Baptist family. In college, when my friends discovered the ROTC boys and listened to their stories, they all wanted to date them. When I listened to their stories, I wanted to join them.

I became incredibly fond of that other road, and I made my mark by following it.

Chapter 2

The Cart Path Less Traveled

*Golf is my life and I love it. I'd
play with rocks if I had to.*
—Margaret Curtis

I had it in my sights. It was white and round and ready to go flying. My grip was strong, my breath under control. "Swing easy. Don't hit the big ball first. Picture finish," I said to myself.

Whoomp! The mushroom went flying! It broke into a dozen pieces, but nothing else on the ground was disturbed. The grass was perfectly untouched. Only the stalk of the mushroom remained.

"Grandpa, I'm ready!" I yelled, holding my finish as if there were a gallery of photographers snapping my picture. I was nine years old.

Grandpa Burton

There's a common misconception that golf is for rich kids. I'm living proof that that isn't always the case. The product of humble beginnings, my father was a construction worker and my mom was a PE teacher.

I was born in Sarasota but spent my childhood near Naples, a beautiful Gulf Coast town in southwest Florida. We were a far cry from the affluent Naples and certainly not regulars in the country club scene. We actually lived in a small town further inland called Golden Gate. I have no idea what it looks like now, but back then we called it the Collier County Boondocks. Directions to our house, which my father built, included, "turn off the paved road." According to Jeff Foxworthy, I guess we were rednecks. A mile-long gravel road gave way to a dirt driveway full of potholes. A cute little house surrounded by a sea of Florida pines sat at the end of the drive.

Behind our house, my father had planted a vegetable garden nearly the size of a football field. We had a plywood coop with lots of chickens and a confused rooster named Foggy. That crazy rooster crowed all day long. We also had rabbits, ducks, and a pig named Fudd.

Next to our house was a tiny guesthouse that my dad built for my mother's parents. My dad was a talented craftsman, a master carpenter. He could build anything, except a relationship with his own children. A hard worker, my dad had a hand in building most of the condos along the southwest Florida coast. But, at the end of a long day, instead of seeking comfort at home with his family, he enjoyed the fellowship of happy hour in town. Instead of hanging out with his kids on the weekends, he played golf with his buddies. We barely saw him.

The guidance and attention I lacked from my father was replaced in abundance by my Grandpa Burton. What a blessing is was to grow up right next to my beloved grandparents.

Grandma Burton was loving and kind, and Grandpa Burton hung the moon. Born and raised in Staten Island, New York, my grandparents had the coolest accents.

"Ya' just in time fa' Easta' Dinna'," they'd say every spring.

Grandma was an amazing cook and an angel from heaven. I could always count on a big hug, a sweet song, and a full belly when I spent time with her. On the weekends, we'd watch *The Lawrence Welk Show* and dance around their living room. At the end of every number, Grandpa would say, "Wasn't that nice," just as if Lawrence Welk had said it himself.

Grandpa Burton was my greatest mentor, my first favorite

veteran. Albion Robert Burton served in the United States Coast Guard in World War II. Achieving the rank of lieutenant commander, he spent most of his service aboard the *Sea Cloud*, a private sailboat that served brilliantly during the war. I loved to listen to his stories about that ship. Every time he talked about her, he pulled out a black-and-white photo of the *Sea Cloud* cruising over white-capped waves, her masts and snow-white sails proudly on display.

After the Japanese attacked Pearl Harbor and the United States entered the war, the navy obtained private yachts to serve within its fleet. They used the ships to conduct patrols and monitor the weather. The owners of the *Sea Cloud* entrusted her to the US Coast Guard, who removed her masts and beautiful white sails and painted her battleship gray. Supplied with a wide range of weapons, she cruised the open water as a weather station. After the war, the *Sea Cloud* returned to her owners, battle-hardened and war-torn, but eager to sail again. Remarkably, she is still on the water, currently serving as a luxury cruise ship.[1]

My grandfather served with distinction in the coast guard during the war. When he returned home to Staten Island, he continued his selfless service in the New York Fire Department aboard the fireboats in the New York Harbor. Later in his life, Grandpa Burton went to medical school and spent the rest of his days healing others as a doctor of chiropractic medicine. He was a miracle worker. My mother remembers watching people arrive at his office being carried on stretchers. After a visit with my grandfather and a chiropractic adjustment, they would walk out on their own two feet.

Because Grandpa Burton was our family doctor, my brother and I were hardly ever sick. If I came home with so much as the sniffles, he'd call me over to take a look at me. He'd have me sit in a chair facing away from him. Standing behind me, he'd gently lay my cheek into his massive hand and tilt my head so my ear was resting in his palm.

"Relax, Wesley Ann."

Crack!

He'd do the same to the other side. Honestly, those adjustments frightened me a little, but they kept me incredibly healthy. After an adjustment, my sinuses would clear, my headache would fade, and I would always feel just a little bit taller.

My grandfather was my first true hero. He's gone now, but his legacy lives on. Sharing the values he learned in his military service, he taught me how to live and who to be. He encouraged me to help people every chance I could. He taught me to make the most out of every day. He also introduced me to a game I would enjoy my entire life. He taught me how to play golf.

Golf with Grandpa

The summer days I spent with Grandpa Burton on the public golf course in Golden Gate remain some of my favorite lifetime moments. When he first took me on the golf course with him, he would send me into the rough to hunt for pinecones and wild mushrooms while he played for real. Pinecones were fun to hit, but I preferred the mushrooms, so I would look for them first. The rounded caps offered a perfect target, the stem a perfect tee. I'd whack every mushroom I found, trying so hard to hit them purely. My effort paid off. Eventually, I found a pretty good tempo and a fairly decent golf swing. Grandpa said as soon as I could hit the top off and leave the stem in place, I'd be ready to hit a real golf ball.

The day I hit that mushroom perfectly, he walked right over to me and said, "That's the swing, Wesley Ann. That's the swing!"

That very day, he took me to the driving range. He took a good look at my swing, made sure I had a proper grip, and told me to swing my club like a pendulum.

"Tick-tock, Wesley Ann. Like a clock," he said.

We hit golf balls until the sun went down. The next day, he took me back to the golf course.

I started at the 150-yard markers, while Grandpa Burton hit from the men's tees. I didn't hit the ball very far, but it was always right down the middle. I got better and better every time we played. As the rounds and the years went by, Grandpa made it tougher and tougher for me. During our summer rounds, he would come up with scenarios. Sometimes, he'd put my ball behind a tree or plug it into a bunker. I didn't realize it at the time, but he was teaching me to practice under tougher conditions than I would actually play. It was an early example of training as you fight, a military philosophy.

I played golf with Grandpa Burton from age nine to thirteen. (When I was thirteen, he and Grandma moved back to Sarasota.) The time spent on the golf course with him was an investment that would pay dividends throughout my entire life. Golf has opened doors for me that I never even knew were there. Grandpa taught me more than just the physical game. He taught me the history of golf, the customs and courtesies. He taught me rules and etiquette that would transcend beyond golf and weave their way into my life. The following are a few examples.

- **"Keep your head down. Swing easy."** Golf is a game of focus. In golf, and in life, it's easy to get distracted. It's also easy to become overwhelmed with too many "swing thoughts." We all have people and tasks pulling us in different directions. It's easy to get caught up in the chatter. In the Army, I learned a great acronym: KISS, for "Keep It Simple, Stupid!" It's a great reminder to ignore distractions and keep your focus. Stay on task. When I got distracted on the golf course or in life, Grandpa Burton would just look at me and say, "Focus on what you know, Wesley Ann. Swing easy and hit the ball."

- **"Always be honest; count all your strokes."** Golf is a game of honesty and integrity. Golf is a sport in which you call a penalty on yourself. If you ground your club in a hazard and your opponent doesn't see you, you still did it and must incur the penalty. If you address the ball and swing and miss, you're supposed to count that stroke, even if no one saw you do it. Having integrity means doing the right thing, even if no one is watching.

- **"Leave the golf course better than you found it."** Golf is a game of respect. It's competitive, for sure, but you never disrespect your opponent or the course you are playing. A proper golfer respects the golf course and takes care of it by fixing divots and ball marks and raking sand traps. Grandpa Burton always used to say, "Walk on these greens with angel feet, don't ever step on your opponent's line, and always leave the golf course better than you found it."

- **"Define your strategy and practice good golf course management."** Golf is a game of judgment. There are eighteen holes in a full round of golf. You play all the holes, one at a time. Before a tournament, Grandpa Burton would tell me to grab a scorecard, look at each hole, and make a plan. He taught me to use good judgment to identify good landing areas and places to avoid. Once I did that, he said, "Use your notes and play the course one shot at a time. Make good choices. You don't always have to hit the big shots. A two-inch putt counts the same as a two-hundred-yard drive."

- **"Never give up."** Golf is a game of perseverance. Never give up! If you totally blow a hole, write down your score, and then forget about it and play the next one. The easiest way to blow a whole round is to get wrapped up in one bad shot or one bad hole. Let it go. Move on to the next one. Grandpa Burton always told me to keep my chin up, even during the worst holes. He told me to go back to the basics and focus on what I know. Scaling back to a three-quarter swing and recalling the childhood memory of hitting mushrooms always got me back on track. I never gave up.

- **"And always remember: picture finish."** Golf is a game that demands sportsmanship. At the end of every round, a golfer removes her hat, looks her opponent in the eyes, and shakes her hand. By doing this, you take ownership of your round and your behavior during that round. It's humbling to shake your opponent's hand at the end of a battle and fun to shake hands with your playing partners after a friendly round. (Plus, it's good practice for the business world. A handshake can tell you a lot about a person.) Grandpa Burton said, "Picture finish" every time I hit the ball. It was his way of getting me to slow down and enjoy the moment. At the end of each round, he would say it again and remind me to shake his hand.

High School and College Golf

With the foundation that Grandpa Burton provided, I went on to play junior golf with the Southwest Florida Junior Golf Association.

We played in golf tournaments every Monday all over the area all summer long. When I was little, our tee box was the 150-yard marker, just like when I played with Grandpa. But, eventually, I moved up to the "big kid" flights and moved back to the ladies' tee. Those tournaments fine-tuned my game and got me ready to play high school golf.

I played on the girls' varsity golf team at Lely High School all four years. We always had a great team, and we traveled all over southwest Florida for our golf matches. I made the all-conference team my sophomore, junior, and senior years and the all-district team my junior and senior years. Our team always earned a spot to compete at the state tournament. We won the state championship my freshman year and came in second my sophomore year. I had the best time playing golf in high school, and I learned so much from my coach and my teammates.

Growing up in Florida, I always dreamed about playing golf for the University of Florida, my mother's alma mater. Cheering for the Gators every football season made me want to become one more than anything. There was just one problem: I wasn't good enough to compete at that level. Only the best of the best golfers got scholarships to Florida. If I wanted to play college golf, I had to find a different path.

The summer before my senior year in high school, my mom and I took a road trip through Florida, Alabama, Georgia, South Carolina, and North Carolina, visiting colleges and golf coaches all along the way. The story was the same for all the big schools—I might be able to walk on a team but probably wouldn't play until my senior year. What fun would that be? I had better luck with the smaller schools. Troy State and Jacksonville University looked very promising, so I kept them in mind. Toward the end of our trip, we visited my mom's aunt and uncle in Asheville, North Carolina. Uncle Bill Dixon told us to hop on the Blue Ridge Parkway, go on up to Boone, and check out Appalachian.

I think my exact response was, "Hop on the what? Go on up to where? And check out … what?"

He laughed. Then, with an all-knowing look about hi... us to go.

After a long and dizzying drive on the Blue Ridge Parkway— I'm talking about nearly one hundred winding, two-lane, count... miles—we finally arrived in Boone. The moment we took that last curvy turn on NC 321 and laid our eyes on that beautiful High Country valley, I knew I was home. I was positively breathless when we drove through town toward the university. Somehow, I knew it was a very special place. I knew I belonged there. I just needed to find out if they had a ladies golf team.

Wandering around the mountain campus, we stumbled upon the athletic department and discovered that they did have a golf team, but the coach wasn't there. In his stead, we spoke briefly with the athletic director. After a short interview, we thanked him, gave him a copy of my golf "resume" and my United States Golf Association handicap sheet, and set out to explore the campus once again. It was so beautiful. The summer air was cool and crisp, not anything like the hot and humid Florida air. With every step, I became increasingly convinced that Boone would be my new home.

By the time we got back to Naples, a message was waiting on our answering machine from the Appalachian State women's golf coach. Not only did he offer me a spot on the team, he offered me a partial scholarship as well. I was on my way to college, and I was going to play golf.

In the fall of 1989, I left the golf mecca of southwest Florida for the beauty of western North Carolina. As a freshman member of the Appalachian State women's golf team, I learned very quickly that mountain golf is totally different than any golf I had ever played in Florida. Uphill lies, I could handle. But side-hill and downhill lies completely killed my confidence. I struggled so much with them.

Okay. Downhill lie. Bend your back knee, leave the other one straight, shift your weight, swing easy, don't top it. Ugh ... too many swing thoughts! Where is the flat lie? I miss Florida. I need Grandpa Burton. Can I just hit those mushrooms instead?

Another challenge was the change in ball flight. In navigating the slopes and the changes in distance they created, I struggled to

Country, Golf
he told
and

b to hit. The thin air of the higher elevations
oo. It took me a whole season, but I finally
mountain golf. All of that, of course, was a
olf is a game of perseverance.

Be Here Now

As a collegiate student athlete, one of my toughest challenges was time management. We had golf tournaments in the fall and in the spring. Juggling golf practice, strength and conditioning, classes, lectures, and study hall, I often wished there were more than twenty-four hours in the day. The best advice I ever received on the subject of time management came from a class called freshman seminar. Not every freshman had to take it and I think it only counted as an elective, but as a student athlete, that class was the best one I ever took.

Cindy Wallace, my favorite teacher of all time, is currently the vice chancellor for student development at Appalachian, but back in 1989, she taught my freshman seminar class. She encouraged us to be present in our own lives and not get caught up in stresses swirling around us. She taught us a lesson called "Be Here Now." I believe she derived the lesson from the writings of psychologist and philosopher Ram Dass (formerly Dr. Richard Alpert), specifically from his book, *Be Here Now*.[2] I never read his book, but I always remembered Cindy's take on the lesson. She encouraged us to live in the moment.

She told us, "When you are at practice, focus on your sport. When you're in the classroom, focus on the lecture. When you are studying, limit the distractions and actually study."

I adopted the "Be Here Now" philosophy and shaped it to suit my life. To me, "Be Here Now" can be broken down into three parts: (1) cherish the past and (2) prepare for the future, but (3) be here now. I even applied it to my golf game: learn from the last shot and prepare for the next shot, but hit this shot. Standing over the golf ball, swing thoughts are abundant. *What did I learn from the last shot? Where do I want to be for my next shot? All of it is important, but nothing happens until I hit this shot.* Ram Dass's concept and Cindy's application of "Be Here Now" helped me focus on and off the golf course. That philosophy got me through college, and it has followed me throughout my entire adult life.

Golf Values

In 2011, I volunteered as a coach with the First Tee Program in Whispering Pines, North Carolina, and I learned their "nine core values of golf": honesty, integrity, sportsmanship, respect, confidence, responsibility, perseverance, courtesy, and judgment.[3]

The lessons I learned from my grandfather are so similar to the lessons young golfers are being taught today through the First Tee Program. That's the beauty of golf. Fashion, equipment, and golf courses will always change, but the core values of the game remain the same. They are as true today as they were when I was a kid. When golfers, young and old, learn these values on the golf course, they permeate their daily lives and, hopefully, make them better people.

Golf is more than just a game. It's a way of life. A background in golf lays a foundation of proper behavior, etiquette, integrity, and courtesy. Golf can also provide an abundance of opportunity. For me, golf has opened doors I never even knew were there. It brought me to and through college. Golf even opened a few doors for me in the Army. In fact, that incredible game is still opening doors for me today. (I'll explain all of that throughout the course of this book).

This I know for sure: traveling through life as a girl named Wesley and a girl who plays golf has been a unique and rewarding journey. I will be forever thankful that Grandpa Burton introduced me to such a wonderful game.

Chapter 3

Train a Child

Train a child in the way he should go, and
when he is old he will not turn from it.
—*Proverbs 22:6 (NIV)*

My family didn't spend Sunday mornings at church, but that doesn't mean I grew up without guidance. As I wrote in chapter 2, I got plenty of guidance from my grandfather. Grandpa Burton taught me much about golf, but he also taught me about life. Long before I ever held a golf club, he taught me a valuable lesson and introduced me to a set of rules I would follow forever. At the tender age of three, I became intimately familiar with the Eighth Commandment: "You shall not steal" (Exodus 20:15 NIV).

One day, my mother and I stopped at the Pik Quik, a little convenience store just down the road from our home. While Mom was paying for her items, I discovered the penny bubblegum on the shelves below the register. Captivated by the brightly colored wrappers and hypnotized by the thought of that sweet treat, I began to stuff my pockets. The cashier cleared his throat and nodded in my direction.

"Wesley Ann! What are you doing?"

I didn't answer, but by the sound of my mother's voice I knew I was in trouble.

"Put that back! That's not yours!"

Tears flooded my eyes and streamed down my cheeks. I was

heartbroken. Not only because I couldn't have the bubblegum, but more so because I had disappointed my mother. She emptied my pockets and hurried me out the door.

When we got home, she gave me two choices. I could go to my room and miss my afternoon viewing of *Sesame Street,* or I could watch *Sesame Street* and deal with my father when he got home. I honestly had to think about it. I loved *Sesame Street*! I never missed it. I had to have my daily fellowship with Bert and Ernie, but I didn't want my father to know I had done something wrong. After a few painful moments of indecision, I turned my back on that magical place "where the air is sweet" and began the slow journey down the hallway to my bedroom, weeping all the way.

That evening, Grandpa Burton pulled me up onto his lap and opened his Bible.

"Wesley Ann, you need to learn about the Ten Commandments."

He read to me from Exodus, chapter 20, and introduced me to God's laws, paying particular attention to Exodus 20:15: "You shall not steal."

Grandpa Burton carefully explained each of the commandments and sent me back to my room to think about my actions. That moment was just one of many lessons I learned from my beloved grandfather. I can't chew bubblegum without thinking about him.

Early Influences

Grandma and Grandpa Burton were good, Christian people. They lived beside us until I was thirteen years old and set a beautiful example. Grandpa Burton read the Bible every day. Grandma Burton prayed out loud and taught me how to talk to God. Every time I spent the night at their house, Grandma Burton led me in my nighttime prayers: "Now I lay me down to sleep, I pray the Lord my soul to keep. If I should die before I wake, I pray the Lord my soul to take."

To this day, I still begin my nighttime prayers that way. But even with such wonderful, Christian grandparents, we still never went to church. My family just didn't go.

My childhood best friend was Jewish. If we had a sleepover at her house and it was time for them to go to temple, I would go with them. During my youth, I spent more time in a Jewish temple than in any Protestant church. I remember those days fondly, especially playing with dreidels and eating chocolate coins with them during Hanukkah.

In high school, I went to a Presbyterian church because it was located in our neighborhood and because my mother worked there. My father had left my mother, my brother, and me by then. We were on our own, living in a tiny apartment in Naples, Florida. My mother worked several jobs to make ends meet. Twice a week, she cleaned Lely Presbyterian Church.

I would often help my mother. We'd scrub the bathrooms, clean the kitchen, polish the wood, vacuum the floors, and wash the windows. I didn't work nearly as hard as she did, but I was able to knock a few things off of her to-do list. Sometimes, after I got my chores done, I'd wander through the church. Following the pictures on the wall and losing myself in the stained glass, I'd end up in the sanctuary. The rows and rows of church pews were inviting. I'd almost hear them call to me, beckoning me to sit down and rest a little while. Seated on the hardwood church pews, surrounded by the musty smell of old wood and furniture polish, I'd stare up at the huge wooden cross suspended from the vaulted ceiling. I would often lose myself in the comfort of that church. It was so peaceful in there.

As a student at Appalachian State University, I often went to Sunday services at the United Methodist Church in downtown Boone because it was near campus. My friends and I would walk there on Sunday mornings. Everyone assumed my family was Methodist because my name is Wesley. I used to tell them that the Wesley Foundation (a Methodist campus ministry) was named after me.

My roommate, Michelle Smith, grew up in a sweet Southern Baptist family. She may not know this, but she served as my

Christian mentor on those Sunday mornings. I watched her as we entered the church. I followed her example and did what she did. One Sunday morning, the congregation sang "Amazing Grace." I had heard that song over the years but never really paid attention to it. On that Sunday, something began to stir deep inside of me as I listened to those words for the very first time.

***

I once was lost, but now I'm found;
was blind, but now I see.
—John Newton, "Amazing Grace"

***

Looking back now, I can see that God was slowly working on me. He is very patient, and I am grateful for that. My faith was definitely a slow build. Growing up going to a Jewish temple because my friends were Jewish and attending Presbyterian and Methodist churches for convenience must sound ridiculous. But everything happens for a reason, and everything happens in God's perfect timing. When the moment was right, He led me to a young man who would lead me to my Savior.

Somewhere I Belong

Isn't it amazing how God knows what we need long before we do? That very thing happened to me during my junior year at Appalachian. I was having the time of my life in college. I was playing golf, doing very well as a student athlete. I had great friends and a promising future. I had joined the Army Reserve Officer Training Corps (ROTC) program (I'll share that story in chapter 4) and was excelling beyond my own expectations. But, even with all the good things in my life, something was missing.

In October 1992, God blessed me with a life-changing encounter with a young man named Larry Bauguess. Larry was everything I never even knew I was looking for: a strong Christian, a warrior, and a gentleman. He would lead me to a faith I had never known and a Savior I never thought I deserved. Larry and I met as army cadets at Appalachian. (I'll share our early days of courtship in chapter 5. For now, I just want to write about the beginning of my Christian walk with him.)

Shortly after Larry and I began dating, he brought me home to meet his parents. Warm and welcoming, Larry's family members are down-home Southern Baptists who are not afraid to share their faith. They love and serve a wonderful God who has blessed them greatly. One of the first things I noticed the first time I walked into their house was a sign on their kitchen wall that read, "As for me and my family, we will serve the Lord."

Larry and I would drive down the mountain from Boone to Moravian Falls to visit his family as often as we could. The thirty-minute drive down US 421 was gorgeous. Hardwood trees were abundant, the land untouched. Larry's family lived in a lush valley just below the Brushy Mountains. Their all-brick ranch house sat on a gradual slope and had a walkout basement. Behind the house, a slow-moving creek marked the perimeter of their land. I loved being there. It was so peaceful, so welcoming.

Cub Creek Baptist Church was just as warm and inviting as the Bauguess family itself. During one of our weekend visits, the sweet Southern Baptist church was hosting a revival. The weeklong celebration brought the congregation closer to Jesus and revitalized individual church members. During revival, many Christian brothers and sisters reaffirmed and strengthened their bond with the Lord.

My life changed forever when we attended one of the revival services. Neal Hatfield[1] was the guest preacher and the man who invited me to meet Jesus. God had been working on me through Larry and his family. Larry provided a beautiful example. He showed me what a Christian was and how a Christian lived. His family did, too. But that night at the revival, it became abundantly clear that I wanted to live that way, too. I wanted a personal relationship with Jesus. I wanted Him to be my Savior.

At the end of his sermon, with our heads bowed and our eyes closed, Neal Hatfield asked us if we were right with God and with

His Son, Jesus. As we searched our souls, he challenged us to find out if we were truly on the right path. Were we walking and talking with Jesus? If not, he said to rise up and come to the front of the sanctuary to kneel and pray.

I felt tears building in my eyes, and I could hear my own heart beating.

I don't know if I'm walking with Jesus. Sometimes I talk to God. Does that count? I don't know if I'm saved. Probably not, I thought.

Before I even knew what I was doing, I was on my feet and walking down the aisle toward the sweet preacher. He met me with a genuine and loving smile. I knelt down and began to cry.

Within seconds, a wonderful lady joined me on the church floor and took me into her arms. She prayed with me. Instantly, I felt safe. I felt like I was home.

"All you have to do is ask Jesus to be your Savior. Just ask him to come into your heart and lead you," she said tenderly.

I gave my life to Jesus that night, and it was the best decision I ever made. A huge burden was lifted. I had been trying to do everything on my own. When my dad left us, I had to grow up very quickly. I had to make things easy for my mom. She was working so hard to provide a home for my brother and me; the least I could do was help her. We worked hard, all three of us. I can't remember a time in high school when I didn't have a job.

I always tried to handle everything myself. I had gotten myself through high school and into college. Engulfed in college debt, I struggled to make ends meet. I secured loans and grants and worked on campus. I had a golf scholarship, but it only covered part of my college expenses. When money began to run out, I accepted an army scholarship and signed my life away to Uncle Sam in order to stay in school. I was completely focused on my own survival, trying to be the master of my own destiny and trying to do it all alone. I never thought I could ask God to take charge, to take my worry, to take my control, to take charge of my life. I never knew I could do that.

The funny thing is that God had been with me all along. He was the one who opened those doors to get me into college. He provided the golf scholarship and the army scholarship. He provided the jobs and the grants. He protected me when I made bad choices. He provided comfort when I was scared and worried. The more I thought I was in control, the less control I actually had. When I look back, I clearly see God's fingerprints all over my life.

That night, at the revival at Cub Creek, I gave it all to Him. He took away my burdens. His love lifted me, and I gave Him full control.

Two weeks after the revival at Cub Creek, I participated in a believer's baptism. I was twenty-one years old. Lifted out of the water as a brand-new woman, I had a new outlook on life. From that day forward, I belonged to Jesus.

Grandma and Grandpa Burton laid the Christian foundation, and the Bauguess family brought me to my current faith. Accepting Jesus as my personal savior was the very best decision I ever made. I am still learning and growing in my faith. Too often, I slip and struggle and try to take back control. But this I know for sure: If I didn't have Jesus to lean on, I never would have made it through Larry's loss. Larry led me to Jesus, who died for my sins, and Jesus gave me strength when Larry died for our country.

Scriptures That Influence My Life

- **"I can do all things through Christ who strengthens me."** (Philippians 4:13 NKJV) This was the first Scripture I committed to memory. For a long time, it was the only one I could remember verbatim. I believe it with my whole heart. I can do all things with Jesus by my side. He gives me strength. He makes me brave. He gives me hope and comfort.

- **"Forgetting what is behind and straining toward what is ahead, I press on toward the goal to win the prize for which God has called me heavenward in Christ Jesus."** (Philippians 3:13-14 NIV) I believe we are here on earth to learn to love Jesus and to learn to love one another. We're here to make the world a better place. Christians are here to be the light in a dark world. We're here to lead others to Jesus. He taught us how to do that. We just need to follow Him. Every day, I do my best to press on toward the goal. This scripture inspires me to keep going and encourages me to never give up.

- **"Also I heard the voice of the Lord, saying: "Whom shall I send, And who will go for Us?" Then I said, "Here am I! Send me."** (Isaiah 6:8 NKJV) More than anything in this world, I want to be a blessing to other people. When I get to heaven, I want God to say to me, "Well done, good and faithful servant." I want Him to be proud of me, and I want to rest assured that I made my tiny corner of the world a better place. I want to live a life of selfless service. I want to make a difference.

- **"Strength and honor are her clothing; She shall rejoice in time to come."** (Proverbs 31:25 NKJV) In recent years, I have been called an Iron Lady. I'm not so sure about that. I just choose to drive on with full assurance that Jesus is by my side. He walks alongside me and offers His strength. I will rejoice when the troubles and trials of this land are behind us. I will rejoice in heaven when I am reunited with the loved ones who have left before me. Until then, I press on.

Chapter 4

Good-bye, Golf Girl; Hello, Commando

> I don't believe you have to be better than
> everybody else. I believe you have to be
> better than you thought you could be.
> —*Ken Venturi*

Ken Venturi was a man I admired and respected. When I was in high school, I worked as the weekend pro-shop attendant at Eagle Creek Country Club, a golf course he redesigned in the early 1980s. Located between Naples and Marco Island in southwest Florida, Eagle Creek was a beautiful oasis nestled in a cypress reserve. The time I spent at that country club inspired me to seek a career in the golf industry. I enjoyed learning from the golf professionals, speaking with the members, and watching the merchandise representatives deliver their best sales pitches. I became friends with the locker-room attendants and cart guys. It really was a fun place to work.

I saw Mr. Venturi at the club from time to time but rarely had the chance to speak with him. I could only admire him from a distance. He had a successful career as a professional golfer on the PGA Tour, but I remember him best as a broadcaster for *CBS Sports*. I spent years watching and listening to him comment on thousands of golf shots made by the best players in the world. He had my dream job. Can you imagine how cool it would be to travel all over the country, watch golf, offer your opinion, and get paid to do it? After graduating from high school, I set the wheels in motion to do just that. I left Florida and headed to college in North Carolina to pursue my dream job as an on-the-golf-course commentator for *CBS*.

I arrived at Appalachian ready to play golf and study broadcast communications. I was eager to find a way to parlay my golf experience into a career in golf broadcasting. In front of the camera or behind the scenes, I really didn't care what job I had. I would run cables if I could work on the golf course for *CBS Sports*. I would have been happy to do all the jobs necessary to climb the ladder up to that broadcasting booth. Right off the bat, I signed up for communications classes and declared my major as soon as I could.

But a funny thing happened on my way to *CBS Sports*—I ended up in the Army.

***
He who plans first plans twice.
—Larry Bauguess
***

My first year at Appalachian was wonderful. I did well in my classes, made a lot of great friends, and played pretty well in our golf matches. I was enjoying my life as a college kid and student athlete.

In 1990, the summer after my freshman year, I served as an orientation leader. Because I could relate to them, the school assigned me to lead the groups of incoming athletes. I spent nearly the whole summer introducing brand-new freshmen and their families to my beloved Appalachian. I gave them campus tours, proctored their admission tests, and helped them register for their first semester classes.

Working with the student-athlete group, I had fun finding out where they were from and what sports they played. I did my best to help plan their schedules and manage their expectations about juggling homework and practices. In addition to the tours, tests, and schedule planning, my groups received an impressive presentation from Captain Bill Duffy, the army recruiter. Along with a brilliant marketing campaign, Captain Duffy explained that the bridge from athlete to soldier was easily crossed. Athletes are already in shape and know what discipline is. Captain Duffy made the Army sound like so much fun. After the third iteration of his presentation, I asked him where to sign.

Intro to Army

The first year of military science teaches rank structure, customs and courtesies, drill and ceremony, and basic soldier tasks. I learned how to shoot a .22-caliber rifle and set up a claymore mine. I learned how to camouflage my equipment and myself. I learned about basic first aid and began to forge leadership skills I never even knew I had. That first year, I learned the army value acronym "LDRSHIP," for loyalty, duty, respect, selfless service, honor, integrity, and personal courage.[1] I had been developing most of those values on the golf course for years, but I liked the way the Army presented them. Those values became my own and continued to shape my character.

When I returned for the second year of military science, I absolutely fell in love with all things army. In the fall of 1991, my classmate and very dear friend, Matt Peaks, knew that I was motivated and wanted to learn more, so he talked me into joining the Commando Club at the beginning of my second year. I really didn't know what I was getting myself into, but I knew that the cadets who wore the Commando tab were the best of the best cadets of Appalachian ROTC. I wanted to learn from them. I wanted to wear that tab.

Intro to Commandos

The Commando Club was not for the weak or faint of heart. If you wanted to join their ranks, the tabbed members would spend considerable time breaking you down before they built you back up. Their goal was to turn soft civilian college students and wannabe soldiers into lean and mean fighting machines. I know it sounds cheesy, but it's true.

Their entire training plan was patterned after that of the US Army Ranger School. The initial challenge, conducted in the fall, was Tactical Training for the Individual Soldier (TTIS), a training event that began at 4:00 a.m. and ended at 4:00 p.m. The purpose of TTIS was to separate the "wannabes" from the "gonna-bes." Tabbed members threw everything they had at us to try to get us to quit. If we quit, they wouldn't have to train us for the rest of the year. Those who survived the twelve-hour intensive training were allowed to continue to train for their tab and pursue their quest to become an elite member of the Army ROTC program. I wanted it—badly.

In the wee small hours of the morning, while the rest of the campus was sleeping, a ragtag bunch of wannabe Commandos prepared to be destroyed. I remember running across campus in the pitch dark, praying I would survive. A few minutes before 4:00 a.m., I stopped to catch my breath in a concrete alley between the library and the psychology building. The ROTC building was around the corner. We were to meet outside at exactly 4:00 a.m. I didn't want to be early, but I didn't want to be late. Either way, they wouldn't welcome me nicely. They would scream at me no matter what. After glancing at my black Ironman watch, I realized the time had come. I left my safe little alley and ran into the hornets' nest.

A tabbed Commando locked onto me like a heat-seeking missile the minute I left the shadows. He was dressed in a Vietnam-era olive drab uniform, wearing thick camouflage paint on his face. In his camo-covered hands, he carried a wooden baseball bat spray-painted black. That thing was wrapped in barbed wire and had a set of deer antlers on the end. His version of a medieval mace was definitely effective. The sight of him running toward me stopped me in my tracks.

"What do we have here?" he screamed.

Standing completely still, at the position of attention, I knew better than to utter a word. He looked me up and down and growled at me. Inches away from my left ear, he told me there was no way I was going to make it through the day. Then, he made me do push-ups until everyone else arrived. He told me I had gotten there too early. A half a breath later, a fellow wannabe arrived, and he screamed at him for being late. Let the mind games begin.

Once everyone arrived, we formed two ranks and began our

ruck run through campus. We ran at least four miles around the university and then marched up the steep, winding road that led to the Broyhill Inn and Conference Center. As we reached the top of the mountain, the tip of the sun peeked above the horizon and we officially began the day.

At the top of Broyhill Mountain, only an inch or two from my face, another tabbed Commando screamed, "Cadet Hobbs, are you as *messed* up as you want to be?"

Hobbs was my maiden name, and he didn't say "messed up." He used a more flavorful word. It was an impossible question to answer. If I had said yes, he would have said, "Oh, you admit you're *messed* up?" If I had said no, he would have said, "Oh, you want to be more *messed* up?"

I was in a no-win situation, so I remained silent.

"Answer me!" he shouted.

Fully knowing I was going to be punished no matter how I replied, I said, "I'm not *messed* up, sir."

With his face even closer than before, he screamed at me, "Don't talk back to me! And don't call me sir! I'm a Commando! Get down! Knock 'em out!"

Right there, at the top of Broyhill Mountain, we continued our day's adventures as the tabbed Commandos unleashed their wrath upon us: Get up. Get down. Roll left. Roll right. High-crawl down that hill. Low-crawl up the other side.

They poured water along a dirt path and made us crawl on our bellies with our faces in the mud. The tabbed Commandos took turns screaming at us. When one became tired, another one would take over.

"Stand up! Get down! Put your face in that mud! Blow bubbles! Roll over! Make a mud angel! Look at me! Don't look at me! Cadet Hobbs, koala-fy yourself!"

Um, what?

Commando Koala-fied

TTIS was the most physically and mentally challenging thing I had ever done—road marching, running, low-crawling, high-crawling, push-ups, sit-ups, flutter kicks until my abdomen tied itself in a knot and I had absolutely no breath left, and then all of that again. The tabbed Commandos got in our faces and screamed at us for twelve hours!

I quickly learned how to compartmentalize my emotions. I learned how to suck it up and take it. I did exactly as I was told. I kept my eye on the prize. And I learned what it meant to be "koala-fied."

"Don't do it! Don't you do it, Hobbs! Don't you dare let go!" the tabbed Commando screamed.

Wrapped around a North Carolina mountain pine three feet off the ground, my arms and legs were begging me to let go, but there was no way I was going to give in. I hugged that pine tree for dear life. Before long, muscle failure began to set in. My hip flexors were on fire, but my arms and legs were frozen in place. I wasn't sure I could let go if I tried.

I surprised myself when I outlasted the patience of my Commando tormentor. After telling me he was bored, he pronounced me "koala-fied" and told me to get down. That was easier said than done. I couldn't move my legs; I could barely feel them. I simply loosened my grip and slid down the tree trunk until I hit the ground. Ouch! That hurt on multiple levels. Somehow, I got my legs to move, and we ran to the next challenge.

As the sun began its downward descent, we made our way back down the mountain. You would think that going down would be easier than going up, but my legs felt like tree trunks and my arms could barely hold my equipment. Every muscle, bone, and joint in my body protested each downhill step. Once we were back at the ROTC department, the tabbed Commandos told us we had made it. Praise Jesus! I hadn't died, but I was too tired to celebrate. All I wanted was a hot shower.

TTIS was an awful thing to endure and an amazing thing to accomplish. I was absolutely exhausted afterward but so proud to have made it through. I savored my success for about a day and a half. Then, I realized that TTIS was only the beginning.

Commandos Lead the Way

The Commando Club met every Wednesday evening for the entire school year. My roommate, Michelle, looked at me like I was nuts every time I laced up my boots, grabbed my army gear, and ran out of our dorm room. Running across campus in full battle-rattle, I always got strange looks from my fellow students. Only another Commando would understand what I was doing and why I was doing it.

Just like the morning of TTIS, the minute I rounded the corner of the psychology building, the tabbed Commandos began to yell. It's pretty ironic, now that I think about it. All the mind games and physical conditioning happened right outside the psychology building. I wonder if the psychology professors ever saw the things we did out there. Maybe they did. What if the whole thing was just some professor's grand experiment? He or she would have plenty of material, that's for sure. The location didn't seem to bother the tabbed Commandos. They enjoyed screaming at us. Making it through TTIS and every Wednesday meeting was a huge accomplishment to me, but it didn't mean much to them. It only meant that I was still there, gutting it out, trying to earn that tab.

Every meeting began with physical training—sit-ups, push-ups, flutter kicks, buddy carries, and so on. Once conditioning was over, the senior members taught us infantry skills and tactics. We wrote operation orders and went on patrols in the mountains above campus. We practiced land navigation, assembling and disassembling our rifles, setting up claymore mines and other booby traps, camouflaging ourselves and our equipment, and using combat life-saving skills.

In the spring, we would rely on all of our training to survive the

Commando Qualification Course (CQC), a three-day exercise. It was TTIS times three. All wannabe commandos would have to pass every test in order to become a tabbed member of the Commando Club. CQC was set up to be just like a mini-Ranger School. We had no sleep. We were subjected to leadership and army skills evaluations around the clock and one meal would have to last for three days.

Wannabe Commandos would go through CQC in buddy teams. The senior club members made the pairings and announced them at the pre-CQC Commando party in the spring of 1992. That's when I found out that my partner was none other than Larry Bauguess. Larry was an outstanding cadet. To me, he was the best of the best cadets in the program. Born to be a leader and destined for greatness, I'm sure he wasn't thrilled to find out they had partnered him with a girl. At that point, only one female had ever successfully completed CQC, compared to hundreds of males over the club's ten-year existence. Even though the girls were allowed to participate, very few even tried. I'm sure the senior Commandos paired him with me just to mess with him. Surprisingly, none of that mattered to Larry. He was a gentleman. He sucked it up and accepted me.

I wish I could tell you that I surprised them all and set the world on fire with my mad skills and super strength. But, sadly, after an entire school year of Commando character building, I didn't finish CQC. I got really sick and had to tap out after only eighteen hours. I left CQC humiliated. I had failed. I had never failed anything until that moment. The worst part was letting down my battle buddy. I felt just awful about it and wondered how I would ever face Larry again. I did the "duffle bag drag" back to my dorm room and cried on Michelle's shoulder.

I thought about quitting the Commando Club. I wondered why I had even signed up for it in the first place. But, reflecting on the entire school year, I realized that I still loved it. I loved the camaraderie, the brotherhood. I had already learned so much; I just had to try again. I chalked it all up as a learning experience and decided to finish the school year with my head held high.

In spite of my poor performance at CQC, I was still one of the best cadets in my ROTC class at Appalachian. That summer, our cadre sent me to the US Army Airborne School at Fort Benning, Georgia, to learn how to jump out of airplanes. Successfully completing that school and earning my Airborne Wings increased my confidence and my value among my peers. It also proved that I really did have the chops for Army service.

Returning to school in the fall of 1992 with renewed confidence and motivation, I signed up for the Commando Club once more. Larry and Matt had made it through CQC and were tabbed Commandos. Initially, I was happy for them. Then, I realized that they would be the ones to "train" me that year, when I would go through all of it again.

***

The definition of insanity is doing the same thing over and over
again and expecting different results.
—Albert Einstein
***

Commando Do-Over

I endured another entire school year of Commando character building. I didn't have to go through TTIS again because I was already koala-fied. But I did have to go to every Wednesday meeting just like the other wannabes. The second year was understandably easier in terms of soldier skills. I got better and better at them. Assembling and disassembling my weapon became second nature. By the spring of 1993, I was highly proficient in first aid, battle drills/react to fire, land navigation, escape and evasion, operational planning, and tactical communication. The second year of Commando conditioning and physical training was just as brutal as the first, but it made me even stronger. This time, I was ready for CQC! Bring it!

We started at the D.D. Dougherty Building (ROTC headquarters) with the normal "conditioning" (screaming, yelling, push-ups, flutter kicks, buddy carries, etc.). After nearly an hour of character building, we dropped our gear and ran up the hill to the Appalachian football stadium for the Army Physical Fitness Test, as if we hadn't done enough physical training (PT) already.

We conducted a standard fitness test consisting of two-minute tests of push-ups and sit-ups and a two-mile run. Just before we took off for the timed run, as if I were an Olympic athlete receiving her gold medal, a senior Commando placed a cowbell around my neck. During the run, I could pass the bell to another wannabe, but if it ever stopped ringing, even for a second, the tabbed Commandos would drop all of us for push-ups or make us run another lap. That bell was so loud. The temptation to hold it in my hand to squelch its ringing was strong, but if I didn't pass the fitness test, I wouldn't pass CQC. On the bright side, when that bell came alive with its clanging, I couldn't hear the Commandos scream at us.

After the fitness test, we stayed outside and began a series of soldier-skills testing. At sundown, we made our way back to the ROTC Department to take a written test. The classroom was blazing hot when we got there. At first, the heat felt pretty nice because spring evenings are awfully chilly in Boone. As we worked, the tabbed Commandos increased the heat and put water on the radiator. The heat and humidity made it ridiculously hard to focus on the test. We could barely stay awake. The moment any of us started nodding off, they would pop our ears with rubber bands to wake us up and then take us out into the hallway for corrective training.

After the written test, still in the blazing-hot room, we received our leadership positions for the overnight mission. We planned our operation, and we wrote and presented the operation order. Then, in our sweat-drenched uniforms, we returned outside for a full night of patrolling. Just our luck—it began to rain freezing-cold, misty, stick-all-over-you, Boone midnight rain.

Our mission was to locate and conduct reconnaissance on an objective on top of Broyhill Mountain and return to report what we found. There were tabbed Commandos all around us, working as an opposing force. We had to move undetected and resist capture or suffer the consequences. With the odds completely stacked against us, we weren't successful in evading our tormentors. They caught us on the way up, and they caught us on the way down. We were punished with the typical corrective training, but we stayed on task, spied on our objective, reported our findings, and accomplished our mission. It took us all night.

The next morning, without so much as an hour of sleep, we had more soldier-skills testing. With each passing hour, testing lane after testing lane, it became harder and harder to stay focused and awake. We spent the early afternoon at Commando Pond, building and crossing rope bridges, conducting survival swims, and making mud angels. We spent the late afternoon at Suicide Hill, low-crawling up and down the massive hill, high above the football stadium, over and over again.

Our only break from Suicide Hill was a "call for fire" station. This was probably the hardest soldier skill I had to accomplish because I really didn't know much about artillery. We stood on a wooden platform that was halfway up the hill and about three stories high, above the practice football field (which is now the Appalachian baseball field). Below us, out on the field, were several big yellow Tonka trucks. We were given a pair of binoculars and told to observe and destroy the enemy target. We had to identify the enemy location and properly call for artillery fire. It sounded something like this: "You, this is me. Fire mission. Enemy tank in the open at grid AB12345678. Over."

A tabbed Commando would run out onto the field to mark the spot where the artillery round landed, which was usually nowhere near the target just to mess with us. My next step was to adjust fire.

"You, this is me. Adjust fire. Add 15 meters. Left 20 meters."

Then, my evaluator would get on the walkie-talkie and tell the locator to take fifteen steps away from our location and twenty steps to the left. I had to repeat my adjustments and "walk the rounds in" three times. Finally, I "blew up" the Tonka target and passed the station.

More soldier-skills testing lasted through the night.

The fun ended in the early hours of Sunday morning. Our last task was a timed orienteering course, which is kind of like a scavenger hunt, only with direction azimuths and distances instead of riddles. Our course zigzagged all over campus. One by one, we found all of our points. Thankfully, the campus was deserted. We looked like two miles of bad road; we didn't smell very good either. With a sprint to the finish, we completed the orienteering course just in time, and CQC was over. We were done. We had made it. We were Commandos!

During the brief graduation ceremony, the senior Commandos pinned our tabs on our foul-smelling uniforms and gave us our certificates. They chose me as Commando Honor Grad. It was a very sweet moment of redemption. I thanked God for seeing me through and for giving me the strength to complete the course and earn my tab.

Once the fun was over, I went home and made a beeline for the shower. The healing water soothed my aching shoulders and washed away three days of grime. Newly clean, I nursed the cuts on my hands and arms and patched up the blisters on my feet. I took a deep breath, plopped on my bed, and settled in for a long-overdue nap.

Just before sleep overtook me, I said another prayer. I thanked God for getting me through CQC and for all that was right in my life. I went from number-one loser the year before to Commando Honor Grad. It pays to press on. I was definitely better than I thought I could be.

Chapter 5

Dog Tags and a Camera

You will see it's me, I believe you could be, be
the right one, you, for every girl like me.
—*Jennifer Nettles and Kristian Bush (Sugarland),*
"Every Girl Like Me"

Of all the girls in the whole world, Larry Bauguess asked me to hold his dog tags and his camera. There we were, standing on the side of US 421 on the outskirts of Boone, with the madcap idea to bungee jump off a construction crane. It was a typical fall Saturday in the high country, cloudy and cool. It was 1992. My first year of Commandos and my failed CQC attempt were behind me, and I had just begun my Commando do-over year. On that Saturday, the football team had an away game, so the town was quiet. We were bored and needed something to do.

As US Army ROTC cadets, we were adrenaline junkies in training. Larry and I, and a few of our classmates, were already Airborne qualified, which meant we had jumped out of perfectly good airplanes over the summer at the US Army Airborne School at Fort Benning, Georgia. There is something magical about exiting an aircraft while in flight. Trusting your equipment to get you to the ground safely, you put your faith in God (and in your training) and jump. I made five jumps that summer. With each landing, I walked a little taller and stood a little prouder. But on that cool Saturday in the early fall, we weren't jumping out of airplanes, and this wasn't an army school.

Our eyes traveled up and down the rickety crane. There wasn't much to it. It was a typical construction crane just like you would see at any job site. I had seen similar cranes a few times in my youth on my dad's construction sites. But this one would hold my fate, and my ankles, in its grip.

Of our pack of seven or eight cadets, Larry volunteered to go first. I wasn't surprised. He was amazing, always highly motivated. Of all the boys in the Appalachian State University ROTC program, he was the one I admired most. Born to be a leader, Larry was completely focused on pursuing an army career. He was driven to be the best at everything he did. He was a North Carolina boy with the coolest Southern drawl. He was smart and funny. At that point, he and I were just friends. Actually, I wouldn't even call us friends—maybe just fellow cadets. I thought very highly of him but doubted he would even give me the time of day.

After the bungee dude gave us his safety briefing, he told Larry it was time for him to get strapped in. Larry looked right at me and grinned.

"Airborne!" he said. Then, he took a step closer to me.

"Hey, Wesley, will you do me a favor and hold my dog tags? Oh, and my camera, too?"

I was stunned. Larry Bauguess was in my personal space, and he said my name. His big blue eyes and crooked little smile made me feel weak in the knees. That was the first time he had had that effect on me. It wouldn't be the last.

I was still harboring the guilt and embarrassment of my less-than-fabulous performance during the spring CQC. When we were Commando buddies, I had let him down. That's something you just don't do. I never thought he would even speak to me again, but there he was standing in front of me, waiting for an answer. Suddenly, I thought, *Maybe he's over my CQC disaster. Maybe I should get over it.*

"Um ... sure," I replied.

He took his dog tags off and carefully placed the chain over my head and around my neck. His hand traveled down the chain and cupped his dog tags. He stared at them for a thoughtful moment and then released them, allowing them to drop to my chest. Then, he handed me his camera.

"Will you take my picture when I'm up there?" he asked.

"Of course," I answered.

Larry was only an inch taller than me, but I looked up to him as if he were a giant. He had beautiful skin, unblemished and young. He wore his dark brown hair "high and tight" like the US Army Rangers, which meant his head was shaved on the sides and in the back. All that remained was a little patch of hair on top of his head. I always thought that little patch of hair looked like a divot I made on the golf course.

As I watched Larry dive from the top of the bungee crane, with the camera at the ready, something stirred inside my chest. My heart fluttered, and I worried for his safety. A lump formed in my throat, and my eyes began to tear. I snapped a few pictures of him descending, rebounding, and hanging by his ankles. I was relieved to see the bungee cord do its job and hold him safely. As he continued to bounce around, a realization hit me—I couldn't wait for him to get off that thing. I wanted him to talk to me again.

Once Larry was back on the ground, he walked over to me, grinning.

"I am so doing that again!" he exclaimed.

I laughed and handed him his dog tags and his camera. I told him I took some good pictures. He told me he'd return the favor.

When it was my turn, the bungee dude strapped the harness just above one of my ankles and led me to the cage that served as the bungee platform. Once we were set, the crane operator lifted us slowly up into the sky. As we were ascending, I saw Larry point his camera at me. I smiled and waved.

What are you doing up here, crazy girl?" I asked myself, silently. *This is nuts!* But I had an audience and had to see it through.

Not to be outdone by my fellow cadet, I let the bungee dude talk me into doing a back dive out of the cage. After he strapped the harness around my other ankle, I rotated into position, grabbed the side beams, and did exactly what you are not supposed to do—I looked down.

"No backing out now," bungee dude said. "Your boyfriend's watching."

"What? He's not my boyfriend."

"He will be after this!"

I looked at him and smiled at the thought. Then, I snapped back into the reality of my task. The bungee dude told me not to jump but to instead fall back and do a "Nestea plunge." I hugged my body and gripped my shoulders with my fingertips. I offered a silent prayer, asking God to forgive me for being stupid and arrogant. I took one last, slow breath.

Then, full of faith and defiance, I fell backward into the cool mountain air.

I tried so hard to keep my eyes open, but I don't remember much of the fall. I do, however, remember the rebound. I felt like my stomach and my heart were in my throat when the bungee cord reached maximum extension and then recoiled and pulled me back up. I bounced around a dozen times before they lowered me back to the ground. That was easily the craziest thing I ever did.

Larry greeted me with a big ol' grin when I reached the ground. "Way to go, Airborne!"

Later in the fall, around the time of the World Series, this same group of cadets went to the Picadilly Pub, a local mom-and-pop restaurant, to watch the Atlanta Braves play the Toronto Blue Jays. I began to notice that Larry and I were often standing together. He would lean his shoulder into mine, and I would lean back against him. We would steal glances and smiles from each other; just looking at him made me blush.

Another night, we all went out to Savannah Joe's, a pool hall and sports bar. My friend Stephanie cornered me in the bathroom.

"For crying out loud, Wesley, you like him, he likes you! You guys just need to get a clue and be together already. Would you go out with him if he asked you?"

"Wow, are we back in middle school?" I retorted. Then, I admitted, "Of course I would. That's Larry Bauguess!"

A Warrior and a Gentleman

Larry and I had our first date on October 24, 1992. The moment I laid my eyes on him, waiting patiently in the lobby of my dorm, I knew my life would never be the same.

He drove us down the mountain to the tiny town of Blowing Rock, where we had dinner at the Meadowbrook Inn. Larry was a perfect gentleman. He opened every door, took my coat when we got to the restaurant, and even pulled out my chair. Conversation came easy for us. We talked all night about sports, music, and the Army.

After dinner, we took a walk along the main street in Blowing Rock. Larry offered me his arm, bent at the elbow. Sliding my hand between his arm and his ribs, I wrapped my fingers around his bicep. Then, he locked my hand in place by gently pulling his arm in toward his body. Larry insisted he walk closest to the road, protecting me from oncoming traffic. Even in our earliest moments, he was a beautiful blend of warrior and gentleman.

We continued to see each other throughout the fall.

One afternoon, Larry called me from the lobby of my dorm and asked me if I wanted to drive down the mountain with him. He needed his mom to sew some patches on his uniform. I'm sure I had to study or write a paper, but I never passed up a chance to see him. We got halfway down the mountain before it dawned on me—I was going to meet his mother.

Suddenly, I became very nervous. I glanced down at my jean shorts, sneakers, and gray Appalachian sweatshirt. I straightened my ponytail and began the search for my lip gloss.

"You look beautiful," Larry said. "Don't worry. They're gonna love you."

The midautumn mountain views and laurel vistas took my breath away as we approached the Wilkes County line. Larry's parents live in a beautiful, creek-lined valley in Moravian Falls, North Carolina, about thirty miles down the mountain from Boone.

Always fond of the road less traveled, I was delighted when we turned off the paved road to get to Larry's house. The crunching of rocks beneath the tires of the old Ford Mustang and the dust trail that followed us gave away the element of surprise. Larry's parents met us in the driveway.

The butterflies circling in my stomach went into full flutter when Larry put the car in park and opened the door. He touched my hand and grinned. Moments later, Larry hugged his parents and turned to introduce me. His mother, Martha, looked surprised and relieved. I wasn't sure why.

The minute we walked into their modest ranch-style home, I could see that this was a family of faith. There was a plaque on the wall that said, "As for me and my house, we will serve the Lord." They spent a lot of time together as a family, most of it in the kitchen. That's where we all settled.

Seated on stools around a peninsula countertop, Martha asked me where I was from. When I told her I was from Florida, she asked me how I ended up at Appalachian. I told her I was a golfer and on scholarship to play for the university.

"How do you have time for golf, schoolwork, and ROTC?" she asked.

It was a challenge, for sure. I had just made the decision to take a year off from golf and focus on ROTC. Juggling my golf practices, strength training, and tournaments against my military science classes and army training was exhausting. I managed it all pretty well for the first two years of ROTC. I was even awarded the Women's Golf Most Valuable Player award at the end of my third year on the team. I loved being a student athlete, and I loved being an ROTC cadet. But as I approached my third year of ROTC, I had to make a decision.

I had already accepted an ROTC scholarship, so I was a contracted cadet. I was committed to the Army after graduation. My performance in my third year of ROTC would have a direct impact on my commission and first assignment. I had to make a tough choice. I decided not to play my fourth year of collegiate golf. I needed to focus on all things army.

Martha offered us something to drink and began to tell me Larry's story. That's when I found out that Larry had been a baseball star in high school. A pitcher with a wicked curveball, he wanted to play for Appalachian. He had his sights set on a life on the baseball field. His dream changed when the coach wanted to send him to a smaller school to play baseball for two years and then have him come back to Appalachian to play his last two years. Larry turned down that idea because he felt led to stay at App. I'm so glad he did.

Baseball at Appalachian didn't work out, but Larry didn't let that get him down. One day, he was walking across campus and saw some guys rappelling down the wall of Broome Kirk Gym. Larry spoke to the guys on the ground and asked what they were doing. They told him about the Army ROTC program and, just like that, he found his new place.

The summer after his freshman year, Larry went to basic training and advance infantry training in the blazing heat at Fort Benning. Larry would serve in the North Carolina Army National Guard while he was in college and then commission into the active duty army when he graduated.

Larry's mom was clearly proud of her son. His dad was, too. While Martha slipped away to sew the patches on his uniform, his dad, John, took his turn telling a few stories of Larry's youth. I heard about high school baseball games, campouts down by the creek, and the time he drove his car through a barbed-wire fence.

Larry's sister, Laura, who was eleven, came in and sat down with us. After listening to the stories, she grinned at Larry and then asked me if I wanted to watch her do cartwheels in the living room.

Of course, I said yes.

Just as the sun retreated behind the mountain, Larry's mother completed her task. Inspecting his mom's handiwork, Larry found it to be perfect. He thanked her and told his family we needed to head back up the mountain.

Outside in the driveway where we first met, Martha hugged me with a sigh of relief. She made sure I knew how happy she was to meet me. Later, I found out why. Larry had called in advance of our visit and told his parents he was bringing home a girl. He asked them to behave.

"This girl is special," he told his mother. "She's in ROTC with me, and her name is Wesley."

Martha didn't know what was going to show up at her house! She expected a giant woman wearing combat boots. She has often told me over the years, usually with a great big smile on her face, how relieved she was that day when she laid her eyes on me.

We all hugged good-bye. Everyone was happy, and I left with a feeling of comfort and peace. As we were backing out of the long driveway, I looked at Larry's family once more. I loved them instantly. I could have stayed there forever.

Part 2

Home Is Where the Army Sends Us

If you highlight everything,
you highlight nothing.
—*Larry Bauguess*

I have always been a note taker. As a visual learner, I hardly ever remembered what a professor said in class if I didn't write it down. Even today, when I read, I have to underline or highlight the important points or I won't remember them. In college, I always wrote in my textbooks. When I studied, I'd always have a highlighter, a pen, and a pencil. I highlighted the text and wrote notes in the margins. I drew pictures, arrows, and stars, anything to help me remember the important things.

One day, Larry and I were studying together. I was ferociously highlighting a page in my history textbook. When I got to the end of the page, Larry looked at it and then looked at me with a puzzled look on his face.

"Wesley," he said, "if you highlight everything, you highlight nothing."

He was right. I thought all of it was important, but by highlighting every word on the page, I had made them all equal. So, really, I highlighted nothing.

It is in that spirit that I write the next six chapters. I'd love to highlight every moment of my military experience and write about every person we met on our military journey, but I simply can't. There isn't enough time or space. And, honestly, I think it would devalue the stories I love the most. In the next six chapters, I introduce you to the places Larry and I called home and reflect upon the moments that shaped my life and continued to build my character.

Chapter 6

Rendezvous with Destiny

Absence makes the heart grow fonder.
—*Thomas Haynes Bayly*

Larry and I married in Naples, Florida, on December 19, 1993. He was already a second lieutenant in the infantry. I was still a student at Appalachian, with one semester to go. During our wedding, we decided to add a twist to a common wedding tradition. When we lit the unity candle, we left the individual candles burning instead of blowing them out because we knew we would have times of separation during our military lives. We knew we needed to be able to stand independently, rely on our own individualism, and rely on God during those times. In our first year of marriage, Larry and I saw each other only ninety-two days.

OBC

After a short honeymoon, I traveled back to Appalachian to finish up my senior year. Larry returned to Fort Benning to continue his Infantry Officer Basic Course. In May 1994, I left my beloved Appalachian as a distinguished military graduate with a degree in broadcast communications and a regular army commission into the Medical Service Corps. I immediately reported to Fort Sam

Houston, Texas, for my Officer Basic Course (OBC). Larry was still in school at Fort Benning.

At OBC, I learned about the Army Medical Department (AMEDD) and their mission "to conserve the fighting strength." It is so important for our soldiers to know that the AMEDD stands ready to take care of them should they become wounded, injured, or ill. As a Medical Service Corps officer, I could choose between two career paths: working in the hospital or working in the field. I definitely wanted to work in a field environment and help provide medical support to the line units, so I paid closer attention to the combat health support lectures.

From the very beginning of our army careers, Larry and I asked to be assigned to the 82nd Airborne Division. Having trained at Fort Bragg and graduated from Airborne School as cadets, we had already fallen in love with the Airborne culture. We wanted nothing more than to become paratroopers in the elite All-American Division. However, as she often does, "Mother Army" set a different plan in motion. She replaced our Airborne dreams with air-assault missions.

***

We have a rendezvous with destiny, our strength and courage strike a spark that will always make men free …
—101st Airborne Division (Air Assault) Song

***

Screaming Eagles

Larry and I were assigned to the 101st Airborne Division (Air Assault) at Fort Campbell, Kentucky. It wasn't the 82nd, but it became a perfect fit for us. The 101st is a unit with a proud history. We were honored to join the Screaming Eagle ranks in the fall of 1994.

Even though Larry had begun his army career a year before me, I arrived at Fort Campbell before him. He had finished his OBC but was still at Fort Benning going through Ranger School, a grueling course that would test his mental and physical strength. The highly coveted Ranger tab was a must-have for all infantry officers. Larry was determined to get his.

I had already earned my air assault wings as an ROTC cadet, so when I arrived at the 101st, the assignment officer sent me straight to my unit. In my first assignment, I served as the treatment platoon leader of the medical company in the main support battalion. The treatment platoon's responsibility was to provide medical care to all classes of patients in the division support area, the area behind the infantry line units and the forward support units. In the field, we set up the division clearing station, which meant we received wounded, injured, or ill soldiers from the forward units and took care of them the very best we could.

Soon after I signed into my unit, I met with the battalion commander. Our meeting served as my initial counseling session, which is a time when the commander lays out the standards of the battalion and makes clear his or her expectations of officers. My commander told me that my unit was getting ready to train and test for the Expert Field Medical Badge (EFMB). Then, he told me not to worry if I didn't get it on my first try.

"Most people don't," he said.

His comment bothered me for two reasons. First, I was kind of offended that he didn't seem to have any faith in me as a soldier or an officer. He didn't know me at all. Second, it made me wonder, *How hard is it?*

Determination replaced my discouragement. The EFMB was as important to a medical service officer as the Ranger tab was to an infantryman. I knew I would give it my all.

Just before I left for the field, Larry called to tell me he had successfully completed Ranger School. I was so excited that he had earned his tab! Then, I realized I would be in the field during his graduation ceremony. I would totally miss one of the most important ceremonies of his career. I was sick about it and told him how sorry I was.

"Go be great," he said. "I'll see you next week when you come in from the field."

A Brief Reunion

We had a break between EFMB training week and EFMB testing week, and I got to go home. Larry was there! Because of OBC, Ranger School, and EFMB training, we hadn't seen each other in months. It was such a blessing to be in the same room with him. After much-needed quality time, I filled him in on everything I had been doing.

I told him all about EFMB training and how similar it all was to Commando training at Appalachian. The EFMB was just as academically, physically, and mentally challenging as our beloved club, but it added very intense and very specific medical skills. I was thankful I could call upon my Commando experience for the grueling training and testing evolution.

Rambling on, I told Larry that the EFMB test began with a written test. It had multiple combat testing lanes, a litter obstacle course, and a twelve-mile road march. During training week, I learned that the EFMB success rate was only 15–20 percent. No wonder my battalion commander had warned me about it.

As I was rattling off everything I had learned during EFMB training week, Larry just looked at me and grinned. He was so kind and patient and seemed content to soak up all of my excitement. Once I finished my rambling, he finally had the chance to talk.

Larry told me a little about Ranger School and said Commando training was nothing compared to what he had just gone through. He told me about the Darby Phase at Fort Benning; the Desert Phase at Fort Bliss, Texas; the Mountain Phase near Dahlonega, Georgia; and the Florida Phase near Eglin Air Force Base. He told me several stories about the formidable Darby Queen (obstacle course), desert survival training, patrolling in the mountains, and waterborne operations in Florida. I hung on his every word.

Then, Larry gave me a gift, a "Dang-it Stump" from the Florida Phase. The stump got its name from the frustration of Ranger candidates during the Florida Phase. As they patrolled in the waist-deep water of the Florida swamps, they often ran into underwater cypress knees. Larry said he and his squad mates constantly whispered, "Dang it!" after they bumped their shins on those hidden stumps and struggled to maintain their footing. The stump Larry brought home represented the physical obstacles he had encountered in Ranger School and still serves as a visual reminder that obstacles can be overcome with the right motivation and endless perseverance.

While I was training for the EFMB, Larry had signed into his unit. Assigned as a Rakkasan, he would serve in the 2-187th Parachute Infantry Regiment. He began his lieutenant time as a

TOW platoon leader in Delta Company. TOW stands for tube-launched, optically-tracked, wire-guided missile. To this day, I know that without looking it up because Larry helped me commit it to memory. He was my husband, but he would always be my teacher and mentor. I loved him for that. Happy with his assignment with the Rakkasans, Larry was eager to get started.

After a very short weekend, I headed back out to the field for EFMB testing week. It was so hard to leave Larry after such a brief reunion.

EMFB

The EFMB test week was definitely more intense than the training week. To earn the coveted EFMB, candidates had to pass the written test and every soldier/medical skill on every combat testing lane. There were no do-overs, no grace for mistakes. The whole thing was like a sudden death-playoff. If I got something wrong, I was going home. All of the EFMB candidates lived together, sleeping and studying on army cots under huge army tents. Hundreds of us began the quest and studied for each lane continually.

I made it through the CPR lane, the medical evacuation lane, and day and night land navigation without any trouble. I even made it through the dreaded and exhausting litter obstacle course, in which four EFMB candidates had to carry a fifth "wounded" soldier on an army litter up hills, down into valleys, across trenches, over a high wall, under concertina wire, and through several more obstacles without causing further injuries to the patient. By the end of the course, my arms were useless and my legs were aching, but we delivered our patient safely to the finish line. The next event was the triage lane, which was the absolute toughest part of EFMB testing.

The triage lane had the highest attrition rate of all the lanes of the EFMB. I had listened to everything the instructors had said during training week and spent most of my time studying for that lane, but I was really nervous. I got more nervous when I learned that several of my medics and some fellow lieutenants hadn't passed. Even one of our doctors had failed it. A doctor! The longer I had to wait, the more nervous I became. When it was my turn, I took a deep breath. I asked Jesus to go through the lane with me and help me focus on what I had been taught.

At the word *go*, my adrenaline kicked in and off I went triaging patients and providing emergency medical treatment. I had three simulated casualties. One lost his leg and needed a tourniquet. One had a significant head injury, and one had a sucking chest wound. I had to provide the proper medical treatment in the correct order. All of this happened under simulated battle stressors, like smoke and artillery and machine-gun fire, to make it as realistic as possible. It was all a blur, but somehow I made it through. I triaged them in the proper order and provided the correct medical treatment. I was a go for the triage lane. I did it! I was a little stunned but so excited and so relieved. Thank you, Jesus!

All I had left to do was the twelve-mile road march the next morning.

As the sun began to rise on the final day of EFMB testing, I realized that there weren't very many of us left—maybe a few dozen out of the hundreds who had begun earlier in the week. I was well aware that the only thing between the Expert Field Medical Badge and me was a twelve-mile walk. Looking forward to that finish line, I wanted my EFMB for sure, but I had an extra incentive. I knew Larry would be waiting for me at the end.

In the solitude of the road march, I took time to talk to God. I thanked Him for getting me through the test. Before every testing lane, I had prayed for wisdom, clarity, and guidance, and He saw me through. During the road march, I asked Him for strength and perseverance. He was with me. I could feel Him. I thanked Him for watching over Larry and me in our days of separation, and I thanked Him for the opportunity to finally be a married couple living under the same roof.

The course was hilly. I enjoyed the downhill stretches and ran every chance I could. I'd lengthen my stride and walk the uphills. By mile eight, I had hot spots on my feet, and my shoulders ached under the weight of my rucksack, but I didn't care. I just kept moving. I wanted to see Larry at the finish line.

Eleven miles down, only one to go. As I turned the corner and began the last mile, I could hear the band playing at the main post parade field. I kept pace with the *thump, thump, thump* of the drums. In the final stretch, just short of the parade field, I saw soldiers, two or three deep, lining the sides of the road. I scanned the crowd, looking for Larry. When I finally spotted him, my heart fluttered. He was at the finish line, and he had never looked so good.

A huge lump invaded my throat, and I could feel tears forming in my eyes. My body was weak from exertion, but I was determined to finish strong. Fighting back the tears, I swallowed hard and tried to breathe deeply. I had just accomplished a huge endeavor. I didn't want people to think I was crying because I was tired or some sissy girl. I just really missed my husband. To see him standing there with those big blue eyes and reassuring smile, after spending most of the year apart, was almost more than I could take. Crossing the finish line, I moved out of the way of the candidates behind me, dropped my ruck, and met Larry's embrace.

The award ceremony took place shortly afterward. My battalion commander, the one who had told me not to worry if I didn't make it, pinned my badge on my chest and shook my hand. It was a great feeling. I couldn't help but think, *He knows me now!* After the ceremony, we were released and given the rest of the day off.

I was as proud of my EFMB as I was of my Commando tab. The Commando tab at Appalachian told everyone that I stood in the ranks of the best of the best cadets. But wearing an EFMB on my uniform as an officer in the real army meant I had instant credibility among my peers in the AMEDD. Better yet, that badge was recognized army wide. I was an expert field medic.

When Larry got home later that night, he rubbed my feet and nursed my wounds. The next week, he would begin Air Assault School, and then he would test for his Expert Infantryman Badge (EIB). He successfully completed both challenges, and for the rest of our army days, we proudly wore our Airborne, Air Assault, and EIB/EFMB badges on our uniforms. We called them our towers of power.

Treatment Platoon

After EFMB testing was out of the way, I finally got the opportunity to get to know my unit and dive into our mission. As I mentioned before, when we went to the field as a company we set up the division clearing station. That means we received patients from the forward battlefield and evaluated their wounds and injuries. We treated and held the ones we could. If they had more serious injuries than we could handle, our company ambulances evacuated them further to the rear of the battle space.

The treatment platoon was the main effort of our medical company. We had an army doctor, a dentist, and an eye doctor; combat medics and nurses; and dental, X-ray, laboratory, and optometry technicians. Since we had two forward surgical squads in my platoon, we also had both general and orthopedic surgeons, a nurse anesthetist, and operating room technicians. As the platoon leader, I was responsible for all of them—and for all the medical equipment.

Our company's most critical task was to accept patients (real and simulated) as soon as possible. So when we first arrived in the field, we immediately set up a place to receive patients, which included a place for triage and emergency medical treatment. Then, we set up one huge tent for our actual medical treatment space and a second tent for our patient hold ward. (For a visual example of what our field treatment area looked like, think back to the TV show *M*A*S*H*.) A third tent went up for X-ray, dental, and optometry. We also dug out a full patient bunker, nearly the size of a one-car garage, complete with overhead cover just in case we needed to protect our patients from enemy artillery. Setting up our medical capabilities was exhausting, but providing exceptional medical support for our fellow Screaming Eagles was worth it.

The most difficult challenge we faced in the field was jumping forward. As a light Infantry/Air Assault Division in the 1990s, maneuver units (like Larry's Rakkasans) constantly moved forward on a linear battlefield. The same was true for the support units. When the infantry moved forward, the support elements followed.

Sometimes, just as soon as we got all the medical capabilities set up, we'd have to break them down, jump forward, and set them all up again. It was like playing leapfrog. The battlefield was fluid, so we had to be fluid, too. We tested our medical support proficiency in the field several times a year and at least once a year at the Joint Readiness Training Center (JRTC). (I'll discuss JRTC later in this chapter and again in chapter 8.)

Larry served as the TOW platoon leader for about the same time that I served as the treatment platoon leader. He enjoyed air assaulting and lighting up the battlefield with his platoon. And he loved being a Rakkasan. I wish I could write more about his Air Assault adventures, but we were so busy with our own units that we barely had time to swap stories. When we were together, we didn't talk about work. We just enjoyed being together. Once we finished our platoon leader time, we moved on to become company executive officers.

XO Time

As the Echo Company executive officer, I was second in command and worked under the impeccable leadership of Captain Brian Gray. Captain Gray taught me how to be the example for our soldiers and how to lead the company in his absence. By sharing his knowledge and investing in his junior leaders, he made the company and those around him infinitely better. Our company truly benefitted from his leadership style.

Staff Time

After my platoon and company executive officer time, I spent the rest of my Fort Campbell days as a staff officer, serving as the division support command (DISCOM) assistant personnel officer (S-1) and the combat health support officer for the main support battalion. Generally, staff jobs are not very exciting, and while that might be true, I did have great opportunities for character building and adventure.

As the DISCOM assistant S-1, I developed an intimate knowledge of personnel actions, especially awards and evaluation reports. This was my first desk job in the Army, and most of my peers would have hated it. I should have hated it, too, because I wasn't out in the field doing fun stuff anymore. But I took that job seriously. I quickly realized that every paper in my inbox had a real person attached to it and that paper was significant to their army career. Paying attention to detail, I made sure that each document got the respect it deserved. Knowing I would get another chance to serve in the field eventually, my S-1 time gave me the chance to take a knee and enjoy decent work hours for a little while.

As the combat health support officer, I was a member of the support operations section of the 801st Main Support Battalion. This section provided logistical support to the entire division. I was responsible for the medical part of that mission. Second only to my time as a platoon leader, my time in support operations was the most fun I had at Fort Campbell. My boss, Major Betsey Riester, was an amazing leader and mentor. She taught me so much about multifunctional logistics.

(In an effort to maintain chronological integrity, I'll pause here to tell you about Larry's first deployment. Then, I'll take you back to support operations.)

Operation Desert Focus

On June 25, 1996, Islamic terrorists killed nineteen American airmen and wounded nearly five hundred others when they detonated a truck bomb just outside Khobar Towers, a military complex in Saudi Arabia.[1] Later that year, the Rakkasan Raiders (Alpha Company, 2nd Battalion, 187th Infantry), were called to Saudi Arabia to provide force protection for US aviation assets at Camp Eagle Town II.[2]

Serving as a rifle platoon leader in Alpha Company, Larry was eager to deploy with his unit and do his part to make the area safer. We didn't join the Army to sit on the sidelines. Ever since we were infused with the Commando spirit in college, we dreamed of the opportunity to serve overseas. The Khobar Tower bombing was a sucker punch and a national tragedy. It made us angry. Larry was thankful to have the opportunity to do something about it. Sadly, we would taste the bitterness of similar sucker punches later in our lives.

In preparation for the deployment, Larry brought home a packet of paperwork. With this being our first deployment, we weren't sure what to expect. Among the papers were an emergency data form, a life insurance form, and a "what if" questionnaire. We had no problem filling out the first two papers; we had seen them before. The third form, however, was new and unwelcomed. It included these questions:

In the event of your death, where would you like to be buried?
Who would you like to be your pallbearers?
What songs would you like to have played at your funeral?
What verses of scripture would you like read?

I did not want to ask these questions or hear the answers. We were young and newly married; surely we didn't need to worry about this. But the leadership said we had to discuss and answer every question. We did the best we could and actually learned a lot about each other through the process.

Larry's answer to one of the questions took me by surprise. I assumed Larry would want to be buried in Arlington National Cemetery in Washington, DC, but when we got to that question, Larry said, "No. I don't want my family to have to travel that far. I want to be buried in the Scenic Memorial Gardens in Moravian Falls, right next to Cub Creek Baptist Church."

I'm glad I asked.

We continued through the entire form. We made a copy of it and put it in our "important papers" notebook that held our birth certificates, marriage license, and military orders.

As Larry prepared for his Saudi deployment, I was preparing for one of my own. My unit was heading to the JRTC at Fort Polk, Louisiana. I would actually leave Fort Campbell before Larry, which made for a strange good-bye. Normally, family members go to the unit headquarters or to the airfield to say good-bye to their deploying soldiers. A deployment send-off is a time-honored tradition. It's patriotic, even romantic. I wanted to send Larry off in proper fashion, but I was leaving first. Our good-bye was anticlimactic, certainly not romantic, but every bit as painful.

The morning I left, Larry came to my battalion area to send me off. Standing a few cars away from the idling bus and careful not to show too much public affection, we kissed and hugged good-bye. My heart sank to my stomach as Larry held me for those few precious moments. I hated knowing that he would be in an empty house right before his deployment, and I hated the thought that our house would be just as empty when I returned home from JRTC. Holding his hand, I told him to be careful. He told me the same. With a pain in my stomach and that familiar lump in my throat, I turned away from my beloved husband and boarded the bus. As we drifted away from each other once again, I put my hand on the window. Larry returned his love with a wave.

While Larry was in Saudi, I volunteered for another JRTC rotation. I think my peers thought I was crazy, but it was so much better than being in that empty house. Though I missed him terribly, the JRTC rigor kept me busy.

Larry wrote as often as he could and told me how proud he was to serve alongside his Rakkasan brothers. Their primary duty was to man the checkpoints at Camp Eagle. His soldiers inspected all the vehicles that entered and exited the safe zone. Larry was steadfast in his mission. It was important work. In their off time, the Rakkasans would do physical training to maintain their fitness and hit golf balls on their makeshift driving range. As always, the game of golf was a great way to build esprit de corps and relieve a little stress.

Back to SPO

Major Riester and I deployed to JRTC twice in four months. Our unit's mission was to stage and push supplies to the maneuver units in the field. My job, specifically, was to track the status of medical evacuation assets; track casualties, medical personnel, and equipment; and push medical supplies to the deployed medical units. Major Riester also taught me about all classes of supply and how to forecast what the troops in the field would need.

At JRTC, I learned about redundant logistics. As a cadet, I was taught not to anticipate commands, but in the logistics world of the real army, it was a good idea to lean forward. We used computer software to forecast what supplies the troops would need and when they would need them. That way, we could go ahead and get the supplies on pallets and rig them for transport before they even asked for them. The supplies would be ready at a moment's notice when the commanders in the field called for them. Once the call came, we would push supplies by helicopter from the logistical package area out to the troops. That gave me an opportunity to serve on the support side of air assault operations.

The logistical package personnel were always looking for soldiers to help hook up loads to the helicopters. They were always busy pushing supplies forward, and I was very happy to help. Many times during those JRTC rotations, I found myself standing on a container, holding an apex fitting or web ring (the part that connects to the helicopter's cargo hook) in my hands. A massive Chinook, which looked more like a flying green school bus than a helicopter, made its approach. Seeing that thing coming straight at me was an incredible rush.

This is nuts! I thought.

As the Chinook got closer, my sling load partner and I crouched into a ready position on top of the container. Fighting claustrophobia and battling rotor wash, we held our breath as the enormous helicopter hovered directly over our heads.

The noise of the rotors was deafening, even through our hearing protection. My partner used the grounding rod and touched a metal fixture on the bird to eliminate the risk of electric shock. Immediately after, I slammed the apex into the cargo hook. Once the load was securely hooked to the bird, we jumped off the container and ran to the safety area. The Chinook bared down and lifted up, carrying the supplies under its belly to the men in the field who needed them.

Onward Movement

The JRTC rotations were over, and Larry returned from Saudi Arabia in the spring of 1997. Larry's mom and dad drove in from North Carolina to see him step off the plane. We hadn't gotten to send him off, but we were there, standing tall, when he returned. There is nothing as patriotic as seeing army superheroes walk out of a military airplane with their gear on their backs. The memory of them marching down the stairs, across the tarmac, and into the hangar brings tears to my eyes even today. I was so proud of them.

Larry was as handsome as ever. His face was golden brown from the desert sun, which made his eyes even bluer. I motioned for his mom and dad to hug him first because I knew once I had my chance, I would not want to let him go. We stayed in the reception hangar for a little while to experience the excitement of a hero's homecoming. Then, we headed home. Finally, our house wouldn't be empty.

Shortly after Larry's return from Saudi Arabia, he went back to Fort Benning, Georgia, for his officer advanced course. We were separated, once again. Always looking out for me, Captain Gray pulled a few strings with my assignment officer and got me into my advanced course a year early so I could try to keep up with Larry. Going to those schools at the same time was a true blessing. It allowed us to move on to our next assignment together.

A Final Fort Campbell Note

As I write this chapter, I do realize that everything I did as a lieutenant in the 101st pales in comparison to the stories of our

Screaming Eagles who have fought and continue to fight in the global war on terror. As excited as I was about all my experiences, I fully understand that I served in a pre-9/11 army. Most of my involvements with casualties and battle losses were simulated, though we did treat a few real-world injuries. We trained as we expected to fight, and I was always ready. On my watch, the call to deploy never came. As I end this chapter, I want to thank all the Screaming Eagles who have served and sacrificed in the name of freedom. We will never be able to adequately repay you. And we will never be able to thank you enough. Air Assault!

Chapter 7

The Land of the Not-Quite-Right

We haven't been in Korea for fifty years.
We've been in Korea one year, fifty times.
—*Captain Dana Rucinski (1998)*

When Larry and I landed at Kimpo Airport in Seoul, Korea, in the spring of 1998, the first thing to hit us was the smell of kimchi. I knew right then and there that it was going to be a very long year. The TV had one channel. There were no commercials, just public service announcements. The *Today* show was on at night, and *The Tonight Show* was on in the morning. We affectionately referred to Korea as the "land of the not-quite-right." It was definitely an interesting place.

We had just completed our advanced courses. Larry went to the infantry officer advanced course at Fort Benning, Georgia, and I attended the combined logistics officer advanced course at Fort Lee, Virginia. Those courses taught us how to be captains and what would be expected of us as staff officers and, eventually, as company commanders.

Early in Larry's advanced course, the infantry assignment manager went down to Georgia looking for a soul to steal—I mean, to work out everyone's next assignment. Each army branch has a group of managers who place officers into their next jobs and help them manage their careers. When Larry met with his manager, he asked to go to the 82nd Airborne Division. The manager told him there were no slots available but he was willing to make a deal.

"If you serve one year in Korea, I'll send you anywhere you want to go afterward."

Sounded like a good deal. So, as a means to an end, Larry volunteered for Korea and asked for Fort Bragg as a follow-on assignment. I did the same.

We stuck with that plan when we got to Korea. Larry received orders to work as a planner in the operations (S-3) shop in the 1-503rd Parachute Infantry Regiment, an Air Assault battalion in the 2nd Infantry Division. Larry was already familiar with air assault operations from our time in the 101st, so his assignment was perfect. I was assigned to the 2nd Infantry (DISCOM), specifically to the division medical operations center. I was excited to work as a medical planner again, especially in Korea's challenging environment.

Because we were married and both on active duty, we could have gone to Korea under the Army Married Couples Program. This would have guaranteed an assignment together, but we would have had to serve two years in country. We were both eager to get to Fort Bragg, so we rolled the dice and went to Korea as individuals and hoped we would be assigned to the same camp. As luck would have it, Larry and I were both sent to Camp Casey. We couldn't live together because of some ridiculous rule (I'll explain later), but our unit headquarters were only a mile apart. We saw each other as often as we could, and since there was only one main road on Camp Casey, we ran by each other almost every day during morning physical training.

Larry quickly settled into his unit and his personal space. He lived in the barracks on the ground floor of the three-floor building. The sterile Army barracks had white tile floors and white walls. His room had a bed, a little kitchenette, and two big wall lockers that he strategically placed to break up his one-room space into a bedroom and a living area. He did have his own bathroom, which was a rare commodity in barracks living. Larry was happy with his room. It was all he needed.

I was not so lucky, right off the bat. My new home was in a

building called the crack house. Its name had nothing to do with drug activity. It got its name because it literally had cracks in the floors, in the walls, and even in the ceiling. We could feel a draft all night, and when it rained outside, it rained inside. It was creepy and full of bugs.

I stayed in the crack house for about six weeks, until a coveted spot opened up in the "super hooch." The super hooch was a three-story barracks building. The rooms were like tiny apartments. Each had a square floor plan with four rooms, one in each corner. Upon walking in the door, the full kitchen was on the right and the bathroom was on the left. It had a nice living space on the far right and a separate bedroom to the left. It was a perfect little one-bedroom apartment and so much better than the crack house.

Larry and I could have easily lived in the same space. It would have been a win-win situation. We could have actually lived together and freed up one of our spaces for someone else. Unfortunately, my command wouldn't let us. They needed everyone to be at arm's reach just in case North Korea invaded. Tactically, that made sense, but still, we were married and had been for four years. It was kind of silly to live so close but have to live apart. We made the best of it, though, and saw each other as often as we could.

Once we were settled into our jobs, Larry and I were happy to serve as staff officers in the 2nd Infantry Division. It didn't take us long to figure out the battle rhythm. We were content to serve our year, mark our time, and earn our spot in the 82nd. We both wanted to command companies in the All-American Division and were well on our way to fulfill our Airborne dream.

He Who Plans First, Plans Twice

The DISCOM personnel officer was reaching the end of his one-year tour and needed a replacement. The clever officer looked through all the Officer Record Briefs of the DISCOM officers. An Officer Record Brief is a spreadsheet that tracks an officer's personnel actions, to include a record of all the jobs he or she has had. It's basically an army-style resume. My experience as the assistant DISCOM S-1 at Fort Campbell sealed my fate. Just as I was getting cozy in the medical operations shop, I was told to report to the DISCOM executive officer. She told me I was the new DISCOM S-1—no discussion, no offer. Tag, you're it! I was not happy.

As the DISCOM S-1, I actually filled two roles: the personnel officer and the adjutant. As the personnel officer, I was responsible for personnel actions (mostly awards and evaluations), officer management (placing the right officer in the right job), and maintaining accountability of all DISCOM personnel (over 2,500 soldiers) during field exercises and alerts. Every so often and usually in the middle of the night, alert sirens would ring all over Camp Casey, and all army personnel would have to report to their units for accountability. We did this to ensure readiness and practice our battle drills just in case the North Koreans attacked, which could have happened at any moment. Lower units would report their personnel numbers to higher units, and those numbers would travel all the way up to us in DISCOM. Then, we would roll them all together and report our numbers to division. Personnel accountability was my most important responsibility.

My secondary responsibility was to serve as the adjutant. The adjutant is an officer who acts as an administrative assistant to a commanding officer. Just as I settled into my new job, the staff began preparing for a change of command. Our senior leader was leaving, and the ripple effects were huge. A change of command calls for event planning and lots of parade practice. It also generates a mountain of paperwork. The DISCOM commander was leaving, so everyone he evaluated had to get a new evaluation report from him. My shop had to work around the clock to process all of the evaluation reports and awards generated by the change of command. It was a busy time.

A brigade-level change of command ceremony is a massive event. We practiced for an entire week. As the adjutant, I played an important role in the change-of-command ceremony. Standing tall on the division parade field, with a 2,500-soldier brigade, the adjutant forms the entire unit and commands the band to sound the adjutant's call. If you've ever seen an army change-of-command ceremony, you'll remember the little guy who has to zoom from the far left side of the parade field and go all the way to the center of the field before the band stops playing. Well, for the 2nd Infantry Division DISCOM change-of-command ceremony in 1998, I was that little guy.

The adjutant's call lasts all of about ten seconds. The division support command sergeant major told me I had to be at my mark, front and center, before the band played the final note of the adjutant's call. And under no circumstances was I allowed to run. I had to walk as fast as I could. I felt, and probably looked, ridiculous. All of my fellow adjutants out there know what I mean. But, praise God, I got to my place before the music stopped and formed the entire brigade without a single mistake. The rest of the ceremony was flawless. I was delighted when it was over.

After the ceremony, the outgoing commander stayed at the parade field to accept well wishes from the crowd, and the new commander hosted a reception at Reggie's, a club on Camp Casey near our headquarters. Hosting the commander's reception was another of my responsibilities. As the event planner, I was responsible for the floor plans, seating charts, nameplates, invitations, military customs and courtesies, Korean customs and courtesies, and the menu. In my role as the adjutant, I became an expert in the art of event planning.

Meanwhile, back in infantry land, Larry was just getting settled in the battalion S-3 shop when the rug was pulled out from under him, too. I think it's funny how you have everything moving in one direction and—*wham*—you get knocked right off course. Okay, I know that even in unstable times God is in charge, but change isn't always easy to accept when we're in the moment. Larry and I were supposed to do our staff time in Korea and then we'd go to Fort Bragg (hopefully the 82nd) to do our company commands.

That was our plan, but as Larry used to say, "He who plans first, plans twice."

A month or two into his time in the 1-503rd S-3 shop, Larry was "volun-told" to take command of the Headquarters and Headquarters Company (HHC). They needed a commander for that unit, and the brigade commander pinned the rose on Larry. This was definitely not his plan. Taking command of HHC changed everything. It gave him credit for command time, restarted the Korea clock, shifted our entire timeline, and caused us to lose our follow-on to Fort Bragg. After allowing himself a moment of grief and grumbling, Larry the warrior and gentleman accepted his new assignment and made the best of it.

As the HHC commander, the battalion staff, the specialty platoons, and the logistical elements fell under his command. Larry's saving grace was the fact that the high-speed scout and mortar sections were also part of the HHC. Having a few *super hooah's* in there with him made it all worth it. He looked forward to going to the field and training with his scouts and mortar men.

Larry invited his mom and dad to come to Korea to watch his change-of-command ceremony. Up to that point, John and Martha Bauguess had never flown in an airplane. John was a long-distance truck driver who never had the need to fly anywhere. Larry called home to tell his parents his wishes, and they agreed to come. After jumping through a few hoops to get passports on time, they embarked on their very first flight, a thirteen-hour one. It was so great to see their faces when we picked them up at the Kimpo Airport in Seoul. They were tired but happy to see us, too. John and Martha enjoyed their time in Korea. I know they were so proud to witness Larry's ceremony. He was honored and proud of them for coming.

Slippery

The coolest member of the HHC 1-503rd family was the company dog named Slippery. That dog was so ugly he was cute! I don't even know what kind of dog he was. Caramel in color and beyond scruffy, he was about the size of Eddie from the show *Frazier*. His teeth were crooked, and he had the craziest under bite. At first glance, you might say that dog was unlovable, but what he lacked in looks he made up for in loyalty, drive, and commitment.

Before the change-of-command ceremony, Slippery would not leave the outgoing commander's side. He matched him step for step. However, during the ceremony when the company guide-on was passed to Larry so, too, passed the dog's loyalty. When the ceremony was over, Slippery was by Larry's side. And he would stay there for the entire year.

Larry had a great whistle. It was very subtle, almost a whisper of a whistle. If Slippery ever wandered off, Larry just did his little whistle and that dog came bounding to him. Slippery went everywhere with Larry. He ran right by Larry's side during company runs. He trained with him and rode in vehicles with him; I even have a picture of Larry and Slippery in a helicopter. He was a great dog who was fit as a fiddle. On the weekends, we would hike up Mount Soyosan, a beautiful mountain outside of Camp Casey with a hiking trail that started right behind Larry's barracks building. It was a pretty tough hike to get to the top, but the view was worth it. Slippery went up with us every time. That dog was the picture of loyalty.

The DISCOM Chicks and a Killer Monsoon

In the DISCOM that year, we had the most amazing group of female officers. Captain Dana Rucinski was the intelligence officer, and Captain Corey Bollinger was the signal officer. Two other high-speed females worked logistics in the Material Management Center, a female major who worked in the transportation office and a medical service captain who arrived a few weeks after me and filled my suddenly vacant medical slot. The seven of us were quite a crew. We called ourselves the DISCOM Chicks.

On the weekends, in the evenings, we would all go down into the local Korean town of Dongducheon and blow off some steam in one of the local clubs. Rare was the night when we didn't belt out "Wide Open Spaces" (a song by the Dixie Chicks) at the top of our lungs. That song meant a lot to us. We really missed the wide-open spaces of America's heartland. Everything in Korea is so cramped, so overcrowded. We longed for home but thrived in each other's company. We would work, travel, shop, eat, and exercise together. I loved those ladies. We had so much fun together. I was so blessed to share that Korea tour with them.

Larry had great men in his company. He especially loved his noncommissioned officers. My beloved husband was an outstanding leader, but he was an even better soldier. He never asked his men to do anything that he wouldn't do himself. He would get right out there with them, going on missions and getting dirty. He loved them, and they loved him.

Larry was blessed to have Lieutenant Colonel Mike Linnington as his battalion commander in Korea. Having served with him in the Rakkasan Brigade in the 101st, Larry already knew he was a great man and an outstanding leader. Lieutenant Colonel Linnington taught his men many lessons, from conducting air assault operations to combating guerilla tactics. But the most valuable lesson his men learned under his command happened during monsoon season.

I awoke to the sound of rain pounding against the windows of the super hooch. The sound reminded me of the heavy rains of my youth in southwest Florida. I rolled over, closed my tired eyes, and let the rain lull me back to sleep with its steady cadence. I love hearing it rain at night—so peaceful, so steady. Sweet white noise. Ah ... sleep.

A half second later, the Camp Casey sirens began to scream.

Are you kidding me? I thought. *What a time for a drill. It's pouring outside. Someone at division has a sick sense of humor!*

We'd had several drills by then, so I was intimately familiar with the alert procedures. I got up, got dressed, and was out the door within a few minutes. Dodging sheets of rain, I went straight to my office to begin receiving the personnel accountability reports.

Sadly, this was no drill. It was a killer monsoon. Before the sirens roared through Camp Casey, the heavy rainfall had already taken its toll on the Korean mountainside. There was so much water falling from the sky that several dams broke in the highlands. The water had rushed down the mountain with such fury that the lower dams didn't stand a chance. The rushing water broke through each dam it encountered and flooded the cement canals that ran through Camp Casey and the city of Dongducheon.

The flooding happened so fast that several soldiers and civilians were pushed into the canals, including one of the assistant division commanders. The brigadier general lived next door to Lieutenant Colonel Linnington in small VIP quarters right at the base of Mount Soyosan. The rushing water overwhelmed the drainage canal and flooded both sets of living quarters instantly. The general had only a moment to escape his building, though he did take time to throw on his beloved cowboy boots.

The escape from his quarters put him into the rush of the water and pinned him to a chain-link fence. The general was a tough man, impressive in size and strength, but the current was unforgiving. He was unable to evacuate any further and in danger of drowning. Once Lieutenant Colonel Linnington escaped his own flooded hooch, he heard the general yell for help. Assisted by a few Delta Company soldiers who were stacking sandbags to help with the flooding, Lieutenant Colonel Linnington pulled the general to safety. Thankful to be alive, he stood on safe ground in disbelief, wearing soaked pajamas and a single cowboy boot.

The day after the harrowing incident, Lieutenant Colonel Linnington gathered his men for a meeting. He told them the general could have died that night and warned everyone that they all had better get their heads on straight because, clearly, no one is guaranteed tomorrow. He told them to have the "if anything happens to me" talk with their wives or parents. He told them to get their paperwork straight and figure out how they will take care of the people they leave behind. The meeting generated some interesting discussion among the men afterward. Larry walked back to the barracks with Captain Frank Jenio, a friend and fellow commander. Along the way, they talked about their wives and families.

Frank told Larry that if anything ever happened to him, he would want his wife, Sherri, to live on and be happy. He would want her to eventually find someone to take care of her and their children. Larry told Frank he would want the same for me. The two of them promised to look after each other's families should anything ever happen to either one of them.

When I saw Larry later that evening, he greeted me with a long and tender hug. We talked about the monsoon and how precious life truly is. Then, we prayed for the people who were affected by the flood. We prayed for the lives that were lost; we prayed for the Koreans who had lost their homes; we prayed for the flooded businesses in Dongducheon; and we thanked God for those who were saved. The next day, Larry and I went to see an army lawyer and drew up our wills.

That Korean monsoon opened our eyes to the reality that we aren't guaranteed tomorrow. Bad things can happen when we least expect them. Serving in the Republic of Korea, we were prepared for a North Korean attack. We trained for that all the time. The plans were drawn and practiced. We knew how to stand up against Kim Jong-il (the dictator of the Democratic People's Republic of Korea, North Korea). But we weren't expecting a killer monsoon. It had caught us completely off guard. We all learned a huge lesson by that.

Family Time

On the heels of the killer monsoon, midway through our Korean tour, I started wondering about our future. Larry and I began talking about having children. We had put off having kids until we were sure we were ready. Actually, Larry had been ready for kids for a long time, but I held us back. I wanted to see how far my army career would take me. But, I'll be honest—when we lost our follow-on to Fort Bragg, my sails deflated a bit. Add to that the monsoon reality check, and I started to shift my focus to what really mattered. I wanted a family. I wanted to have kids. Those feelings grew rather quickly.

Larry and I both had a deep respect for dual military couples who started families and stayed on active duty. That is a very hard thing to do. I had friends at Fort Campbell who would drop their kids off at day care at 5:30 a.m. to make it to work in time for physical training. They wouldn't see their kids again until after work, usually after 6:00 p.m. God bless them. That's really tough. As Larry and I began to discuss starting a family, we talked about how we would manage it. Neither of us wanted to get out of the Army, but we also didn't want a day care to raise our kids. If we were going to have kids, one of us would have to stay home with them.

One night, Larry came to my room and said he would get out and stay at home with our future children. He had the whole thing mapped out. He told me I had a bright future in the Army and that he was willing to follow me wherever my career took us. I considered that for about thirty seconds, smiled at him, and kissed his face. It was a very sweet offer but not what either of us really wanted. He was the Airborne Ranger, the army hooah. He was the one with the brighter future.

After careful consideration and lots of prayer, I sent in my request for release from active duty. It was approved. I would separate from the active duty army in May 1999.

When my tour ended, I had to leave Korea even though Larry would be there for three more months finishing up his command. As we suspected, Larry's follow-on assignment changed because of his HHC command. We learned that he lost the Fort Bragg follow-on. Instead, he would be assigned as an observer-controller at JRTC at Fort Polk, Louisiana.

I left Larry in Korea in April 1999 with a heavy heart. We were used to times apart, but we never liked them. I always got this awful feeling in the pit of my stomach and a lump in my throat when I was away from him. Spending three full months with my mom in Naples, I tried to busy myself by running in the morning, helping her at home during the day, and hitting golf balls in the afternoon. Every moment of my time at home was coupled with pangs of guilt for being stateside while Larry was still in Korea.

As Larry's tour came to a close, we decided to invite his sister, Laura, to accompany me back to Korea for his change-of-command ceremony. She had just graduated from high school and would attend North Carolina State University in the fall. The trip to Korea was our graduation gift to her.

Returning as a civilian, I saw Korea through a different lens. I appreciated it much more as a tourist than I had as a soldier. Laura definitely had an interesting experience, too. She is tall, with beautiful blonde hair and big green eyes. The Koreans loved her! Boldly, they stared at her when we rode the trains. Some of them would touch her hair and look deeply into her beautiful eyes. It was funny. Laura took it in stride and smiled kindly. She was a good sport.

Laura and I wore sundresses to Larry's change-of-command ceremony. On that beautiful July day, it was a luxury for me to sit in the stands as a lady instead of standing on the field as a soldier.

I might just get used to this army wife thing, I thought.

Larry passed the guidon and the company responsibilities to the next commander, pleased with a job well done. Just as expected and right on cue, Slippery's loyalties shifted to the new HHC commander. Losing that goofy dog broke Larry's heart. He was so sad to see his devoted friend walk away, step for step, with a new master. That dog never even looked back.

After the ceremony, Larry had a few things to wrap up. I showed Laura the very interesting city of Dongducheon, kimchi smell and all, while Larry finished out-processing. We bought a few last minute souvenirs and spent one more night in Korea. The next day, we headed down to the Kimpo Airport in Seoul for the last time. We boarded the plane with our hearts fully satisfied by a successful tour.

As the plane lifted off, Larry looked out the window and then said to me with a sideways grin, "I hope you didn't forget anything because we're not going back there to get it."

Chapter 8

Bayous, Babies, and Broken Hearts

One, two, three, four! Hey!
Somebody, anybody start a war! Hey!
—*Old army cadence*

As an army cadet in the early 1990s, I remember singing and running to that cadence. We meant it. We were fired up, young, and conceited. Trained to fight, we wanted to go. We wanted to serve. At a Commando party in February 1991, I remember seeing a world map on the wall with pins in various places. One pin stuck right in the heart of Boone had a tag that said, "Where we are." Another pin stuck in Baghdad had an identical tag that said, "Where we want to be!" The bravado among the Commando ranks was limitless. I kept that motivation throughout my active duty army time. I was fit to fight. I was ready to go, but I didn't realize how ridiculous that cadence was until war found us ten years later.

Larry and I left Korea in the summer of 1999. We took a little time off to visit with family and then made our way to the JRTC at Fort Polk, Louisiana. Several of our peers referred to Fort Polk as the armpit of the army, mostly because it's hot and sticky and sometimes stinky and because it's pretty much in the middle of nowhere.

Honestly, Fort Polk wasn't so bad. Louisiana is a great state. It's beautiful, actually, and rich in culture and character. Geographically,

Fort Polk's surrounding area didn't have much to offer, but if we fanned out a bit, we could find things to do in Alexandria and Natchitoches (the setting of the movie *Steel Magnolias*). Venturing out a bit farther, we could explore New Orleans, Baton Rouge, and Beaumont, Texas. We enjoyed our time at Fort Polk. We learned a lot about the Army and about ourselves, we enjoyed the family time, and we made great friends. During our stay in the Bayou State, our faith in God would be tested, twice.

JRTC

The Joint Readiness Training Center is a critical entity in the Army's war-fighting arsenal. It provides realistic battlefield conditions and scenarios for US Army divisional units (usually light-infantry, brigade-sized elements) and gives them the opportunity to train as they fight. At JRTC, units can fight in an urban environment or out on the open range in an area called the box. Units can test their weapon systems under harsh conditions with live-fire exercises. JRTC goes to great lengths to provide the most realistic environment possible, to include dealing with civilians on the battlefield and embedded media. They even provide a brutal opposing force, the "Geronimos" of the 1-509th Parachute Infantry Regiment. At JRTC, units test their commanders, staff officers, and soldiers under stressful wartime situations. With a critical eye, the JRTC observer/controllers (OCs) evaluate their planning, tactics, initiative, and judgment.

Larry was assigned as an OC for JRTC Task Force One. Since he had commanded a company already, he was considered a branch-qualified captain, which meant he was qualified to evaluate another company commander. At JRTC, he would observe and critique infantry company commanders during their rotation. The OCs evaluated the Blue Force's performance and then presented their findings during after-action reviews in an effort to teach, coach, and mentor the units. The OC task force conducted the after-action reviews openly so they could all learn from their performance and make them even better. I think the entire concept of JRTC is brilliant.

Once we got over the fact that we were not at Fort Bragg, we realized Larry's assignment as an OC was a blessing. He would get the chance to observe company commanders, executive officers, and battalion commanders in almost every brigade in every army light-infantry division while they negotiated a JRTC rotation. Can you imagine the benefit of such an opportunity? It would be like going "under the ropes" during the practice round of every major golf tournament on the PGA Tour for three years in a row, watching and listening to the top ten players in the world and hearing the advice of their swing coaches as they negotiate every shot. Larry was there to observe and evaluate these high-speed units, but he was the one who got the benefit of all those lessons learned. That experience was priceless.

A typical JRTC rotation lasted twenty-eight days from the initial planning at the staging base to the final after-action review. The OCs were involved in the majority of the process. Larry would be in the field about three and a half weeks each month. He would get to come home every three or four days for a refit, which meant he could come home to shower, eat, and sleep for a few hours, and then he'd be gone again. I missed him while he was out in the field, but the non-rotation time made up for it. Between rotations the guys would be home a lot. Most of the time, they would go in to work in the morning to prepare for the next rotation and be home by lunchtime. That was really nice!

Who Am I?

While Larry was enjoying his time at JRTC, I was having a little identity crisis. I had spent the previous nine years as either an army cadet or an army officer. Once I left the active duty army, I found myself asking, *Now what am I?* I answered my own question with, *I'm just a wife.* I hated that. I felt like a doofus when people asked, "What do you do?" or "Where do you work?" I would offer that I had just come off active duty, but then they would always ask, "And what are you doing now?" I'd try to come up with something remarkable to say, but cleaning the house, exercising, and preparing meals sounded so empty.

Larry and I were trying to start a family, but it didn't happen instantly. While I was on active duty, I often stressed out about getting pregnant. If I was a few days late, I'd bargain with God pretty heavily for more time without kids. I found it ironic that when I actually wanted to get pregnant, I didn't. I thought about getting a job or going back to school, but I didn't want to get neck deep in something and then find out I was pregnant. So I wallowed in self-pity, tried to wait patiently for God's perfect timing, and listened to all of the cool stuff Larry was doing. He was jumping out of airplanes and doing all this high-speed JRTC stuff, while I was just hanging out, rearranging the furniture for the twelfth time, and trying to figure out who I was and what I was supposed to be doing.

We lived on post in a tiny apartment across the street from Warrior Hills Golf Course. There was a walking and running trail that went all the way around the golf course. One day, I woke up and realized that I didn't need a label. I didn't need to define my existence. I just needed to live as a child of God. I needed to support my husband and enjoy my surroundings. For crying out loud, there was a golf course right across the street! What was I so upset about? Letting go of my self-pity, I embraced the extra time I had. I filled my days taking care of the home front, exercising, and hitting golf balls. It was really nice to be back on the golf course. It became my happy place.

A few months into our Fort Polk assignment, I finally met some really great ladies whose husbands were also OCs. During the rotations, we would get together for fellowship, exercise, and road trips. Several of us joined a church group at Fort Polk for fellowship and Bible study. Some of the ladies were fitness nuts. Together, we would exercise several times a week. It was nice to maintain some level of fitness because, even though I was no longer on active duty, I was still in the Army Reserves. I needed to stay in shape. While the guys were in the field, we would often make day trips to Alexandria, where there was a mall, a Hobby Lobby, and a few decent restaurants. I thank God for those ladies. Their fellowship was priceless.

Baby Bump

One day, in the middle of February 2000, I started feeling kind of funny and thought, *Could it be?* Without telling Larry, I went to Bayne-Jones Army Community Hospital to take a blood test. A nurse called me at home the next morning. She congratulated me, set up my first prenatal appointment, and tried to end the phone call. It all happened so fast; I was stunned and a little confused.

"Wait, are you sure?" I asked.

"Blood tests don't lie," she replied.

Just like that, my life changed forever. I got off the phone and immediately dropped to my knees and prayed. Thanking God for this incredible blessing, I asked Him to prepare me for motherhood. I asked Him to help me take good care of this precious child. I was so happy.

Later that morning, I went to the store and bought a bunch of little baby gift bags and a few baby items. I placed them on the dining room table and waited for Larry to come home for lunch. He walked in and didn't even see them. I called him into our little dining room area and grinned. He looked at the bags and looked at me.

"Get out of here!" he said with a big ol' grin.

"It's true," I replied.

He gave me the sweetest hug and kiss and then dropped to his knees in front of me. He placed his hands on my belly and started talking to the baby right away. He was going to be a wonderful father.

Air Assault Baby

On the morning of September 6, 2000, Larry was heading out to the field for another rotation. He kissed me (and my growing belly) good-bye and said he'd be home in a few days for his refit. That day, I went for a long walk, drove into town to run a few errands, and relaxed most of the evening. When I crawled into bed that night at around ten o'clock, I felt a funny little pop. I wasn't due for another month, so at first I overlooked it. Then, I started feeling some moisture that couldn't be ignored. I got up and did what most first-time moms would do—I called a friend.

Christine Mullen had three kids. She had hosted my baby shower and coached me through my entire pregnancy. She was a wonderful mother and I was scared, so she was definitely the right person to call. Her husband, Nick, was an OC with Larry.

Christine drove me to the hospital and sent a message through unit channels to my sweet husband. The doctors debated about whether to keep me at Bayne-Jones or to medically evacuate me to a larger hospital in Shreveport. Since I was only thirty-six weeks along, they didn't want to take any unnecessary risks. They decided to keep me, which was a relief because I knew Larry would be on his way as soon as he got the message. I didn't want him to drive in to Fort Polk only to find out that I was in Shreveport.

Christine entertained me until Larry arrived, which wasn't very long, actually. He must have broken the land-speed record because he was there in no time. When he walked into the hospital room, a rush of emotions overtook me. My eyes welled up and I started to cry, though they were happy tears. Larry always brought me such comfort. I was so relieved and so happy to see him. He held my hand, caressed my face, and kissed my forehead. As Larry took over the support duties, I saw my angel Christine slip out the door.

Ryann Jessica Bauguess arrived at 11:01 a.m. on September 7, 2000. She was tiny at five pounds and eleven ounces but such a beauty! Bound to be a protective daddy, Larry was the first to hold her. A moment later, he gave her to me. She had tiny hands, itty-bitty feet, and the sweetest little face. I fell in love with her instantly. The nurses took her to the nursery and did their thing, leaving us beaming with pride and relief. We looked at each other, amazed that we were actually the parents of that precious child.

Larry stayed close to Ryann, providing over watch protection.

I rested in the recovery room. After a few hours, I started to sense that something was wrong. They hadn't brought her to me. I was a newbie mother, but even I knew that mothers and babies needed to bond right away. My heart nearly stopped when Larry came in and said that Ryann was having trouble breathing and they were running tests.

"What does that mean?" I asked.

Against the nurse's orders, I got out of bed and walked with Larry to the nursery. I had to see my Ryann. They had her in a separate room, away from the other babies, with this horrible contraption over her head. It looked like her tiny head was on a cake plate with the glass dome over it. Straight from a nightmare, she was screaming, and I started crying. In a moment of panic, I lifted the dome off her head. I couldn't stand it. I wanted to comfort my child. The nurses immediately yelled at me and told me to leave her alone.

"Leave her alone? She's my baby! Do something to comfort her!" I pleaded.

Honestly, I wanted to beat the life out of those nurses. How dare they yell at me for wanting to comfort my own child? Could they not see her? Could they not hear her cries? Larry did his best to calm me down. He whisked me away, held me, and told me she would be okay. Once I caught my breath, I realized that Ryann needed the oxygen that the awful dome provided. I also realized that the nurses were doing the best they could for her. I had no choice but to accept the circumstance and await further news.

Larry and I sat in the waiting room and began to pray. We prayed out loud, and we prayed silently. I felt so helpless, so scared, and so sad. I felt like a failure. What kind of mother would I be if I fell apart in the first hours of motherhood? I was ashamed of my actions and sorry that I had yelled at the nurses, but at my core I'm a protector and a fixer. I was once a soldier who made things happen, but I couldn't do anything to help Ryann. I just had to wait. One of the hardest things in the world to do is wait.

Finally, we heard some news, though at first I wasn't sure it was good news. The medical professionals at Bayne-Jones decided to medevac Ryann to Lake Charles Memorial Hospital in Lake

Charles, Louisiana. Before we could even process their decision, the medevac team was already preparing Ryann for the flight. They were awesome. They took the time to explain everything to us and took that awful dome off Ryann's precious head. They let me hold her for a few seconds and kiss her before they put her in this little incubator/bed. They quickly secured her and wheeled her down the hall. Watching as the distance between us steadily increased, I was absolutely numb. With every step they took away from me, I felt as if the air was being sucked right out of my chest. I couldn't believe this was happening.

Larry was a pillar of strength through all of it. A few minutes after we got back to my hospital room, we heard the medevac helicopter fire up. The landing pad must have been directly over us. The sound of the rotors carried through the otherwise silent night. Larry and I stood at the window, praying for Ryann. Peering out the window, the helicopter came into view and then disappeared into the midnight sky. Larry gently wrapped his arms around me and kissed my cheek.

"That's my girl!" he whispered in my ear. "On her first air assault mission and she's only eleven hours old."

We were scared and exhausted, but as former Screaming Eagles of the 101st, we just had to laugh at that. We held each other by the window for a few silent moments. Then, Larry kissed my forehead and told me he had to go to Lake Charles. I agreed. Ryann needed her daddy. He drove so fast that he nearly beat the helicopter. In fact, he got to the Newborn Intensive Care Unit (NICU) before Ryann was all set up. He had to wait to see her.

The next morning, I told my doctor I was leaving. My mom had arrived from Florida overnight. Together, we promised the doctor that I would take it easy. He didn't want me to go so soon, but, considering my resolve, he gave in to my wishes. After receiving his instructions, we made an appointment for the next week and left the hospital. Mom and I went by our apartment to grab a few things, and then we got on the road to Lake Charles.

Altogether, we spent eleven prayerful days in the NICU at Lake Charles Memorial Hospital while Ryann recovered from aspiration pneumonia and a few other things I couldn't pronounce or clearly understand. We learned that during her delivery, Ryann had been hit with a one-two punch. Because she arrived early, her lungs weren't completely developed, and during her delivery she took a breath before she should have. The combination of the two was too much for her to handle. So she needed this amazing NICU team, a bunch of scary tubes, and a wall full of monitors to help her fight for her life.

In spite of the bumpy road and dramatic entrance to the world, Ryann made a full recovery. On the eleventh day, we were allowed to take her home. God blessed us with that amazing NICU team and gave us our precious child back with a clean bill of health. We were so thankful.

When we got home, there was a "Welcome Home, Ryann Jessica" sign on our door, lovingly made by one of our army neighbors. In the morning, Larry added a sign of his own. It read,

Dear Friends I have not met,

I was born on 7 Sep 00. I spent the last 11 days in the ICU at Lake Charles Memorial Hospital. I am looking forward to meeting you all very soon, but for the next few days, I would like to spend some quality time with my parents.

Thank you, Ryann.

Ryann was a beautiful baby, and Larry was a wonderful daddy. We kept her inside for her first few weeks. When we thought she was strong enough, we started to venture outside. We loved to take Ryann out for long walks. We would bundle her up, put her in the stroller, and walk on the track around the golf course. Larry would often pack a rucksack and throw it on his back. He was always trying to make himself better, physically and mentally. I absolutely loved our sweet little family.

Jumpmaster

As a member of the JRTC, Larry was on jump status, and he would be the first to admit that he was a "jump chaser." When we graduated from Airborne School, we only had five jumps. We hadn't been in a jump unit until Fort Polk, so Larry had some catching up to do. He tried to get on every jump available. At JRTC, the OCs jumped out of all kinds of aircraft: fixed-wing, rotary-wing, anything. If it flew, Larry would jump out of it. Once he had logged enough jumps, Larry got a slot for jumpmaster school.

Jumpmaster school was very demanding. Academic and hands-on, the course required a lot of memorization. Jumpmasters are the subject-matter experts for everything related to an airborne operation. They plan the operation, inspect the parachutes of fellow jumpers, deliver the prejump guidance and safety brief, and send paratroopers out of the aircraft. They have a huge responsibility.

The toughest part of jumpmaster school is the jumpmaster parachute inspection. I can't tell you how many times I was "inspected" while Larry was in that course. Larry would bring home a jump harness, strap me in, and then inspect me as if I were on the next chalk. Larry was so committed to earning his jumpmaster status that he even practiced on Ryann. She would just lie there and giggle, but he would go through the motions and recite all the checkpoints. All of that practicing came in handy—Larry graduated with no problem at all. I was so proud of him.

OPFOR

One day in early 2001, Larry came home from work and told me that he had an opportunity to interview for a second company command. The 1-509th Parachute Infantry Regiment (the JRTC opposing force unit) had a few company commands opening up, and the battalion commander was beginning the search for replacements. Larry wanted to throw his hat in the ring, and I supported him completely. My husband was at his best when he was working directly with troops. This was a great opportunity for him. We prayed about it and gave it to God. On March 21, 2001, Larry took command of Delta Troop, 1-509th Parachute Infantry Regiment, America's only airborne armored cavalry troop. Ryann was seven months old.

Larry's time in command of Delta Troop was awesome. I dare say, at the risk of offending anyone Larry served with before or since, that year in Delta Troop was the best of his entire career. He had so much fun! He absolutely loved the men he led. They were 19-Deltas (cavalry scouts), and they were totally cool. Infantry scouts are a special breed. By the nature of their jobs, they are out front. They are the eyes and ears of their units and take huge risks. Cavalry scouts are even more special because, well, they are cavalry! But this cavalry scout unit had a special mission as the opposing force on the Fort Polk battlefield. They were airborne and had armored vehicles. They got to be the enemy in tanks. Ruthless in their mission and haggard in their appearance, they got to beat up the best units the Army had to offer. All I heard for a solid year was, "Kill BLUFOR" (Blue Forces, or friendly forces), and boy, did they. (At the risk of insulting your intelligence, I will tell you that they didn't actually kill anyone. All of this was simulated through the use of multiple integrated laser engagement system [MILES] gear. I'll explain that technique in the introduction to Part Three).

Larry was an outstanding leader. He always led from the front and never asked his men to do anything that he wasn't willing to do himself. As the cavalry troop commander, he made the plan and briefed the plan. He (and his sergeants) trained the men, and he went out there with them. Larry wasn't the type of commander to sit in the headquarters and monitor the fight. He was out there doing the fighting. He was killing BLUFOR and having the time of his life.

I ran the cavalry troop family readiness group for Larry. The cavalry ladies were every bit as cool as their cavalry scout husbands. We too formed a special bond, and I was honored to serve among their ranks, even for just a year. Those ladies had been there for quite a while. They were tightly knit, but they welcomed me as one of their own. During the rotations, we would check in with one another. We'd get together for social events and information meetings, and then we would plan a huge lunch for the men every time they returned from the field.

I enjoyed Larry's command of Delta Troop every bit as much as he did. I will always have a special place in my heart for cavalry scouts and their ladies.

September 2001

Our sweet girl had her first birthday on September 7, 2001. Larry's mom and dad came down from North Carolina to celebrate with us. When Ryann opened her presents, she pushed the actual toys aside and played with the wrapping paper and boxes instead. Then, she enjoyed a special birthday cupcake. I've seen other one-year-olds devour cupcakes and cover themselves with icing in the process, but Ryann was incredibly neat and downright dainty as she ate her sweet treat. It was a wonderful day.

John and Martha stayed a few more days and visited with us. We gave them the grand tour of Fort Polk and truly enjoyed their company. They loved spending time with our sweet Ryann and spent nearly the whole visit on the floor with her and her toys. John and Martha are the most wonderful people I know. John is funny, and Martha is warm and so easy to talk to. She always gave me fabulous parenting advice. I am so very blessed to have such good Christian in-laws.

On the morning of September 11, 2001, John and Martha rose before the sun and got ready for their long drive back to North Carolina. Larry had already been to physical training and got back in time to send his mom and dad on their way. After that early morning good-bye, we began preparing for our day. Larry showered and got ready for work. I woke Ryann and fed and dressed her. She was enrolled in a little Mother's Morning Out program at a local church in Leesville, just outside of Fort Polk. It was a sweet little program and perfect for us, as Ryann attended for just three hours on Tuesdays and Thursdays.

That Tuesday morning, a few minutes before 9:00 a.m., we were scurrying around getting ready like any other day. Ryann and I were sitting on the couch, getting ready to put her shoes on, when something on the TV caught my eye. The *Today* show was showing footage of a plane that had crashed into the North Tower of the World Trade Center. I rose to my feet, still holding Ryann, and stood there in disbelief trying to comprehend what I saw. I called for Larry. He was in our bedroom, lacing up his boots.

"Larry? Someone just flew a plane into a building in New York City. How do you make a mistake like that?"

Larry came into the living room just as the second plane flew into the South Tower.

He looked at me and immediately said, "I've got to go. Stay home today."

He kissed us both and raced out the door.

Like all Americans on that tragic day, I was absolutely stunned. My heart sank like a lead balloon. I didn't know what to think. As soon as Larry left, I locked the door and returned to the couch with Ryann on my lap. I hugged and gently rocked her. I couldn't take my eyes off the TV screen. I could barely breathe and didn't move for hours. Larry called and said they were watching everything at work. He told us how much he loved us and said he would be home when he could. I told him to be careful and that we loved him, too.

Hours went by, and I barely moved. I was so stunned at first that I couldn't even pray. But then I realized that's exactly what I needed to do. I couldn't do anything else, but I could pray. With Ryann on my lap, I began to pray out loud. I prayed for the people in the towers, the lost and the trapped. I prayed for the first responders, the firefighters, the police officers, and the families. I prayed for all of New York. Later, as the stories developed, I prayed for the Pentagon and for the flight that went down in Pennsylvania. I just prayed all day; otherwise, I felt helpless and numb.

I could go on and on, of course, describing how I felt that day, but my feelings are insignificant compared to those of the New Yorkers who survived and of those who lost loved ones in the towers of World Trade Center, in the Pentagon, and in Pennsylvania. Even as I type this, I'm not sure I'm qualified to write about 9/11, but at the same time, I realize that we are all connected. Our country was sucker-punched that day. We all lived through it. We were all affected by it. We all have our own stories about where we were and what we did. And even though I witnessed the 9/11 tragedies from the safety of my own home, with my precious child on my lap, the events of that horrific day would lead to the global war on terror and would later bring tragedy to my family. It's all connected. We were all affected.

***
... but we also glory in our sufferings, because we know that suffering produces perseverance.
—Romans 5:3 (NIV)
***

I am proud of how we joined forces as compatriots. We stood together. We loved our nation through the darkest day since Pearl Harbor. We haven't forgotten—well, most of us haven't. I believe we gain strength from adversity and wisdom from challenges. With our hearts and minds safely nestled in our faith in God, we can get through anything.

Fort Knox

In the interest of lightening the mood before I end this chapter, I have to include my favorite Geronimo story. Before leaving his opposing force command, Larry and his men traveled up to Fort Knox, Kentucky, to fire their tanks. They were there for about a week. During some downtime, Larry came up with a team-building exercise. He sent his men on a scavenger hunt, similar to those on the TV show *The Amazing Race*. Pretty cool idea, right?

There they were, scurrying all over Fort Knox, snapping photos of landmarks while wearing their olive-green, Vietnam-era uniforms and boonie hats and sporting their modified grooming standards, which meant they could grow beards. Let's just say they caught the attention of a few MPs.

I was at home playing with Ryann when the phone rang.

"Hello?"

"My husband just called me from jail!" yelled one of the Geronimo wives.

"Oh, my goodness! I'll call Larry."

"He's with them!"

"What?"

"The entire troop has been arrested. The provost marshal at Fort Knox is holding all of them. Your husband got all of our men arrested!"

Wow, was she mad! As she was telling me what she knew, another call came in. I answered the other line, and it was another wife calling to tell me what had happened. This happened several times that night. Finally, Larry called.

"Hello, beautiful. How are my two girls?"

"We're fine. How are you?"

"Outstanding! We had a great day! Good team building."

"I heard. Is this your one phone call from the slammer?"

Larry laughed. "So, you've heard about our little adventure."

"Several times. Got a few phone calls this evening. What happened?"

Larry proceeded to tell me all about their scavenger hunt. The provost marshal had rounded up every last one of them and put them in a holding cell. He kept them there for hours. Larry and his men were used to their own appearance; at Fort Polk, it was common to see a soldier in olive greens and a boonie hat. But at Fort Knox, they looked like foreign fighters. In the wake of the tragedy of 9/11, the military police didn't hesitate to apprehend every one of them.

The provost marshal spoke with the post commander at Fort Polk and, believe it or not, all was forgiven. Larry laughed about the whole thing. And the wives, who were convinced their husbands' careers were over, eventually laughed, too.

Growth and Character Building

While we were stationed at Fort Polk, we experienced great joy and great sadness. Our faith was tested. Ryann's entrance into this world threw us for a loop, but God led us through that storm and blessed us in the aftermath. One year later, our country was attacked. That one rocked us all. But, just like we always do, we persevered. God is good, all the time. At Fort Polk, Larry and I enjoyed the good times, and we stuck together through the bad. He had the time of his life running around with his Geronimos. He learned so much from all the units and all of the JRTC rotations. I learned how to be an army wife and a new mother, and we both drew closer to God. We learned to rely on His strength instead of our own. For us, it was a time of growth and character building. The reward for our faithfulness was realized in the early spring of 2002, when Larry and I received two surprises. We were finally going to Fort Bragg, and we were going to be parents once again.

Chapter 9

Fortress Bragg, Finally

Like the sound of a siren song, oh
Carolina, ya keep callin' me home.
—*Eric Church, "Carolina"*

I absolutely love North Carolina! From the mountains in the west to the coastal flats and beaches in the east, this state has it all. I love the change of seasons. The fall colors, especially in the mountains, are breathtaking. The winter is mild. If we're lucky, we'll get some snow in January and February. We don't get much, just enough to throw snowballs and build a snowman or two. The spring is so beautiful with the redbuds and dogwoods in bloom. The summer is just as hot as Florida's and plenty humid, but it doesn't last nearly as long. I may not have been born in North Carolina, but I got here as soon as I could.

Calling Carolina Home

It took us nine years to return to North Carolina after we received our active duty army commissions. At every turn, Larry and I asked Mother Army to send us to Fort Bragg. Every time, she sent us somewhere else. Finally, in May 2002, she sent us home, though our ultimate goal of serving in the 82nd Airborne Division still eluded us.

In the spirit of taking one for the team, Larry accepted an active component/reserve component (AC/RC) job on Fort Bragg, hoping he would get the chance to serve in the All-American Division eventually. This was certainly not the job of his dreams, but it got us stationed where we wanted to be. In the AC/RC world, active duty leaders acted as teachers, coaches, and mentors to reserve units. The reserve units would come to Fort Bragg as part of their mobilization plan in preparation for deployment. Similar to his duties as an OC at Fort Polk, Larry and his team would take the deploying units out to the field and to the firing ranges to evaluate their aptitude and wartime readiness. In the grand scheme of things, his function was important because some of those reserve units needed a lot of extra coaching. But Larry didn't want to prepare units to deploy; he wanted to deploy. As much as Larry disliked his AC/RC job, it had decent hours and offered us wonderful family time. And Larry did enjoy working with the sergeants and fellow captains on his team.

Two significant events occurred in our AC/RC time (2002–2004) at Fort Bragg. One was joyous and wonderful. The other was tragic and so very sad.

Baby Bundle Number Two

Driving from Louisiana to North Carolina seven months pregnant wasn't my favorite thing to do, but I was so happy to be settled in our new home before the baby arrived. As you'll recall, we had our share of drama with Miss Ryann, so we didn't take any chances with the new baby. I was ready just in case she decided to arrive early. Sure enough, not to be completely outdone by her big sister, Ellie Grace Bauguess decided to bless us with her presence three weeks early. She made her grand entrance into this world on July 23, 2002.

I started having minor contractions at lunchtime. I wasn't nearly as nervous this time around, and it was so different because I had Ryann at home with me. Careful not to alarm her, I called Larry at work. He came straight home to assess the situation. Without a moment's hesitation, he drove us to the hospital on Fort Bragg. The nurses at Womack Army Medical Center monitored me for an hour or so and then let me go back home, ruling it a false alarm. A few hours later, though, I just knew it was time. Larry called his mom, who lived only three hours away. Martha hung up the phone, hopped in the car, and headed our way. A trusted neighbor kept Ryann until Mamaw arrived.

Larry and I settled in at the labor and delivery ward, but we wouldn't be there long. Ellie was tired of waiting and ready for her grand entrance. She arrived so quickly that we didn't even have time for an epidural. I'll be happy to never do that again. But my sweet Ellie, a beautiful and healthy baby, was worth it. From her first moments in this world, I knew she would be quite a character. She was strong, and she was gorgeous. God had blessed us with a healthy baby girl. We were so relieved and so grateful.

The nurses brought Ellie to me right away. This time, I got to keep her, which was a totally different experience from Ryann's arrival. Snuggled up, safe and secure in my arms, she was mine. She wasn't hooked to any machines, and there was no scary dome. She was healthy and breathing on her own. Cooing and staring at me with her big blue eyes, she was the picture of health. I was so thankful.

Martha brought Ryann to see us in the hospital the next day. I noticed that her fingernails were freshly painted bright pink as she bounced into the hospital room. Ryann hugged me and her daddy but wasn't sure what to think of Ellie. She retreated to Mamaw and clung to her for the rest of the visit. It would take some time for her to warm up to her little sister.

The next day, Larry and I brought Ellie home and settled into a wonderful little family of four. Ryann was very helpful to me, but she still didn't pay much attention to Ellie. She loved it when her baby sister slept because she could have me all to herself again. I was mindful to give them each their mommy time. Weeks turned into months, and when Ellie began to scoot and eventually crawl, everything changed. She would set her sights on Ryann and just had to be near her. She wanted to do everything her big sister did. Ryann slowly began to like that idea. She began to see Ellie as a playmate and even as a friend.

Taking Care of Our Own

The second significant event that occurred during our AC/RC time was the untimely death of one of Larry's noncommissioned officers. One of his master sergeants suffered a fatal heart attack in his home late one night. Larry was assigned as the casualty assistance officer, so his job was to take care of the family, offer assistance during the funeral and memorial services, and guide them through the mountain of paperwork that followed. Serving as a liaison between the family and the Army, Larry would also help them make sense of the survivor benefits and entitlements.

Newly assigned as the casualty assistance officer, Larry came home to change into his Class A uniform (the army green business suit) for his first meeting with the master sergeant's widow. That first meeting with the surviving family members had to take place within twenty-four hours of the service member's death. Back then, casualty assistance officers were offered a forty-five-minute training video about how to do their job, handed a folder full of paperwork, and told to go be great. It wasn't the most thorough preparation.

"Wesley, I have no idea what I'm getting ready to walk into. That video was a joke," Larry said as he straightened his tie. "How do you comfort a family at a time like this?"

"Larry, you are a good, good man," I said. "Follow your heart. Treat them the way you would want us to be treated."

He smiled and kissed me good-bye. Larry was a good Christian man. He was a warrior and a gentleman. I knew he would serve them well.

Larry was a wonderful casualty assistance officer and a good friend to the master sergeant's family. He was by their side as they navigated the paperwork jungle, and he was there for the funeral. Having traveled down to Georgia, Larry told me that he was deeply moved by the strength of the family and by the church service. During the service, the preacher declared, "God doesn't make mistakes!" That sermon stayed with Larry. Those words had quite an impact on him. He believed that, too. Larry believed that God has a plan for all of us and that He doesn't make mistakes.

I don't think God does bad things to people. All of our days are numbered. No one lives forever. I believe those who die young accomplished their missions on earth and have been called home. They will never grow old. They will never suffer. They are in a perfect place of peace. It's just really hard on those of us left behind. But I also think God blesses us with the strength we need to get through those tough times. I believe in the saying, "If God leads you to it, He'll lead you through it." I think He gives us little building blocks of experience throughout our lives. If you turn around and look back, you'll see them. Hopefully, it will all make sense. I believe God is very present in our lives; you just have to believe He's there. He is present in my life, for sure, and He was present in Larry's life, too. God led Larry during his service as a casualty assistance officer, seeing him through the difficult time and difficult mission. He learned so much, and I did, too. We were both stronger for it.

Larry served the master sergeant's widow every day for nearly six months, and he maintained contact with her for more than a year after that. I was very proud of him. He didn't look at his casualty assistance officer time as an additional duty or a tasking. He took that mission seriously and deeply cared for that family. During that service, Larry discovered many flaws in the casualty assistance program. He documented all of it in his little green notebook and prepared an extensive after-action report to identify shortcomings in several on-post agencies. I think Larry made the system better. He tried to, anyway.

Larry's casualty assistance officer experience raised several questions about our own mortality, which led to conversations about final wishes and life planning. The whole thing reminded us that none of us are guaranteed tomorrow and prompted us to make the most out of every day.

XVIII Airborne Corps/Iraq Deployment

In May 2004, Larry's AC/RC tour was finally over. He was reassigned to the XVIII (18th) Airborne Corps headquarters. This was definitely a step up from AC/RC and one step closer to his beloved

82nd. The XVIII Airborne Corps was the higher headquarters of the All-American Division, and Larry thought it was his best chance to get his foot in the door. If he did well at corps, maybe they'd get him a slot at division. Larry was assigned to the G-3 Future Operations section. It was a desk job—typical staff officer work—so he didn't absolutely love it. But he did really like the guys he worked with, and he loved and respected his leaders.

We learned fairly quickly that the XVIII Airborne Corps was scheduled to deploy to Iraq in January 2005. Our family time became much more significant in the face of the one-year deployment. Ryann was four years old, and Ellie was two. Hoping for a sweet daddy–daughters bonding moment, I asked Larry if he would tell the girls about the deployment. I thought it would sound better coming from him. In true Larry fashion, he prepared a military-style briefing and a notebook, though he did keep it age appropriate.

One night, he got down on the floor with Ryann and Ellie and showed them the notebook.

"Girls, I have something to show you," he said.

Helplessly in love with their daddy, they gave him their undivided attention. The first page had a picture of President George W. Bush. Larry explained that he was our president and also the commander in chief.

The girls looked at him funny, so he pointed to the picture of the president and said, "This is Daddy's boss." They seemed to get that, so he turned the page.

"Daddy and some of Daddy's friends are going to a country called Iraq to help the people over there."

He pointed to the second page, which was a world map. Larry had drawn arrows to mark where each of us would be. One arrow pointed to the eastern shore of North Carolina, and he wrote, "Mommy, Ryann, and Ellie will be here." The other arrow pointed to Iraq and said, "Daddy will be here." They didn't really understand that, but Larry was prepared. He turned the page.

The next page had a hand-drawn illustration. Larry had drawn a house, complete with green grass and little stick figures of Mommy, Ryann, and Ellie on the left side of the page. Ryann and Ellie giggled as they pointed to themselves. Blue waves symbolized the ocean in the middle. A tent, a stick figure of Larry, and brown sand were drawn on the right side of the page. Larry explained to them that Daddy would be far away helping the people of Iraq for one whole year. He told them that Daddy would be away for every holiday and every birthday, one time. He thought that might help put it in perspective. The girls seemed satisfied with his explanation and then asked if they could go play. Attention span maxed out. Briefing done. Mission complete.

The night before Larry deployed was like any other. He asked for lasagna as his send-off meal. It was so good. Once we were all completely stuffed, Larry cleared the table and did the dishes while I gave the girls a bath. After that, he started packing his gear into his rucksack; a big, black footlocker; and a duffle bag. That's right—the night before he deployed, he started to pack. It never failed; he always waited until the last minute to put his things together. Whether we were packing for a family trip, a month-long field problem, or a one-year deployment, he waited right up to the deadline.

"If you wait until the last minute, it only takes a minute," he would say.

Larry packed according to the published packing list but added a few personal touches. He packed a baseball and two gloves, hoping he'd find time to play catch over there. He decided to take his bat, too, just in case there was time for batting practice. Packing that bat alongside all his other gear wasn't an easy task. He had to pack and repack several times to get it just right. He finally had to place it diagonally in his footlocker and pack everything else around it. I just smiled in awe of his perseverance.

With their jammies on and ready for bed, Ryann and Ellie marched into our living room and offered Larry some coloring books and crayons to take with him. He promised to color pictures for them and send them in the mail as often as he could. Placing them securely into his footlocker, he closed the lid and let Ryann lock it. I kissed the girls good night, and then Larry walked them to their room to tuck them into bed.

Masters of bedtime delay tactics, the girls asked for a bedtime story. Larry grabbed Dr. Seuss's *Hop on Pop*, snuggled up with them, and began to read. Unable to resist the urge to spy, I sat on the floor in the hallway right outside their bedroom and leaned against the wall. He was so good with those girls, such an animated storyteller. He was an amazing daddy.

When he finished the story, he gave the girls each a big hug and a kiss and said he would see them tomorrow. He explained that he wouldn't be at home when they woke up, but Mommy would bring them to his work to say good-bye. They were so tired that they probably would have agreed to anything, so they kissed him good night and fell fast asleep.

As he quietly left their bedroom, Larry found me, with misty eyes, on the floor in the hallway. He sat down next to me, held my hand, and told me everything would be okay.

"Wesley, it's just a year," he said. "Every holiday, one time."

We said good-bye to Larry at Green Ramp on January 24, 2005. Green Ramp is a huge airplane hangar on Pope Air Force Base, just outside of Fort Bragg. Paratroopers stage there before a deployment or a parachute jump. Larry's mom and dad, his sister Laura, and her husband Ben came to see him off. Sitting on the plywood benches, we had a few wonderful family moments. Trying to keep the mood light, we told stories and played "I Spy" with the girls.

When the leaders began the manifest call, we knew it was time to say good-bye. Each soldier sounded off when he heard his name and then grabbed his gear, took time for one last hug, and headed out to board the plane. We watched Larry walk out the hangar door and onto the tarmac. He turned back to give us a smile and a little wave. He was so handsome. His smile still made my heart flutter. We stood motionless in the hangar and watched the XVIII Airborne Corps soldiers board the plane. My eyes welled up, and my throat tightened.

One year. Every holiday, one time.

"It can't be over until it starts, so here we go," I said to myself.

Letters from Daddy

Larry's first letter home was dated January 28, 2005. He wrote about his journey to Iraq, stopping in New York, Rome, and Kuwait along the way. Then, always coaching, he told the girls to ask me to show them all of those places on the map. Larry wrote to us every day. Some letters were long and some were very short, depending on his workload.

In his next few letters, Larry told us a little about his workplace. He said he was getting used to the battle rhythm. The XVIII Airborne Corps was operating as the Multinational Corps in Iraq. Its headquarters was located in one of Saddam Hussein's former abodes. Larry said the palace was huge. He and his fellow majors worked on the joint operations floor. In the great big room were rows of desks on multiple levels, like bleachers in a stadium. He worked as a fragmentary order writer, which means he wrote updated orders for the maneuver units. Larry wasn't crazy about working behind a desk when others were patrolling the streets and kicking down doors, but he didn't spend all of his time on the joint operations floor. He did get to go out several times, including several trips to Tikrit.

The girls and I were getting used to our own battle rhythm at home. Ryann was in prekindergarten, and Ellie was in a little preschool class at our church. We had plenty to do to fill our days, but we sure missed Larry. We heard from him more often than I ever thought we would. He called almost every day.

Larry sent us letters and beautifully colored pictures from the coloring books Ryann and Ellie had given him. He was so funny. I could just picture him in Iraq, this tough infantryman, coloring pictures for his daughters. He said it was a good stress reliever. The guys Larry worked with teased him at first, but then they asked if they could color pictures for their kids, too. Our girls loved it! We hung every picture on their bedroom walls. By the end of the deployment, their room was covered with pictures from their daddy. We still have most of them.

Larry also started a tic-tac-toe game to maintain a connection with us while he was in Iraq. He drew the tic-tac-toe board in crayon on a piece of notebook paper and mailed it home. The girls would make their move, and we would send it back. The mail was taking about two weeks each way, so every game would last several months. It was a great way to pass the time. The girls loved getting that tic-tac-toe letter in the mailbox. We played four or five games during the Iraq deployment, and Larry let them win every time. The girls loved that, too!

I can't tell you exactly what Larry and his fellow soldiers did while they were in Iraq, but I do know that they did great work. Our soldiers helped a lot of people, and they left Iraq better than they found it. I am very proud of them all. I recently found a letter from Larry dated January 30, 2005, which was election day in Iraq. Unsure of how the media was covering that historic day, Larry wanted to report to us what he witnessed. He said he was so proud to be in Iraq at that time, and he was proud of the Iraqi people.

In the letter, he wrote, "Everyone who does not exercise their right to vote in the U.S. should have been here today."

If an incident happened at a polling location, the people would take cover, tend to the wounded, and then get back in line. They were so dedicated, holding fast to the dream of democracy. Larry said it was amazing. He was grateful to witness it. My heart breaks now, though. Our soldiers and our allies did such good work over there. It's such a shame to see it all fall apart.

Homecoming

Larry and the XVIII Airborne Corps returned home in January 2006 after a remarkably successful Iraq deployment. The girls and I met him at Green Ramp and beamed with pride when we saw him march into the hangar with his unit. The excitement in the hangar was electric. We couldn't wait to hug him. As soon as the commander said, "Dismissed," family members rushed in to find their soldiers. It was such a joyous moment!

Larry's hard work in Iraq didn't go unnoticed. The XVIII Airborne Corps chief of staff, Colonel Jim Huggins, was well aware that Larry wanted to go to the 82nd. Larry must have impressed his boss because, upon his return from Iraq, Larry learned that his next assignment would be a field grade position in the 82nd Airborne Division. Finally, he would get his chance to serve in the All-American Division. Praise God! Patience and perseverance finally paid off.

Chapter 10

Living the All-American Dream

The 82nd Airborne, to defend what's right we have
sworn ... yes the 82nd Airborne ...
will be there!
—*82nd Airborne Division All-American Chorus,*
"We Were There"

I absolutely adore the 82nd Airborne Division and will love them forever. Paratroopers of the All-American Division have participated in military campaigns from World War I and II to Vietnam, Granada, and Kuwait to the global war on terror in Iraq and Afghanistan.[1] They are America's Guard of Honor. They have my undying love because when they were needed, they were there, every time. I would love for every American to listen to the 82nd Airborne Division All-American Chorus sing the song "We Were There." You can find several renditions of it on YouTube. Listen to the words, and you'll receive a fabulous history lesson. If this song, and the service and sacrifice it represents, does not move you, you might want to check your pulse and take a good long look at your level of patriotism.

2 Fury

Larry reported to the 82nd Airborne Division in April 2006. It took us thirteen years, but we were finally members of the All-American Division. Assigned to the 4th Brigade Combat Team, whose motto was "Fury from the Sky," Larry served as the battalion executive officer for the 2-508th Parachute Infantry Regiment. In that position, Larry was the second in command and served as the commanding officer's chief of staff. It was his job to make sure the staff officers of the battalion did their jobs, but he also made sure they had everything they needed to perform well.

Larry was an awesome teacher, coach, and mentor. His men respected him for that. He didn't just bark orders and tell them what to do. He showed them, always striving to make everyone around him better. For the rest of the spring, Larry became one with the battle rhythm of his new unit. He enjoyed getting to know the paratroopers of the "2 Fury" battalion.

In true army style, once you get the hang of something, it changes. Summertime is change-of-command time at Fort Bragg. For 2 Fury, that meant welcoming a new battalion commander. Actually, nearly every battalion and most of the companies changed leadership that summer. The brigade was changing leadership, as well. A whole new crew of commanders was coming in—new blood, fresh motivation, lots of changes.

Larry was eager to get to work with his new commander, Lieutenant Colonel Tim McAteer. I was motivated, too. As the battalion executive officer's wife, I wasn't exactly sure what my role would be in the family readiness group, but I knew I wanted to help take care of our military families. In the spirit of camaraderie and to map the way forward, Lieutenant Colonel McAteer and his wife, Shon, invited us to their house for dinner shortly after the change of command. They were a great couple and a wonderful family.

Shon and I got along very well right from the start. She had served on active duty, too. We both loved the Army and looked at leadership in similar ways. But Shon had accepted a teaching position for the fall and wasn't sure she would have the time to fully dedicate herself to the battalion family readiness group, so she asked me if I would like to run it. I thought about it for a moment and felt led to accept.

Running a battalion family readiness group required a pretty hefty time commitment. Leaders would have to attend monthly meetings at division headquarters to receive information about upcoming events, after which we'd go to the brigade meeting. Brigade would filter through the division information and offer brigade-specific guidance. We would then take all the information from both meetings and lead our battalion meetings. Information rolled all the way down to each member of our unit family. Information dissemination was the most critical aspect of military family readiness. We had to push the message down to the user level as quickly as possible.

Hitting the Ground Running

Keeping up with the workload of the 82nd Airborne Division is like trying to drink water from a fire hose. For the remainder of 2006, the battalion would conduct a summer training camp for the cadets at the United States Military Academy at West Point; take a trip to Afghanistan; conduct a JRTC rotation at Fort Polk; and prepare for their upcoming deployment in support of Operation Enduring Freedom Eight. That's right—as soon as we got our feet on the ground in the 82nd, we learned about their February 2007 deployment to Afghanistan.

Larry enjoyed the summer at West Point, especially since the weather was significantly cooler there than at Fort Bragg. The West Point summer camp reminded him of our college ROTC days. We had such a good time as army cadets learning soldier skills, patrolling through the woods, and negotiating obstacles to get to the objective, and he enjoyed providing a similar experience to the West Point cadets. The camp also offered a bonding opportunity for the paratroopers and leaders of 2-508. At the end of the summer, they all came together for a pig pickin' to celebrate a job well done.

Larry didn't actually stay at West Point the whole summer. About midway through, he and other battalion leaders began the plans for their October JRTC rotation and their subsequent deployment to Afghanistan. At one point that summer, Larry flew from New York to Louisiana for a JRTC planning conference. Then, he flew to all the way to Afghanistan with several other leaders to perform a predeployment survey. During the survey, our leaders walked the land that would become their outpost and inspected the existing infrastructure. They took pictures and began developing their logistics and force protection plans for the deployment.

While Larry was busy jetting between New York, Louisiana, and Afghanistan, the girls and I had an adventure of our own. We were moving to a brand new house. We said good-bye to our tiny three-bedroom, ranch-style duplex (circa 1950) on Lemuy Street and said hello to a brand new house about a mile away. We didn't move far and remained on post at Fort Bragg, but an army move is an army move no matter the distance. Our new house was a two-story townhouse with four bedrooms. We were delighted with the extra space, and the move actually went very well. After a long and crazy summer, Larry came home to a totally different house.

2 Fury Family Readiness Group

When the troopers returned to Bragg that fall, they began training for their upcoming JRTC rotation and their follow-on deployment to Afghanistan. The paratroopers were extremely busy training for combat. They focused on weapons training, marksmanship, soldier-skill proficiency, and airborne operations (jumping out of airplanes). The staff was busy writing operation orders and pulling together all the logistics necessary for the rotation and the deployment. While the battalion was getting themselves battle-ready, so, too, was the family readiness group.

In early fall, Lieutenant Colonel McAteer and I had our first family readiness group leadership meeting and developed our family readiness training plan for the battalion. We used a training matrix, much like the soldiers use, to help prepare our families for the deployment. The matrix had a deployment timeline and included tasks such as collecting contact information for our paratroopers and their family members. This was not to invade their personal lives; it was to help us disseminate important information to our families during the deployment. We needed to make sure our personnel rosters were current and had correct contact information for each family member. The matrix also advised us to offer organizational and communication classes to our company group leaders and encouraged us to schedule fun activities for the family members to help relieve some of the stress and worry that comes with a yearlong deployment. In order to accomplish all of the tasks on our deployment matrix, we needed to create a steering committee and schedule monthly meetings.

In September, we brought the company commanders and company family readiness group leaders together to form the steering committee and share our group training plan. We would continue to have steering committee meetings every month thereafter. During the meetings, we went over the battalion calendar and discussed the unit's upcoming events. We planned classes, discussed communication strategies, and worked on our unit rosters.

In a nutshell, our job in running a family readiness group was to take care of families. We would provide as much information to the family members as we could. We'd provide fun activities as distractors and stress relievers and do our best to come together to inspire endurance during a wartime deployment. When deployed soldiers know their families are taken care of at home, they are able to completely focus on the battlefield. I recognized this and promised to do everything I could to help make that happen.

Getting Real

While family readiness groups, in general, like to focus on planning fun events for their families, not everything in that world can be fun and uplifting. One of the items on the deployment matrix was the highly emotional, yet realistic, task of preparing for casualty operations. No commander ever wants to admit that he may not bring everyone home. The ultimate goal, of course, is to bring all service members home alive and well. But Larry would be the first one to say, "Hope is not a method." Facing a twelve-month deployment and thinking that we wouldn't suffer a significant injury or a loss would be just plain foolish. I knew we needed to be prepared, just in case.

For our October steering committee meeting, just before the unit deployed to JRTC, our battalion asked the division's casualty assistance office to give us a class on casualty notification and assistance. The instructor walked us through the notification procedure for a fallen soldier. Communication travels through official channels from the battlefield back to division headquarters. Division will assign a notification team, which consists of an officer and a chaplain. The notification team will notify the next of kin in person. For the battle injured, it was a little more complicated, but the instructor said it is common practice for the injured soldier to call home him- or herself, when and if he or she is able to speak. In the case of the severely injured, a phone call will come from a commander or a medical professional. All of this was good information to know, but no one ever wanted to experience it.

Care Team

Later in October, our brigade leadership coordinated a care team class for the battalion family readiness group leaders. A care team is a small group of family readiness group members who serve a unit family who has suffered a tragedy, such as a loss or serious injury or illness. Care team members serve within the home of a new widow or the spouse of a severely injured soldier. Delicately, they answer the phone and receive visitors, gifts, and flowers. With an abundance of compassion, they protect the family, provide comfort, and keep the household running.

An army community service instructor conducted our class.

She gave us an overview of what a care team was and why it was important. She told us it was something we had to do, but she really didn't tell us how to build a program. It reminded me of Larry's casualty assistance officer experience when we first got to Fort Bragg when they showed him a video and said, "Go be great." After the army community service class, the care team concept weighed heavily on my heart. I knew I had to build one; I just needed to figure out how to do it well.

I looked through the class materials at home the next day. The official definition of a care team, as stated in the Army Community Service Operation Ready Care Team training class, is, "A group of trained individuals from the unit's FRG (family readiness group) that support individuals/families for a determined period of time after a trauma or crisis."[2]

The commander was responsible for the overall Care Team Program, but it would be the ladies of the family readiness group who actually served in this capacity. I continued looking through the care team papers and found one quote (from the Army War College, Spouses' Project of 2004) that put the entire program in perspective:

> Responding to a tragedy is an overwhelming experience. We will always feel inadequate when faced with the emotions and the enormity of what has happened. That is why we must think about it now. We must be as prepared as possible ... we owe the soldier that much.[3]

Providing comfort to a family in a time of crisis was a huge responsibility. I was overwhelmed just thinking about it. But there was no time to be fearful. I knew we had to build a care team program for our battalion. We had to train our ladies to be able to serve a family in need. We couldn't just fly by the seat of our pants. We needed to be prepared. Maybe if we were totally prepared, it wouldn't happen.

Hitting Home

With a heavy heart, I will tell you that the 82nd Combat Aviation Brigade suffered a horrible loss shortly after our brigade care team class. That unfortunate event really hit home. In a delicate moment, I got the opportunity to ask one of the Combat Aviation Brigade family readiness group leaders how the family was doing and if the unit was providing a care team. She told me the family was doing as well as could be expected and was receiving help from their unit care team.

"I feel horrible for asking at a time like this, but would you share some of your care team procedures with me?"

"I'd be happy to," she responded.

A few hours later, she sent me eight e-mails full of care team products, which included training slides, nearly a dozen corresponding handouts, and the entire contents of something she called the family binder. She had received all of it from a friend of hers in the 101st. It was a perfect "how to" package. I thanked her for her compassion and generosity. Then, I went to work.

I read through every bit of information she had sent me. I don't think I even slept that night. During the course of the next few days, I dissected the information, adjusted a few things, and made it our own. I tailored the slides and the supporting handouts to fit our unit, and I built our own family binder. The family binder was a notebook that would stay in the home and become the go-to guide for all information. It had several sections and included a telephone message log, gift and flower delivery logs, a meal plan matrix, and a section for important family information.

Once I finished all the care team products, I laid my hands on them and prayed, asking God to protect our paratroopers. I asked Him to go with them to JRTC and to Afghanistan. I nearly begged Him to bring them all back home again. I told Him I never wanted to actually use any of the care team materials. I never wanted to stand up a care team for any of the 2 Fury families. With my head bowed and my eyes closed, I gave it all over to God. I put it all in His hands. Then, I stood up and put everything on the shelf and waited for the right time to present the Care Team Program to the battalion family readiness group.

Stealing Moments

In preparation for the JRTC rotation and follow-on deployment, Larry was working really long hours. Though I missed my husband, I never complained. I was just glad he was living his dream serving in the 82ⁿᵈ Airborne Division. He was a battalion executive officer, working with great noncommissioned officers and young officers, and jumping out of airplanes. It just doesn't get much better than that. He was as happy as a pig in mud. And I was happy, too. I'd take him coming home at 10:00 p.m. every night if he came home happy.

Having said all of that, the hours away from us took their toll on Larry. He didn't want to be away from us for as long as he was, but the mission dictated his hours. He would be up most mornings by 4:30 a.m. He was already at work when the girls woke up for school. By the time he came home at nearly ten o'clock every night, the girls were already fast asleep. He never saw them awake. To remedy this, we would bring him lunch and dinner on a regular basis. He had to see his girls, and we had to see him. I would make him something at home or zip through a drive-through, and we'd deliver his meal to him at the battalion. Sometimes, he would meet us in the parking lot. Sometimes, we'd go into the conference room and eat together, and other times, I'd make a full pan of lasagna so he could share it with his guys. Those days, we'd only get ten or fifteen minutes with him, but it was so worth it.

Larry's workload and crazy busy weekdays led us to value the rare moments when he was home. We spent every moment of the weekends together and really protected that time. He would play with the girls all day on Saturdays. They loved to climb on him and wrestle. Sometimes, we would all cuddle up together to watch a movie or a football game. It didn't matter what we were watching as long as we were together. In the evenings, Larry and I would sit on opposite ends of the couch and rub each other's feet. Ryann and Ellie would see this and climb up on our laps and start rubbing each other's feet, too. It must have looked ridiculous, all four of us on the couch rubbing each other's feet, but it was relaxing and good bonding for all of us.

JRTC

The battalion deployed to JRTC in late October. Just as JRTC offered the troopers a practice deployment before the real one, it offered the same for the family readiness group. It gave us a chance to test our rosters by making phone calls and sending out e-mails. We quickly discovered that e-mail was much more effective and way faster, but we still maintained a phone roster as the secondary method of communication.

We had our first battalion steering committee meeting without the commanders in the first week in November. After we checked on everyone and discussed the calendar, I introduced the care team concept. Speaking softly, I looked each of them in the eyes to make sure they were with me. Then, I told them that we needed to prepare ourselves to serve our families in the event of a serious incident or the death of one of our troopers. Every one of those ladies nodded in agreement. Not one of them looked down or broke eye contact with me. That told me that these ladies were tough.

After showing them the care team slides and explaining the family binder, we decided that we would train our ladies ourselves. Once they were trained, they would become part of a battalion pool, standing ready to serve as needed. I would train the company family readiness group leaders first. Then, we would open the class up to all the adult 2 Fury family members who wanted to serve.

Presto Change-o

The paratroopers of 2-508 had a successful JRTC rotation. Larry called me shortly after the exercise ended. He didn't have much time to talk, but he wanted me to know how proud he was of the battalion and said he was ready to go to war with them. I was delighted to hear they had done so well. I told him we did great, too, and that the family readiness group was developing strong bonds. Our phone call was brief, but Larry said he would call again. His next phone call came a few hours later.

"Are you sitting down?" he asked.

"Uh-oh. Is this a good thing or a bad thing?" I replied.

Bracing for the worst, I hopped up on the kitchen counter, took a deep breath, and told him I was set.

He paused for a moment and said, "We're moving."

"Get outta here! I just got this house settled. I literally just unpacked the last box."

"No, no, no. Not physically moving. I'm moving to a new battalion."

Momentarily, I was relieved, but Larry did not sound happy. I asked him if he was going to 1-508, the other infantry battalion.

"No. Are you ready for this? We're going to the special troops battalion."

"I'm sorry—the what?"

Larry repeated himself, but I told him I didn't understand. He told me that the 4th Brigade Special Troops Battalion was composed of engineers, military intelligence, military police, chemical recon, and signal elements. However, the battalion would be landowners in Afghanistan. They would have to provide their own force protection and would go out on missions looking for bad guys, just like the infantry battalions. Since the 4th Brigade Special Troops Battalion isn't an infantry battalion, Colonel Martin Schweitzer, the 4th Brigade Commander, wanted their operations shop (S-3) to be infantry heavy. Larry was tagged to be the battalion operation officer (S-3) and given the mission to build an infantry presence in that battalion.

I took all of that as a compliment. Larry was a strong leader and a brilliant tactician. I was so proud of him and proud that Colonel Schweitzer saw that in him. Then, I realized what the move meant for me, and I became selfishly angry. I had done so much work for the 2-508 family readiness group. We were really starting to bond, and I loved the group leaders. I couldn't believe I had to walk away from those ladies. For a moment, I thought about staying with 2-508 but realized that would be a poke in the eye to the new battalion. Eventually, I accepted the move, but I didn't say anything to anyone until Larry came home from JRTC.

Wanting to leave a strong legacy, I built a thorough continuity book for the next 2-508 family readiness group leader. The two-inch binder had a table of contents and multiple sections. I wrote about everything we had done since early summer and included a list of the agencies and units with whom I had been working. I was hoping the book would help with the transition. When we left the 2-508, a new leader hadn't been identified, and I felt really guilty for leaving them that way. I wasn't sure what the new battalion would mean for me. But I made a promise to myself that I would still do everything I could for 2-508. That battalion will always have a special place in my heart.

"Hey, Kool-Aid"

The new battalion was a different world for us. Having always served in an infantry unit, Larry was used to infantrymen who were squared away, in word and deed. He really hadn't ever worked with female soldiers, even though he was married to a super-squared-away one. Culture shock hit him right in the face when he walked into the 4th Brigade Special Troops Battalion headquarters for the very first time. As Larry entered the building, a young female soldier was walking out. Being the gentleman that he was, Larry held the door open for her.

She said to him, "Thanks, man," and walked on by.

Thanks, man? Larry came unglued. For those of you who do not understand proper military bearing, "Thanks man," isn't it. Though Larry was often laid back when it came to military bearing and military courtesies, he couldn't let that one go. The new battalion didn't exactly make a great first impression on Larry, but Larry certainly gave that unfortunate female soldier a lasting impression of him.

I think it goes without saying that Larry was less than pleased with the entire situation. But, in true Larry fashion, he got over it just as quickly as he had gotten under it. He let himself be mad for about a day. Honestly, I was mad, too. Then, we met Lieutenant Colonel Steve Baker, the commander of the Diablo Battalion, and everything was right in our world again. To know Steve Baker is to love him. He's a great leader and a brilliant engineer with the mind of a warfighter. He's humble and genuine; his paratroopers knew that he cared for them. Recognizing that Lieutenant Colonel Baker was a warrior and a gentleman, we figured he and Larry would get along just fine.

Newly committed to the battalion, Larry began to build an outstanding S-3 shop. Knowing that they would be landowners in Afghanistan, Larry was determined to get his men and women battle ready. The battalion's area of responsibility would be Forward Operating Base Gardez, in the Paktia province. Larry said it was a high-traffic area for the Taliban, who used that area to travel between Afghanistan and Pakistan. Larry was committed to block the pass. He was convinced that they were going to make history.

Larry got his shop ready both mentally and physically. One of the S-3 captains once told me about a road march they conducted during morning physical training. About halfway through the road march, Larry made them stop. Thinking they were taking a break, the troopers dropped their rucks and prepared to rest. Instead, Larry made them carry one another up and down a hill, over and over and over again. He told them that they never knew when they might have to carry their buddy off the battlefield. He was getting them battle ready.

When we were reassigned to the battalion, I wasn't sure where I would fit in. Major Ken Ratashak was the battalion executive officer, and I quickly learned that his wife, Shanna, had just taken over as the battalion family readiness group leader. Shanna is wonderful. She is so funny and has a sweet and tender soul. Once we got our feet on the ground at the battalion, Shanna asked me if I would like to help her. Delighted to have the chance to continue in that role, we decided to lead the family readiness group together. We quickly developed a wonderful partnership.

Shanna let me take the lead with the Care Team Program. Agreeing that it was a critical aspect of the group, Shanna began to recruit ladies for our battalion team. Just like 2-508, we taught our company family readiness group leaders first and then extended the class to the battalion ladies. Leading up to the deployment, Shanna and I had several meetings with Lieutenant Colonel Baker. We briefed him on all of our family readiness group plans, and he always supported us. We were going to have a great partnership with him, as well.

As Larry continued preparing the 4th Brigade Special Troops Battalion for their deployment, he began to realize something weird about their unit name. Even though he had gone on the predeployment trip to Afghanistan as a member of 2-508, he paid attention to what the other battalions in the brigade were going to do. He recalled that the 4th Brigade Special Troops Battalion of the 82nd Airborne Division was replacing the 4th Brigade Special Troops Battalion of the 10th Mountain Division. He found that confusing. Every time someone said, "4th BSTB," others would wonder, *Which one?* Realizing that several army divisions have a 4th Brigade Special Troops Battalion, Larry decided to make a change.

He started calling his group the 508th Special Troops Battalion because they were members of the 508th Parachute Infantry Regiment. Larry changed his letterhead to reflect the name change and put "508th STB" on all of his briefing slides. Lieutenant Colonel Baker knew he was doing that and agreed that it was a good way to provide clarity. Larry's idea spread like wildfire, and soon enough all the paratroopers were "drinking the Kool-Aid" and calling themselves 508th STB. I started calling it that, too, and soon the family readiness group ladies followed in kind. It was pretty cool.

Predeployment Stress

The reality of the deployment started sinking in when we got back from the Christmas holidays. It was January 2007, and block leave was over. We only had one month left with Larry. He was working late hours again, and we didn't see him very much. Taking him lunch and dinner was the only way the girls could see him during daylight hours.

In mid-January, the battalion conducted a huge predeployment briefing. Shanna and I spoke about the family readiness group. She talked about group meetings, family rosters, and the events calendar, and I gave a "once-over-lightly" about care teams. We wanted to tell our families that our battalion was ready to serve if something should happen to one of our troopers or family members. On that subject, we chose our words carefully. We wanted the troopers to know that we had total confidence in them and believed they would be completely successful. We just wanted the troopers and their families to know that we were committed to take care of our own in the event of a tragedy.

The weeks leading up to the deployment went by way too fast. As a family, we were really busy. One weekend before he left, Larry found the time to update the notebook he had put together before his Iraq deployment. He kept the first half of the book the same. President Bush was still on the front page. The Iraq maps and pictures were in there, too. Behind them, he added a few new maps of Afghanistan and drew the arrows again. He talked to Ryann and Ellie about the deployment in his special Daddy way. Showing them the maps, he told them this time he was going to help the people of Afghanistan. He even said he was going to help find Osama bin Laden and stop him from hurting anyone else.

Larry was so good with those girls. He was always a warrior and a gentleman, even with four- and six-year-old little girls. He wasn't home much in those days, but when he was he put everything else away and dedicated himself to us. He was such a good daddy and wonderful husband.

The days leading up to a deployment can be very stressful. Larry was still working crazy hours. We barely saw him, and he wasn't even deployed yet. One Saturday night, I let the stress monster get the best of me. I lost my cool over something one of the girls did at the dinner table. I don't even remember what it was. Larry calmly intervened and suggested I go upstairs to catch my breath. Sensing that I was coming unglued, we both realized that a little quiet time would do me good. When I reached our bedroom, I threw myself on the bed and burst into tears. I cried so hard that I couldn't even breathe. Honestly, I didn't even know what I was crying about; I just needed to let it out.

After Larry gave the girls their bath and tucked them into their beds, he came in to tend to me. I was still sobbing. This was not like me. I was an army veteran, for crying out loud. I was tougher than most. That night, though, wrapped up in his arms, I told Larry I was scared.

"What if you don't come back?" I asked, quietly. "What if something horrible happens? What if you get really hurt? What if the Taliban captures you? What would they do to you?"

I filled the room with "what ifs."

Larry said to me, "Wesley, God will be with me, and He'll be with you, too."

He had such a peace about him. He always did. He held me and kissed me and comforted me. His warmth gave me strength. I slowly started to feel better as he rocked me in his arms.

Then he said, "I am coming home to you, Wesley. I promise."

The Last Minute

In preparation for the deployment, all the paratroopers had to update their paperwork: wills, powers of attorney, emergency data forms, and life insurance forms. All of this is incredibly important. Larry was so busy in those last few weeks that he didn't have time to do his updates. He made sure his soldiers were squared away, but as a leader, he just couldn't find the time. He finally got it done the day before he left.

"If you wait until the last minute, it only takes a minute," he announced as he walked in our front door, carrying updated power of attorney and emergency data forms.

He also had new insurance paperwork and a new will. As I placed the new forms in our important papers notebook, I saw the page we had filled out way back in 1996, when Larry had deployed to Saudi Arabia. I studied it for a few minutes.

"Larry, do we need to update this?"

"Nope," he said. "It's all good."

I sat at our kitchen table in silence as he scurried around packing the last bit of his gear. Noticing my stillness, Larry stopped what he was doing and sat down next to me. He put his hand on my leg and looked me in the eye.

"I'm coming home, Wesley. Just file that stuff away."

I did as I was told.

I helped him with his last-minute packing. Then, we went up to bed for what would be the last time.

Saying Good-Bye

The next morning, February 3, 2007, Larry was up and at work before the rest of us even started to rise. At around eight o'clock, I woke the girls, dressed them, and prepared breakfast. Just like every other Saturday, they nibbled on cereal and mini muffins while watching the *Disney Channel* and then played with their toys. Larry's parents arrived at around eleven o'clock. They wanted to be there for Larry and for us.

The day was heavy, the air was still, and the tension was thicker than it had been on Larry's previous deployments. He hadn't even left yet, but my heart was aching already. The cold, gray February sky matched my mood.

We were at home, waiting for him to call to let us know when to come to battalion for the final farewell. When Larry had deployed to Iraq, we got to go to Green Ramp and actually watch them board the plane. This time, we were only allowed to say good-bye at the unit. Honestly, I'm not sure which is better. I think it may be easier to say good-bye in the battalion area because then it's done. It's like ripping off a bandage; you just do it and move on. But on the other hand, maybe it's harder because you know that your paratrooper stays in the hangar at Pope Air Force Base for hours before he gets on the plane. That is precious time you could be spending together. You could have one more kiss, one more hug, one more touch. Knowing you are so close and yet so far away is really tough.

By midafternoon, Larry called to tell us it was time. While he was drawing his equipment from the arms room, I took the girls and Larry's parents to the battalion headquarters building. John and Martha met Lieutenant Colonel Baker and some of the men and women who worked with Larry. Every one of them had such wonderful things to say about Major Bauguess. John and Martha were beaming with pride. After Larry drew his weapon, we met him outside and walked with him to turn in his rucksack.

Before long, it was time to say good-bye. My heart ached as Larry hugged his mom and his dad, and the air was literally sucked from my chest as I watched him kneel down to hug and kiss the girls. After a long moment with his girls, he stood and looked at me.

I could see tears in his eyes. That was the beautiful blend I loved so much—warrior and gentleman, strength and compassion; a true hero embodies both. I was so proud of him. He and I hugged and kissed and held each other close. Soon, the girls and Larry's parents joined in. We all huddled close for a group hug and stayed together as long as we could. We all had tears in our eyes. We didn't want to let him go.

Then, the dreaded white buses arrived.

My heart was breaking and yet beating awfully fast. I hated that moment. I didn't want to say good-bye. We walked to the line of buses together and had time for one last hug and kiss before Larry turned and walked toward his bus. We watched him climb up the stairs and find his seat. As the buses pulled away, we blew him kisses and waved until they were completely out of sight. My heart felt like it weighed twenty pounds.

We stood in the empty lot until the numbness wore off and we realized how cold it had become. We didn't even notice that the sun had set while we were standing there. I scooped Ellie up and reached for Ryann's hand. With Larry's parents, we walked back to our cars and went on home.

Chapter 11

Afghanistan

Keep it up! Keep it up!
Keep that super spirit up!
Keep ... it ... up!
—*Lely High School Cheer, 1986–1989*

I was a cheerleader in high school. I always feel the need to add to that by saying, "In my high school, cheerleading was a sport." Seriously, it was. We ran. We did push-ups and sit-ups. Our cheerleading coach was married to a football coach, so she knew how to condition us. Groomed into a pretty fierce competition squad, we participated in the National High School Cheerleading Championship at Sea World in Orlando, Florida. We were awesome!

As cheerleaders, our job was to motivate the team and to entertain and inspire the crowd. We cheered our hearts out for our boys during football and basketball season. Each and every one of us knew the sports for which we cheered. We knew the rules; we followed the game. We prayed; we yelled; we fought for victory.

I never could have predicted how much my experience as a cheerleader would help me as a US Army soldier, but it did. Think about it. As a cheerleader, I learned how to yell not from my throat but from my diaphragm. When you yell from your throat, your voice doesn't last very long. But when you belt it out from your gut, you yell loudly, your throat never hurts, and your voice lasts all day. As a cadet in ROTC and later as a lieutenant and captain, I could call army cadence all day long. I never got tired of it. As an army officer, I was a cheerleader for my soldiers. I motivated them and cheered for them during physical training tests. I rooted for them in every situation. I brought them up when they were down, proving to them time and time again that I was their best ally.

In military life, the competition between different branches of service is fierce. Just watch the military academies play each other in football every fall and you'll see what I mean. The Air Force calls army soldiers "grunts" or "ground pounders," and the Army calls the Navy "squids." During the Army/Navy game, we always want to "slam the squids!" Competition is just as thick between the army divisions and army branches. The 82nd competes with the 101st and the 10th Mountain Division. Infantry competes with armor and field artillery. Whatever army division and whatever army branch you serve, you become their best cheerleader. You can hear it in the cadences.

***

Eighty-second ... patch on my shoulder! Pick up your 'chute
and follow me! Airborne Infantry!
—82nd Airborne Division Cadence

***

My experience as a high school cheerleader served me well as an army wife, a mother, and a family readiness group leader. Often, I became the standard-bearer and motivator for our unit family and, of course, for our actual family. During deployments, cheerleading was an essential task. As a family readiness group leader, it was my job to keep those on the home front motivated. A yearlong deployment was no joke. It was my job to remind our families that it would be a marathon, not a sprint. It was my job to cheer them on for the long haul.

Battle Rhythms

Larry spent the first few days in Afghanistan transitioning with the 10th Mountain Division's 4th Brigade Special Troops Battalion. They had a few days of overlap before the 10th Mountain soldiers returned home. He was definitely glad they were calling themselves the 508th Special Troops Battalion by then. That would have been way too confusing. Once the 10th Mountain left, Larry and his troopers settled into their jobs very quickly because they had to be ready for the Taliban's spring offensive. Larry was convinced that they were going to catch Osama bin Laden or at least put a hurting on his team of jihad extremists.

Larry loved his job and the paratroopers with whom he served. It didn't take them long to get used to the battle rhythm, though it did take a little while to get all the computers up and running. We didn't hear from him much in that first month, only a phone call or two. By March, though, Larry was able to e-mail us almost every day. Falling into a battle rhythm of our own, I would e-mail him at night right before I went to bed. Then, like clockwork, I'd have a response from him in the morning. At night, I would send him a review of our day, and in the morning, he would tell me how much he loved us. He couldn't really talk about his days, even though I would have loved to hear every detail.

12 March 2007

Wesley,

I love you more than you will ever know. Thank you for being my wife and the mother of our beautiful daughters. I am very proud of you. Thank you for all that you do. I still believe and I tell people here, that you have a harder job than I do. I thank you for keeping the home front in one piece. Thank you for all that you do for the families of not only the Diablo BN, but for the entire TF Fury. It does not go unnoticed, even though I do not say thanks enough. Thank you. Wesley, I love you with all that I am. Please give our daughters a kiss on the cheek tonight and tell them that I love them.

I love you very much!

Larry

Larry was so good at writing to everyone in our family. He made a point to acknowledge each of us and never ended an e-mail without saying, "I love you." Larry had told me once, "We are living the history that our children and grandchildren will study in school." I saved every one of his e-mails so we could bring that history to life for them someday. That's also the reason I'm writing this book. We really are living the history that future generations will study. We need to document it now and make sure it is taught correctly.

Friday Talks

Our battalion rear-detachment commander, Captain Collin Kilpatrick, told us that the battalion was setting up an Internet workstation that would allow the battalion leadership in Afghanistan to talk with the leadership at Fort Bragg. The workstation would go live every Friday morning, and Shanna and I were invited to attend each one.

During the workstation meetings, Lieutenant Colonel Baker would give us a "state of the battalion" address and then let us tell him what the family readiness group was doing at home. Nowadays, we're all used to video conferencing, but back then we didn't have that capability at the battalion level. I was super impressed that we could talk to our guys in Afghanistan at all. We couldn't see them, but we could hear them very clearly. Sometimes, I even got to hear Larry. And if we were all set up before Lieutenant Colonel Baker was ready, Larry and I would get a brief chance to talk. Shanna and Ken would take advantage of those rare opportunities, too. We were thankful for those special moments.

Once we got the hang of it, we opened the Internet workstation to the company family readiness group leaders. Several of them would come to listen to the weekly report. Lieutenant Colonel Baker always gave us a very thorough, often humorous, rundown of the battalion's actions for the week. He would only tell us the news that was unclassified and could be repeated to our unit family members. Diligently, we would take notes and then send out an e-mail to the company family readiness group leaders. They would pass the information down the chain to their family members. We did this every week of the deployment. It was a wonderful way to stay connected with our deployed paratroopers.

The brigade had set up a similar system. After our Friday Internet workstation session with the battalion, we would go to the brigade headquarters to listen to the brigade commander, Colonel Martin Schweitzer, give us the weekly wrap-up at the brigade level. He would start with a report about the two infantry battalions and then report on the field artillery battalion and the cavalry squadron. Finally, he would get to the support units.

At both the battalion and the brigade Internet workstation, the commanders would cover the family readiness group business first and then let us ladies go. The army leaders would stay for the official business. The brigade ladies would usually hang out at brigade a bit longer to check on one another and enjoy some fellowship. We had a great group of ladies, and we all got along really well. We would often share our experiences, ideas, and best practices. It was such a blessing to serve with those amazing ladies.

Every Friday evening, I would pull out my notes from the battalion and brigade Internet workstation meetings and start drafting an e-mail message to the company family readiness group leaders. Shanna and I called these messages our Friday Talks. A standard Friday Talk e-mail read like this:

16 March 2007

Hello Ladies and Gentlemen!

    I hope you are doing well and are looking forward to the weekend. We were able to talk with LTC Baker and able to listen to COL Schweitzer today. LTC Baker sounded great, as always. Our Paratroopers are doing a fantastic job. They are doing so well that they have the attention and appreciation of the Brigade Commander.

COL Schweitzer said today that our Paratroopers have "caught the biggest fish" so far. That's great news! They captured a key bad guy and liberated a population center. He also told the story of an Afghani child, who arrived at one of our humanitarian drop sites. He was out in the snow and had no clothes on. Our Paratroopers cleaned him up and gave him clothes. He was very grateful and the Troopers were incredibly proud to help him. Our men and women are doing great things. I'm so proud of them.

LTC Baker wants to say to the FRG Leaders "thank you for all that you do." He said that it is so nice that the Paratroopers can focus completely on their jobs, knowing that their families are being taken care of at home. You, too, are doing great things. Thank you so much.

I have just one more thing. We really need to let our families know that the mail has gotten completely backed up because people are sending boxes that are *too big*. Big boxes stop little boxes and letters from going forward. This has the attention of the Brigade Commander and he has asked the FRG leadership to get the word out that we can only send *shoe-box sized boxes* over there. Please do what you can to get this word out.

I hope you have a wonderful weekend. Thank you for all that you do. Take care!

~Wesley~

Shanna and I adhered to Larry's "living the history" philosophy and tried to put as much detail into these Friday Talks as we could. We sent out a Friday Talk e-mail every week for the entire deployment.

Lieutenant Colonel Baker continued to walk us through everything the battalion was doing overseas. He told us that our paratroopers were doing great things in the name of freedom. He told us that they were "catching bad guys, conducting border meetings, building relationships and functional teams with the local

population and government and even building roads and schools."
He also let us know that the warmer weather allowed the "bad guys"
to resurface. He was trying to delicately prepare us for the Taliban's
spring offensive. But he also said that our paratroopers are highly
trained and fit to fight. He said, "We will slap them back into their
holes!" You've got to love Lieutenant Colonel Baker.

Larry's daily e-mails continued.

5 April 2007

Hello Wesley,

Just got back in from out and about. Did you get to see
the picture of the camels? In the time we were out, I saw
at least 5 sets of camels. I think someone took a picture
of me over near them. I will try to find it and send it also.

I love you very much. Thanks for being my wife. Thanks
for being the mother of our two beautiful daughters.
Thanks for all that you do at home. I can't wait to be
back there with you and the girls. Give each of you a big
hug for me. Please be careful and take care of each other.
If you can, please send a couple of coloring books. I got
the crayons in my first care package. Thanks again.

I love you very very much!

Larry

Just as he had when he was in Iraq, Larry loved to color pictures
for the girls as a stress reliever. And, boy, did we love to receive
them! He also loved going "out and about." He was definitely not a
sit-behind-the-desk kind of officer. Early in the deployment, Larry
and I came up with a code phrase when we communicated by phone
or e-mail. If he ever said to me, "Tomorrow's going to be a good
day," that meant he was going out and I would say an extra prayer.
He said that a lot during this Afghanistan deployment and, at this
point, they had only been there for two months.

Larry was a great historian. He was very good at documenting everything and especially loved to add pictures. He followed up his e-mail with pictures of the camels he mentioned and also a picture of a herd of goats. Dingy and gray, the goats were walking on a dirt road that hugged a rocky mountain. Right in the middle of the herd of goats walked an Afghani girl. She was beautiful. Her hot-pink headdress was a breathtaking contrast against the sea of gray and brown tones. That picture had such strong symbolism. Amid all the bad news we've heard throughout this global war on terror, there is good news. There are wonderful stories of beauty and blessings. Our troopers were there to help those beautiful diamonds in the rough.

April was a very busy month for the Diablos in both parts of the world. Our weekly Internet workstation meetings with Lieutenant Colonel Baker and Colonel Schweitzer continued.

On April 6, Lieutenant Colonel Baker said they were "busier than a one-legged man in an a**-kicking contest! Busy is good, helps the time go faster."

He also offered us a reality check by acknowledging that the honeymoon was over and the troopers were feeling it. The families were, too. In the beginning of the deployment, the troopers and the family members were running on adrenaline. But we all know that doesn't last. Sooner or later, reality sets in. We all began to realize just how long a year would be. So in the Friday Talk message, I put on my cheerleading skirt and reminded the families that we needed to help one another. Shanna and I would often write, "We are in this together. We can do it!" Larry must have felt that way, too. In his morning e-mail a few days later, he wrote, "Remember: this is a marathon, not a sprint. You need to pace yourself and do your best ... one day at a time."

Soldier Bird

In mid-April, we had a sweet little distraction at our house. We were blessed with new neighbors. A little bird family built a nest on our front porch, up high in the corner above our porch swing. We enjoyed watching them through our front window. Every day, we spied on the eggs, eagerly waiting for them to hatch. Then, one day, we heard peeping and were blessed with three baby birds.

A day or two later, we saw the mama bird in the nest tending to her babies. We were so impressed by what happened next. The daddy bird returned to the nest and fed the mama. She immediately turned and fed the babies. That was so cool. Then, while the daddy was guarding the nest, another bird arrived. Boldly, he hopped on the ledge toward the nest. I guess he got too close for the daddy's liking, because the daddy bird ruffled his feathers and chased the bird away. Ryann and Ellie looked at me with their big blue eyes wide open, full of amazement. I told them that the daddy bird was protecting the mama bird and the babies.

"Like our daddy protects us," Ryann said. "That bird is a soldier bird!"

"Ryann, you are exactly right!" I said as tears collected in my eyes.

Care Team Mission

From February to April, we continued to build our Care Team Program and train our volunteers. During each care team class, we went through the slides, discussed the purpose of the family notebook, and reviewed the contents of the supply bin. The supply bin contained everything from water bottles to paper products—anything the care team or a family might need. We also discussed potential scenarios. Every situation would be different. We tried to be realistic and honest with ourselves. In a family readiness group, as in any organization, communication is key. Being able to talk through the casualty notification and assistance process actually made everyone a little more at ease. We were steadily building a sizable battalion pool of care team volunteers.

On April 12, 2007, we conducted a care team class in the conference room at our battalion headquarters. Ten ladies listened with compassion and strength. Each of them agreed to serve as a member of our battalion care team if so called. As the ladies filed out of the classroom, Captain Kilpatrick entered with a troubled look on his face. I soon found out why.

Our brigade lost two paratroopers that day in two separate incidents. My heart broke for the troopers and their families. Neither soldier was in our battalion, but one of the widows was. She was an army specialist serving on our rear detachment. She was a brand new mother, in fact; she had just had a baby. Her husband deployed with 2-508 Parachute Infantry Regiment, our old battalion. Lieutenant Colonel Baker had allowed her to stay at Fort Bragg so that sweet baby didn't have two deployed parents at the same time. A young soldier, a young mother, a young widow—my heart broke for her.

I was completely numb when I left battalion. I drove home to gather a few things and try to keep myself together. Captain Kilpatrick called me thirty minutes later. The notification was complete, and the young widow was going to allow the care team to help her. Because the fallen paratrooper wasn't a member of our battalion, I felt obligated to call the 2-508 family readiness group leader and ask if we could provide the care team for his wife, since she was ours. The leader was thankful for the help. I immediately called two of the ladies who had attended the class that morning. I knew the training would be fresh in their minds, and I hoped that would inspire them to agree to serve now that the moment of truth was upon us. They humbly agreed, got back into their cars, and headed straight to battalion.

Meanwhile, I recruited my dear friend and neighbor, Keli Lowman, to pick up the girls at school that afternoon and keep them for me. I had no idea how long I'd be, but Keli assured me she'd keep them as long as I needed her. When I talked to Keli, I couldn't tell her why I needed her help. I had to respect the confidentiality of the family. We weren't allowed to mention anything to anyone outside of the care team.

A true friend, Keli didn't ask for an explanation. She just said, "Go. Do what you need to do. Don't worry; I've got your girls."

That's the kind of friendship she and I had. It was priceless.

The care team members met at battalion at about two o'clock that afternoon. The three of us looked over our care team checklist and inspected our supplies. After we received all the required information from Captain Kilpatrick and did all our checks, we looked at one another and said, "We can do this."

We left the battalion area and headed to the family's home. During the very quiet ride, my heart began to ache. Insecurity and reality set in. There was nothing I could do to make this situation any better. I couldn't fix any of it. I couldn't bring her husband back. I couldn't bring the father of her sweet baby girl back. I wasn't even sure what to say to her. This care team thing briefed well, but in the moments before we arrived at her house, I seriously doubted the entire concept. What were we going there to do? Would we be any help to her at all? All I could think to do was pray.

I prayed for the rest of the drive. Keeping my eyes on the road, I asked God to give me strength. I prayed for wisdom and hoped that I wouldn't say the wrong thing. I prayed for patience, compassion, and understanding. I prayed for that beautiful family. I prayed for God's strength for them. I asked Jesus to wrap His arms around them and comfort them the way only He can do.

We arrived at the house around three o'clock. We got out of our cars, exchanged reassuring glances, and walked up the driveway. Standing on the front porch, the three of us looked at one another once more.

"We can do this," I said to them.

Then, I half-smiled, took a deep breath, and rang the doorbell.

Quiet Compassion

We respectfully and quietly served the sweet young widow during daylight hours for four days. Each day, we had a new team of volunteers. We answered the door and kept a log of visitors. We answered the phone and kept a message log. We played with her baby and took care of her dogs. We coordinated meals, received flowers, and kept the house tidy. We provided a witness for her initial meeting with her casualty assistance officer, which can be overwhelming. We took notes and kept the family binder current with every bit of information. Most importantly, we let her know she wasn't alone. I hoped that our presence brought her some degree of comfort in those early days.

As a care team, we stayed with her until she left for her husband's funeral. By definition, a care team supports a family for a "determined period of time," usually about three or four days. Our mission was to bridge the gap between notification and extended family arrival. Once her family was in the picture, we faded out. But we continued to check on her. She was constantly in our prayers and would always be a member of our battalion family.

That care team experience was incredibly humbling for me. I knew all along that it was possible for us to lose someone, but I never expected it to actually happen. I had heard about battle losses since this global war on terror began, but when it affects your unit this closely, it is the harshest of all reality checks. My heart went out to this young widow. She didn't ask for this. She never expected to be a widow in her twenties.

The whole thing made me think about Larry, our marriage, and our family. I realized how blessed I was but how fragile life truly is. This was another harsh reminder that no one is guaranteed tomorrow and that freedom isn't free.

In true army fashion, Shanna and I met a few days after we shut down the care team for a quick review. We talked about our experience and evaluated our performance. We reviewed our actions. What went well? What could we have done better? We also checked on each other, actually looking into each other's eyes. Serving on that care team was an emotional experience. It paled in comparison to the emotions and grief that the family was going through, but compassion fatigue is a very real thing. Shanna and I needed that moment to come alongside each other, cheer each other up, and remember that the deployment was a marathon, not a sprint. We still had a long way to go.

Driving on with Heavy Hearts

Shanna and I attended the next battalion Internet workstation meeting and slowly found our battle rhythm again. Out of respect for the family of the fallen paratrooper, we didn't write about our care team mission in our Friday Talk message, but we did speak to Lieutenant Colonel Baker about it. He was grateful that we had represented the unit and done our best to wrap our arms around our young soldier and her family.

During the brigade Internet workstation meeting, we found out that Colonel Schweitzer had just visited our deployed battalion. He told us that the brigade was doing great things.

"The enemy is not able to do what it has done in the past. It has been phenomenal," he said, referring to all the accomplishments of the entire brigade task force.

Then, he said that our battalion continues to amaze him by what they are accomplishing. He was very impressed by the 508 Special Troops Battalion Paratroopers, and he told us that everyone loves "the Baker man."

"I cannot talk about Lieutenant Colonel Baker without smiling. It is phenomenal. Even the enemy loves him. The enemy has turned themselves in [to Lieutenant Colonel Baker], because even they want to be on his team!"

His comments made us all laugh out loud. I'd believe it. I could just see it—a long line of Taliban fighters waiting to turn themselves in to Lieutenant Colonel Baker. His enthusiasm is infectious, and he is a superb leader. Everybody loves him.

That day, the brigade commander closed his comments by recognizing the efforts of the company, battalion, and brigade family readiness group leaders.

"Thank you is not enough, but thank you anyway," he said in closing.

Getting through a deployment requires an incredible amount of teamwork. Obviously, the paratroopers suffer the brunt of it. They are the ones in harm's way. They are carrying the burden of this global war on terror and trying to rebuild a third-world country.

They are sacrificing their lives and bodies to cover us in a blanket of freedom. But the families serve, too. It was nice to hear that the brigade commander recognized what we were doing on the home front. A few comments like that went a long way. Colonel Schweitzer may not have been aware of it at the time, but he was a pretty good cheerleader, too.

Pens for Progress

Since the early days of the deployment, Shanna and I had been trying to figure out ways to help our battalion with its mission. On the rare occasions when we could talk to our husbands, we would ask how we could help in a tangible way. I asked Larry if they would like us to supply them with candy to hand out to the children they saw on their patrols. He wasn't so sure that was a good idea. He was concerned about their dental hygiene and didn't want to make things worse by giving them a bunch of sugar. Instead, he told me a story about one of his recent patrols.

Larry and his men were out and about one day. As they reached a village, Afghani children ran to them and, before they knew it, they were surrounded. The children were friendly and fascinated by our American soldiers. The quagmire of kids wouldn't leave their sides, which kept the troopers from continuing their patrol. A few of the kids locked their eyes on the map markers that Larry had tucked in the little pen pockets in the sleeve of his uniform. He said he had to give some of the kids his markers in order to keep moving and continue their walkabout.

"Wesley, don't send candy. Send us pens and map markers."

Shanna and I took that idea and ran with it. We organized a pen drive called "Pens for Progress" at two schools in the Fort Bragg area. We presented the idea to the school principals and explained that the kids could bring in pens, pencils, and markers, and we would ship them to our soldiers in Afghanistan. The principals loved the idea!

Shanna and I made it easy on the teachers and staff by supplying each classroom with a collection bag and retrieving the collected pens each day. We ran the program in both schools for two weeks. The response was overwhelming. We were blessed with wonderful participation from both schools. We were so excited!

While we were in the midst of the pen drive, I received an e-mail from our brigade family readiness group leaders. The e-mail said that a *CNN Headline News* reporter and camera crew were coming to Fort Bragg in early May in search of some "good news" stories. The e-mail asked for ideas, so Shanna and I pitched our Pens for Progress program. The news crew picked it up.

The morning of May 11, 2007, the *CNN* producers and crew met us at McNair Elementary School on Fort Bragg to tape our daily pen collection. Shanna and I met with the producers before the collection, and they interviewed both of us on camera. We told them about Pens for Progress, how we had gotten the idea, where the pens were going, and what it meant to us to do something to help our troopers and the children in Afghanistan. Then, we got to meet the CNN reporter. It was Robin Meade! Back then, her morning news show was called *Robin & Company*. She was fabulous! Down to earth and approachable, she revealed a heart of compassion and an appreciation for our soldiers and their children. We really enjoyed talking with her.

We had arranged to have one student from each classroom collect their pens and bring them to the cafeteria. Ryann and Ellie each got to represent their first grade and prekindergarten classrooms. After lining the kids up in the hallway, the crew filmed them walking into the cafeteria with their collection bags and pouring out their pens into a huge basket. Then, the children sat at a cafeteria table and talked with Robin.

The kids were fantastic! They all did a beautiful job answering Robin's questions and expressed that they were happy to help the children in Afghanistan. Toward the end of the segment, Robin had all the kids gather around the basket to look at the hundreds of pens and markers they had collected. It was a very sweet and proud moment.

Robin and her crew told us they were coming back to Fort Bragg for a special Memorial Day broadcast. She would run all of the good news stories then. We were grateful and incredibly blessed to have our little Pens for Progress story included in such an endeavor.

Later that morning, Shanna and I attended the Internet workstation meeting at battalion. We told Lieutenant Colonel Baker about our experience with Robin Meade. Pleased with the story and grateful that the pen drive was successful, he said he couldn't wait to receive all the pens and markers.

Carrying on the energy of the happy day, Lieutenant Colonel Baker told us that the battalion was going to host a "Sunday Fun-day" in Afghanistan to celebrate Mother's Day. He said they would be having great food and a few fun events, like a basketball tournament, camel races, and donkey rides. What a great opportunity for them to blow off some steam and build upon their esprit de corps right there in the middle of a war zone. They deserved to have a fun day.

Later that night, an e-mail from Larry popped into my inbox.

11 May 2007

Wesley,

It is so great to hear your voice on Fridays. Thanks for the photos of the "Pens for Progress." I hope I get to see it on TV. Please tape it if you can. I am so proud of you. Thanks for all that you do back there. It does make my job easier over here. I do miss you very much though. I think of you and the girls ALL of the time. Thank you for being my wife and the mother of our two beautiful daughters. Attached is a photo of me with the boys on patrol (I am behind the guy with the Pepsis). I will send a few more tomorrow. I love you Wesley, very much. Please take care of yourself and be careful.

I love you very much!

Larry

That night, I had a moment of reflection. I realized that I was doing exactly what I had been groomed to do. God had blessed me with wonderful skills and talents, and He had blessed me with a wonderful education. As a family readiness group leader, I was using my bachelor's degree in communications and my master's degree in administration every day. And I was using my active duty military experience to relate to the paratroopers, commanders, and families of this awesome division. I was so pleased and thankful. I was in a great place. I thanked God for putting all those pieces together for me. I was so proud to be able to serve in such a meaningful way.

Mother's Day

The next day, my mom, the girls, and I drove up to Moravian Falls to spend Mother's Day with Larry's family. Laura, Ben, and their daughter, Leah, were there, too. We love them all so much. On that beautiful springtime Saturday, we went down to the creek to throw rocks, play in the water, and catch crawdads. Larry's uncle Frank had hung a tire swing on one of the old creek-side oak trees. We stayed down there all afternoon.

On Sunday, we went to church. Cub Creek Baptist Church always does a sweet tribute to mothers on their special day. I was glad we were there. It was such a blessing to spend Mother's Day with my daughters, my mom, my mother-in-law, and my sweet sister-in-law. They are the most wonderful ladies ever.

On our way back home to Fort Bragg on Sunday evening, my cell phone rang. It was Larry! He called to wish me a happy Mother's Day. Hearing his voice was the best part of an amazing day. He asked about our weekend and about everyone at church. I told him about playing in the creek and about the church service. Then, I asked him about their Sunday Fun-day.

"It was good. I got to ride a camel," he said.

"A camel? Really?"

"Yes. It was a pretty good day. The troopers had fun, but my Fun-day was cut short. Our neighbors are not playing nice with others," he said.

He had to go back to his office and work the rest of the day. He told me to check out a few news stories online when we got home and that I would know what he was talking about.

"But," he said, "tomorrow's going to be a good day."

"Oh, okay."

That got my attention, though I knew I couldn't ask for any details.

Larry asked to talk to my mom, so I passed the phone to her. She and Larry spoke for a few minutes. Then, both girls got their turn to talk to Daddy. Just as I got the phone back, we were disconnected. We were driving on US 421 between Greensboro and Sanford, and sometimes the signal disappears. I was heartbroken because I hadn't gotten to say good-bye and tell him that I loved him.

A few minutes later, the phone rang again. *Thank you, Jesus!*

We were in nowhere land and I was afraid the call would drop again, so I quickly said, "I love you, Larry, with all my heart. Please be careful and keep doing great things! I'm so proud of you!"

"Not as proud as I am of you!"

"I love you, Larry!"

"I love you, Wesley, with all my heart! Happy Mother's Day."

Then, we said good-bye.

When we got home, we unloaded the car, put the girls in the bath, and then got them to bed. They had school the next morning, and it would come fast. After I tucked them in, I went downstairs to check my e-mail. There were two e-mails from Larry, one for the girls and one for me. He attached the picture of him riding the camel. He was waving to the camera.

13 May 2007

Ryann and Ellie,

   Look at what Daddy got to ride in Afghanistan. Take care of Mommy and Grammie for me. I love you both very much!

Love,
Daddy

13 May 2007

Wesley,

Happy Mother's Day! I love you with all of my heart. Thank you for being my wife and the mother of our 2 beautiful daughters. You are the best thing that has ever happened to me. I am sorry that my job takes me away from you and the girls. I promise I will make this up to you all. Thank you for allowing me to be a Paratrooper in the US Army. I am very proud of you and all that you do for me, our children and all of the Troopers of this BN. I miss you, but love you so much more. I hope that you had a great Mother's Day. Please take care of yourself. I love you Sweetheart!

Larry

Part 3

Freedom Isn't Free

Freedom is never more than one generation away
from extinction. We didn't pass it to our children in
the bloodstream. It must be fought for, protected,
and handed on for them to do the same.
—*President Ronald Reagan*

I can't tell you how many times I "died" when I was in the Army. As ROTC cadets, my classmates and I learned battle drills while patrolling in the mountains of Boone. React to contact. React to indirect fire. React to ambush. We did those battle drills over and over again until our responses became muscle memory. Good training led to foolish arrogance. We felt like we were ready for anything, but we could never avoid the confounded creativity of our cadre.

"Sniper, two o'clock! Hobbs, you're dead!"

"Oh ... man!"

Almost every time I was in a leadership position, they would let me plan the mission, brief my squad, conduct rehearsals, and lead them out of the wire. We'd usually make it to the listening halt, but as soon as we were moving again, "Bang!"

"Hobbs, you're dead! Peaks, you're squad leader now!"

They weren't picking on me. They did that to everyone. As squad leaders, we would do all the planning, gather the logistics for the mission, and lead the rehearsals. They would "kill" us just as we began movement to evaluate how well we had prepared our soldiers and how well they drove on without us.

The ROTC battalion didn't have a lot of funding for simulated grenades and pyrotechnics, so during training events we had to improvise. One time, during a field training exercise at Fort Bragg, one of my classmates asked a cadre member if we could use pinecones as grenades. He allowed it.

While on patrol, our squad encountered enemy soldiers in a bunker. My fellow cadet took his pinecone grenade out of his pouch, threw it toward the enemy position, and yelled, "Grenade!" The pinecone hit a tree limb and bounced back, landing right in the middle of us.

"Boom!" yelled the cadre. "You're all dead!"

Lesson learned.

When I was a lieutenant, we practiced war games using multiple integrated laser engagement systems (MILES). It was a lot like laser tag. We had sensors that looked like black mini muffins on our suspenders and around our Kevlar helmets. Lasers in metal boxes were attached to the front of our M-16 rifles.

Before a MILES exercise started, we were given casualty cards, sealed in orange envelopes. If we were hit during the exercise, an ear-piercing alarm went off. Dropping to the ground, we had to open one of our MILES cards to find out how badly we were wounded. The card gave instructions to both the casualty and the medic.

MILES combat training served a good purpose. It helped us to train as we fought. It stressed both battlefield leadership and medical evacuation procedures. We used this system while we were in the 101st at Fort Campbell and during JRTC rotations at Fort Polk. By the end of those field exercises, units were exhausted. Systems were tested. MILES casualties were abundant. Commanders would announce end of exercise, and, just like that, the war game was over. The wounded were healed. The dead would rise. We would regroup, refit, receive our evaluations, and prepare for the next mission.

Now that our nation has experienced more than fifteen years of war, one thing is certain: there is no end of exercise in the real world. There is no magic end-of-exercise wand. Battle losses are not simulated. You'll find no MILES gear on the battlefield, no pinecone grenades. Battle losses are real. Husbands and daddies who are killed in action are gone—forever. They don't come back. The wounded are still wounded. They have real injuries, visible and invisible. Their lives and their families have changed forever. This is the reality of war.

Families of our wounded and of our fallen live with a daily reminder that, though it absolutely is worth fighting for, freedom isn't free.

Chapter 12

Breathless

I am sorry that my job takes me
away from you and the girls.
—Major Larry Bauguess

Sergeant Major Isaac Ragusa placed a black pouch in my hand. It was small and had the words "United States Army" printed in gold just below the drawstring closure. With my heart in my throat, I looked at that bag and then looked at the army leader. He was tough, usually a ball of fire, but at that moment he was kind, humble, quiet.

By army regulation, a fallen soldier is to be escorted home by a service member of equal or greater rank. Sergeant Major Ragusa was Larry's operations sergeant major. He may have been junior to Larry, but he was his right-hand man, his battle buddy. He had defied the regulation. Determined to bring Larry home to his family, he dared anyone to tell him to stand down. There was probably a dustup, but Sergeant Major Ragusa had won the battle. He did his duty. He brought his major home.

I admire Sergeant Major Ragusa for that. I was so grateful that someone cared that deeply for my Larry. Later, I learned that Sergeant Major Ragusa hadn't left Larry's side for a single moment. He sat next to him for the entire trip back to the States. They wouldn't let him into the coroner's office at Dover Air Force Base, for obvious reasons, but he stayed right outside until the procedure was done. Then, he brought Larry home, to a tiny airfield in Wilkes County,

North Carolina. Sergeant Major Ragusa did not break contact with Larry until he delivered him home to us.

Not wanting to view the contents just yet, I tightened my grip on that little black pouch and turned my attention to the tiny airplane. Silently, I watched the funeral detail pull a flag-draped casket out of the belly of the bird. Slowly, carefully, respectfully, they carried the casket across the tarmac toward a massive, empty hangar. Empty. That is how I felt at that moment. It was as if my heart and mind disconnected from each other. I couldn't think. I couldn't feel. Like the hangar, I was completely empty.

After the detail disappeared into the cavernous hangar, I glanced down at the pouch. With weak and unsteady hands, I opened it. Inside, I found Larry's Department of Defense ID card, his dog tags, and his wedding ring. Immediately, I took off my wedding rings and put Larry's ring in their place, and then I slid my rings back on top of his, locking it onto my finger.

Wedding rings represent an endless love. They are symbols of a promise made to the one you love that you will honor and cherish them as long as you both shall live. As long as you both shall live—it wasn't supposed to end this way. I kept thinking, *This can't be real.* I was touching Larry's ring, mindlessly spinning it around my finger. I wasn't supposed to have it. He was supposed to have it. *This isn't happening.*

***

This can't be happening to me, this is just a dream …
—Gordie Sampson, Hillary Lindsey, and
Steven McEwan (Carrie Underwood), "Just a Dream"
***

I thought about the girls. Ryann and Ellie were so sweet, so innocent. How could something like this happen to them? How will they ever know how awesome their daddy was? Who will teach them to play catch? Who will teach them to drive? Who will put the fear of God into the young men who come calling for them? Who will stand with me at their high school and college graduations? Who will walk them down the aisle?

At that moment, Ryann and Ellie were playing at Mamaw's house with a trusted friend. At their tender ages, they couldn't comprehend what was happening. They couldn't process our loss. I could barely process it. I just knew that somehow, someway, we would love each other through it.

When motioned to come forward, Larry's mom and dad, his brother and sister, my mother, and I walked, slowly, toward the hangar. Sergeant Major Ragusa told me I could go in first. I felt guilty going in before John and Martha, but I heard Larry's voice telling me to lead the way. The brightness of the beautiful May morning turned horribly dim as I entered the empty hangar. Skylights in the metal roof provided the only light. The chill and the dampness hit me as I approached the casket, now open, a hazy beam illuminating it.

Lord God, I'm so sorry for the man in this box. I am sorry for his family, but please let it not be Larry, I bargained as I walked alone.

My stomach cramped and the air was sucked right out of my lungs when I realized there was no use in bargaining, no use in denying. No more questioning. No more hope that this was a horrible mistake. It was Larry. Physically, there was no doubt. It was Larry, but it was not my Larry. My Larry was full of life. My Larry was a wonderful husband, a loving and amazing daddy. My Larry was a warrior and a gentleman. That was not my Larry. And, yet, it was.

I bowed my head and accepted Larry's presence in that awful box as truth. There was nothing left to do but pray. I thanked God for giving us Larry for as long as we had him. I thanked Him for the wonderful moments. I thanked Him for giving us two beautiful girls who will carry on their daddy's legacy. Then, I asked God to help us figure out how to live without him. I asked Him for His strength. I asked Him for His guidance. At that moment, I asked Him for His breath.

I touched Larry's forehead. I rubbed it gently, the way he used to rub mine. I bent down and kissed the top of his head. I whispered, "I love you." Then, I walked away, brokenhearted and breathless.

The Patriot Guard

Full-sized American flags were flowing in the breeze and reflecting off the glass of the limousine as we pulled to a stop in front of the church. Our nation's color bearers that day were the proud members of the Patriot Guard. Most of them were Vietnam veterans who had taken a personal vow to never let an American soldier come home without a proper welcome, especially our fallen soldiers. Their presence filled me with doses of pride and strength I so desperately needed.

Earlier that morning, we saw them staging in the parking lot of the local Food Lion when we drove to the funeral home. I pointed them out to Ryann and Ellie.

"Girls, look at all of those motorcycles," I said, pointing out the window. "That's the Patriot Guard. They are here to honor Daddy and protect us."

The night before Larry's funeral, we hosted the viewing and the visitation at Reins-Sturdivant Funeral Home in Wilkesboro. It was exhausting, but the number of people who came to honor Larry truly blessed us. The next morning, we were back at the funeral home for a few quiet moments before heading to the church. Family and close friends gathered with us. Just before we departed, I was given a few moments alone with Larry.

Seated on a little couch across from the flag-draped casket, I talked to him as if he were standing in front of me. I told him I was proud of him and always would be. I promised to follow his example. I promised to take good care of the girls. I promised to give them a great childhood and a good education. I promised to raise Ryann and Ellie as good Christian girls and encourage their believer's baptism. I promised Larry I would do my best to set a good example for them. I promised to keep his memory alive by telling our stories and quoting him often. I promised to honor his memory and love him forever.

Then, I said good-bye to the love of my life.

I reflected on those promises as we traveled to the church. Ryann and Ellie were seated on my right and my left. I knew I needed to be strong, but the smooth ride in the limo helped me drift into numbness. I had cried to the point of dehydration in the days between our notification and the funeral. I barely ate and hardly slept. I was absolutely exhausted and had no idea how I would get through that very sad day.

My numbness slowly thawed when I glanced out the window and saw how the good people of Wilkes County were reacting to the funeral procession. Instead of becoming annoyed by the long line of cars crossing their path, delaying their day, they stopped their cars and paid their respects to a hometown hero. Some of the people got out of their cars; some of them even saluted. That meaningful gesture gave me a much-needed dose of energy. Wilkes County is a very special place.

The girls and I sat a little taller and looked out the window with renewed curiosity. It was actually a beautiful day outside. I hadn't noticed before. The sky was clear and Carolina blue. It was springtime, so the trees were a rich green and the roadside wildflowers were in full bloom.

As we neared the church, we saw local firefighters and first responders lining the street. In my dehydrated state, I didn't think it was possible, but my eyes filled with tears once again.

The limo pulled to a stop in front of the church between two lines of patriot guardsmen standing at attention, each of them holding an American flag. We sat there for several moments taking in the sight of our nation's colors and the veterans holding them proudly. Our driver told us we could wait in the car while they transported Larry, but I wanted to be outside. I wanted to stand for him.

"Thank you," I whispered to the closest patriot guard as the girls and I left the vehicle and walked toward the church. The quiet professional gave no verbal response. He just nodded his head with a look of compassion and pride. The strength of his character and commitment was visible in his posture.

Wrapped in the security and comfort of the patriot guard, we watched as the funeral detail carried Larry from the hearse to the sanctuary.

Honoring a Hero

I struggled with this chapter, for obvious reasons. I don't think it's necessary to chronicle Larry's funeral, to reveal every moment. It was a private, sacred service, with full military honors. The funeral itself was highly emotional, but it was impressive and respectful. Homer Greene, the pastor of Cub Creek Baptist Church, called that day "the coronation of Major Larry Bauguess." People respectfully rejoiced because he was in heaven. I suppose I should have rejoiced, too. But I wanted him here. The girls needed their daddy.

On the outside, I was completely put together—an Iron Lady, they called me. I wanted to be strong for the girls. I wanted to be strong for Larry. On the inside, though, I was a jumbled mess full of conflicting emotions. I was so proud of Larry, so honored by him. I was thankful and relieved that he was in heaven. He will always be young. He will never be hurt again. He will watch over us from above. But we needed him home. How would we ever go on without him?

I remain incredibly grateful to all of our family and friends who attended Larry's funeral. High school, college, and army friends traveled great distances to pay respects to Larry. Several of his old commanders were there, and Larry's big, beautiful family was there, of course. Under different circumstances, it would have been wonderful to visit with all of them. At times, I found myself excited to see the friends we hadn't seen in years. But then I remembered why we were all together. I was a mixed bag of emotions, once again.

Breathlessness

After the funeral, we went back to John and Martha's. That sweet little mountain-valley ranch house had always filled me with comfort, but that night, alone in Larry's childhood bedroom, curled up on the bed, my heart hurt so much that I thought I was going to die. I cried so hard and exhaled so deeply that I thought I would never be able to fill my lungs again. The most basic human function escaped me. I couldn't breathe. It was as if I had forgotten how. I was breathless for what seemed like an eternity. Our entire married life flashed before my eyes. I saw Larry as clearly as if he were in the room with me. I saw Ryann and Ellie, so sweet, so innocent. Then, I saw Larry fade away, leaving the three of us standing alone. I was in so much pain that I actually wanted to die.

Then, as if God Himself said, "Nope. Wesley, it's not your time," my breath returned. In His gentle way, He reminded me that all I had to do in those early moments was breathe in and out.

The next day, needing to get out of the house in search of fresh air, I took the girls for a walk. We stopped to throw rocks at the creek. The mindless repetition of launching those stones brought me comfort and reminded me how wonderful a routine can be. Breathe in and out. Pick up a stone and throw it. Do it again. Don't overthink it. Just do it.

In that quiet moment, I heard my grandfather's loving voice: "Focus on what you know, Wesley Ann."

I picked up a rock and threw it.

Building upon that moment, I heard Larry offer a nugget of his wisdom: "She'll get over it, just like she got under it."

He used to say that when one of us got upset about something. It was his way of saying tough moments would pass.

My brain flashed back to my ROTC Commando days, and I heard a growl: "There is no way you are going to make it through this day!"

Shaking away that awful voice, I searched for another and found the sweet voice of our pastor's wife, Clella Lee. I let her voice surround me with the words of the hymns she had sung at Larry's funeral just the day before.

> In Christ alone my hope is found; He is my light, my strength, my song. This Cornerstone, this solid ground; firm through the fiercest drought and storm. (Stuart Townsend and Keith Getty, "In Christ Alone," 2001)

> On Christ, the solid rock, I stand; all other ground is sinking sand, all other ground is sinking sand. (Edward Mote, "My Hope is Built on Nothing Less," 1834)

All those voices, thoughts, and songs came together to bring me strength. I didn't know how we were going to move on without Larry. Every day would be a struggle. But I knew how to be a mother, and I knew how to look after our precious little girls. I could focus on that. I knew I could lean on Jesus. I knew He would give me strength. He could get me through anything. And I knew, just like in Commandos, that the best way to get me to do something is to tell me I can't. It wouldn't be easy, but I knew we could get through Larry's loss with the right perspective and motivation.

I also knew the army life, and I knew I was good at it. Our daily routine back at Fort Bragg was something I knew. Even though we had only been gone a few days, I missed our military community and began to crave it. We needed to go home. The girls needed to sleep in their own beds, and I needed to get my feet back underneath me. We needed to figure out what our new normal looked like, and we needed to do that at Fort Bragg.

Chapter 13

Critical Decision Point

The truth of the matter is that you
always know the right thing to do.
The hard part is doing it.
—*General Norman Schwarzkopf*

When I was a second lieutenant, serving in the 101st, my company commander told me something I have never forgotten. Grooming me as a future commander, Captain Brian Gray said, "Lieutenant Bauguess, in life you always have two choices. You can choose the easy wrong or the hard right."

On the golf course, we are faced with those decisions every time we play. Do you fix your divot, or do you leave it for the guy behind you? Do you fix your ball mark on the green, or do you simply walk away?

Of course, choosing the "hard right" means you fix your divots and your ball marks—every time. But some players don't. Their self-centered nature allows them to just walk away. "Someone else will fix it," they say to themselves. It's a character flaw.

According to army doctrine (FM 101-5 "Staff Organization and Operations," chapter 5), "Decisions are the means by which the commander translates his vision of the end state into action. Decision making is both science and art."[1]

In 1998, between our Fort Campbell and Korea assignments,

168

Larry and I attended an army school at Fort Leavenworth, Kansas, called the Combined Arms and Services Staff School. That's where young captains learn how to be staff officers. We learned how to write operation orders at the battalion and brigade levels. Our instructors taught us problem-solving techniques and the military decision-making process. Within that process, we learned how to develop different courses of action for military missions and how to build a decision matrix to help us determine which action to choose.

We had to identify three or four courses of action for each mission. Our instructors always made us include "do nothing" as one of our plans. They told us that, in some cases, doing nothing is a valid option. It may not be the preferred technique, but it is always an option. I suppose doing nothing could make sense, but it feels like we'd be choosing the "easy wrong."

Once we decided on a course of action, we had to build and brief the actual plan. We always used a map during our briefings. More often than not, we would have to discuss a critical decision point on that map, which marked a place and time where the commander anticipated he would have to make a decision, based on the elements on the battlefield. Considering the unit's mission, the enemy in the area, the terrain features around him, the number of troops available, and the timeline, the commander would have to make a decision about how to proceed. Wise commanders based their decisions on these factors. Sometimes, commanders had too much information, and other times, they didn't have enough. But, regardless, a decision had to be made, and that decision would have a direct impact on the outcome of the mission.

The Hard Right

"Thank you, Mrs. Bauguess," the gate guard said, returning my ID card.

Mrs. Bauguess, I thought as I offered him a half-hearted smile. *Am I still Mrs. Bauguess? Am I still married? I still feel married.*

The drive from Moravian Falls to Fort Bragg had been relatively

169

quiet. The girls dozed in the back seat; Mom and I rode in silence, alone in our thoughts. We stopped at the Pizza Hut in Spring Lake to grab a pizza. I didn't feel like cooking. I was exhausted. Larry's funeral had taken every last bit of strength I had.

As we drove through Fort Bragg, I made mental notes. Everything looked the same. Driving down Randolph Street, we saw a lady jogging and a group walking on the track. As we circled the Iron Mike statue, we saw a family walking their dog. The Officer's Club and Ryder Golf Course were still there. Golfers were practicing on the putting green as we drove by. Driving through the Normandy Neighborhood, we saw children playing outside and a mom and dad working in their yard.

My head and my heart were at odds. I felt equal parts of calm and frustration seeing that everything looked the same. My head found comfort that all was calm and right on Fort Bragg, but my heart couldn't believe that everything was calm and right when our world had been flipped upside-down.

We took a familiar left onto Zabitosky and then crossed the All-American Expressway. My heart picked up its pace as we turned right onto Bastogne Drive and approached our neighborhood. That familiar right-hand turn from Bastogne onto Virginia Place made me feel better. I just wanted to be home. I needed to breathe. I needed to be enveloped by the safety of our own home.

I focused on our house as it came into view on the left side of the street, but something else caught my eye. A gaggle of ladies had gathered on the right. The sight of them all together on Kristina Torres's porch made me smile.

As I drove past them and pulled onto our driveway, I knew that this was my critical decision point on the battlefield map. I could go in the house with Ryann, Ellie, and my mom and close the door behind us. I could choose the easy wrong, shut us in, and keep the rest of the world out. Or I could choose the hard right and walk across the street to face my sweet neighbors, hug them, and even with a shattered heart try to be normal for a minute.

I sent my mom and the girls inside with the pizza. With a

humble smile on my face, a lump in my throat, and tears in my eyes, I walked across Virginia Place.

Those ladies greeted me with open arms and wide-open hearts. In an instant, I knew we would all be okay. Most of them had attended Larry's funeral. All of them had proven themselves to be loyal and true friends. We were so lucky to have such wonderful friends living all around us. We visited for a few minutes. Then, I told them I needed to go inside to check on the girls. Assuring them that we would be back out after dinner, I walked across the street with a tiny boost in confidence.

Thoughtful Gifts

Our living room looked more like a florist shop than a residence. As I walked through our front door, the aroma of evergreen and gardenia circled me. Floral arrangements and plants sat on every flat surface in our house. A few more sat on the floor. I meandered through the living room, looking at every one of them. I took note of each card and smiled when I saw whom it was from. The arrangements were so beautiful. The sight of them and the love and support they represented brought me peace and strength. I will never forget how they made me feel.

A small gardenia bush gave off the most powerful scent and reminded me of my grandmother. For years, Grandma Burton had tended to a beautiful gardenia bush in front of their Florida home. It was a love/hate relationship. In her strong Staten Island accent, she called it her "Ga-damn-ya" bush because that thing grew so big and so fast, she could never keep up with it.

Next to one of the flower arrangements was an envelope addressed to me. I held it for a moment, opened the flap, and pulled out the card. On a yellow background, the cover displayed a drawing of vertical brown lines, maybe two dozen, curved and gathered in the middle with twine, and tied off in a bow. The inside of the card read, "Sticks in a bundle are harder to break." The card was from

Kristina Torres. It was a perfect visual example of the strength and loving support I received my sweet neighbors.

After my little stroll through that strange indoor garden, I walked deeper into the house toward the kitchen. I found Mom, Ryann, and Ellie seated at the dining room table already feasting on the pizza.

"Mommy, did you see all the flowers?" Ellie said with delight.

"Yes! Can you believe that?"

I sat down with them and smiled, fully taking in this beautiful trio. Caught up in a vortex of emotions, I was indescribably sad but so lucky to be surrounded by such wonderful people. I knew how lucky I was to be the mother of these two precious little girls. I was so lucky to have my mom by my side. And I was so lucky to have such wonderful friends and neighbors. How could I be so hurt and so thankful at the same time?

I couldn't eat, which wasn't a surprise. I ate very little over the course of that horrible week. I forced down a few tiny bites and then excused myself. Everyone else stayed at the table.

My legs were dreadfully weak as I climbed the stairs. I knew I needed to do some exercise, but that would have to wait. I walked into our bedroom, which was the hardest place in the house for me. It was so cold and empty. Walking beyond the bedroom into the bathroom, I paused to look at myself in the mirror. My eyes were puffy, yet my face appeared thin. My body looked thin, as well—worn out. Considering what we just had just gone through and realizing that I had hardly eaten a thing all week, I guess I should have expected that.

In the midst of my self-examination, I noticed a very clean smell. I looked down at the countertop and saw that it was perfectly clean. The floor was clean, too. Walking deeper into the bathroom, where the shower and commode were, I found a sparkling toilet and recently mopped floor. The shower curtain was closed. I was actually a little frightened to open it because I knew how dirty it had been when I left.

Reminiscent of *Psycho*, I reached for the shower curtain and pulled it open. I was horrified to find it spotless. Someone not only saw how dirty my shower was, but they cleaned it and put up a new shower curtain. I was truly mortified, out-of-this-world embarrassed. I wondered who had done it. I knew I had to first apologize and then thank them profusely. The whole scene made me laugh out loud.

I pulled myself together and went back downstairs. The girls had finished dinner and were helping Grammie clean the table. I asked them if they wanted to go outside to play.

"Yes!" they squealed.

Sticks in a Bundle

As the garage door lifted, I caught a glimpse of my neighbors, still outside, just as they said they would be. Helmets on, the girls zoomed down the driveway on their pink Barbie scooters. With a nudge from the gradual slope, I walked across the street to face the person who had cleaned my nasty shower. It was Amy St. Peter. I started laughing and shivered a little when I told her how embarrassed I was. She laughed in return and agreed that it was pretty gross. She couldn't help but tease me a little. We all laughed and cried and then laughed again.

I thanked them all. They all had a hand in beautifying our house. Keli had brought in and arranged all the flowers and plants. Amy had done the cleaning. Kristina, Jennifer, and Chantell had helped, too. They were awesome and so funny. We were so lucky to have such wonderful neighbors. I believe it's worth mentioning that all those ladies had deployed husbands. I represented their worst fear as army wives and, yet, they embraced me and loved me all the same.

As the warm spring evening progressed, several other neighbors joined us outside. One sweet lady came over to see how we were doing. She told me she was so happy to see us out because she had no idea how to approach us otherwise. That validated our decision to go outside. By doing so, we extended an invitation to our neighbors. We gave them permission to talk to us and treat us just as we had always been treated before. We had always played outside. All the kids played on the street. It was so normal, so routine. I found comfort in doing the normal and routine things. That night, we stayed outside until dark.

After we said our "good nights" and "see you tomorrows," we headed inside. I gave the girls their bath, read them a story, and tucked them into bed. I kissed them and hugged them and told them how much I loved them, and then I sat in the rocking chair until they fell asleep.

Avoiding my empty bedroom, I went back downstairs and piddled around. I made a cup of hot tea and settled in front of my computer to check my e-mail. Soon enough, I was staring at my inbox, disappointed and heartbroken because there were no e-mails from Larry. There would never be another e-mail from Larry. Out of pure curiosity, I Googled Larry's name and several articles popped up. Feeling like a watchdog wanting to make sure Larry was properly respected, I clicked on one of them. I made it halfway through the article from the *Winston-Salem Journal* before grief swallowed me whole. Submitting to the pain, I laid my head down and wept.

Later that night, lying on top of our bed and staring out the window, I reflected upon the day. I was so hurt and so empty. I was exhausted from the drive and the endless emotional roller coaster. I still couldn't imagine living my life without Larry. I wondered what it was like in heaven. I wondered what he was doing. Was he with Grandma and Grandpa Burton? I wondered how he could be there and leave us here. How was I going to raise these girls without him?

Just as I started to really feel sorry for myself, the image of my neighbors standing on Kristina's porch flashed into my mind. The visual image of those amazing ladies, my sticks in a bundle, made me smile. I closed my eyes and thanked God for them. I thanked Him for their comic relief and for my clean shower. I thanked Him for bringing us home safely and for carrying us through the whole week. I thanked Him for His never-ending strength and for always pushing me toward the hard right.

Chapter 14

Steps of Faith

For we walk by faith, not by sight.
—2 Corinthians 5:7 (NKJV)

A second little black "United States Army" pouch sat on my desk. My casualty assistance officer left it with me after one of our meetings. That officer was a source of strength and comfort during Larry's funeral. He made all the arrangements on the Army's behalf and coordinated directly with the funeral home so I didn't have to. After the funeral, he faithfully led me through the paperwork jungle of early army widowhood. He proved himself an invaluable friend as we settled Larry's estate and set up benefits for the girls. As army wives, we lean on our husbands to navigate through government bureaucracy. As army widows, we lean on our casualty assistance officers. I'm so thankful God blessed me with a good one.

After staring at the little black pouch for several minutes, I conjured the courage to pick it up and pull open the drawstrings. Inside, I found Larry's dog tags, his memorial bracelet, and a mysterious camera. The dog tags, I knew all too well. Running my fingers across the cold metal plates, I traced the indentation of his name, social security number, blood type, and religion. Larry's dog tags represented his life and reminded me of our bungee jump in Boone.

I reached for his bracelet, a cold metal cuff that read, "For the boys who don't come home." My stomach soured at the irony.

Larry wore that bracelet all the time. He never took it off. Memorial bracelets are treasured items among the military ranks. They are sacred. Soldiers wear them to honor one another and to remember those who made the ultimate sacrifice. I put his bracelet on my wrist.

I had never seen the camera before. I wasn't even sure it was Larry's. I stood up from my desk and took a few steps while I inspected the silver camera. Pacing in anticipation, I slid open the battery hatch and found not only batteries but also a memory card. I was surprised the Army had left that in there. I closed the little door and, out of pure curiosity, pressed the power button. The camera came to life and focused on my feet.

I clicked the image review button but really had no expectation of finding any pictures. *Surely the Army sterilized this card before giving it to me.* After a thoughtful pause, as if the camera was unsure of itself, it revealed an image of bearded men in strange uniforms. I studied their faces and then pressed the button to see if there were any more images. There were several. As I thumbed through the images, I saw 82nd Paratroopers I recognized, as well as Afghani and Pakistani men I did not. Larry was only in one image, which led me to believe that he was the photographer. When I saw a schoolhouse in the background, I suspected the photos were from the peace meeting in Pakistan.

Standing by my desk, lost in that camera, I was desperate for answers. I thumbed through the photos over and over again. Why did this happen? What happened exactly? Why Larry? Foolishly, I hoped the pictures would speak to me, but only silence and confusion remained.

I put Larry's items back in the little black pouch, tucked them away in my desk, and sat back down in quiet reflection. In those early days of widowhood, my attention span was very short. I wanted to know the details but could only accept information in small doses. Overwhelmed by the fact that I faced a future without my best friend, my most trusted advisor, the love of my life, I could only process a few things at a time. Larry wasn't there to help me brainstorm, war-game, or make any decisions. I couldn't believe our children would live every day of their lives without their daddy, their coach, their mentor. How were we ever going to survive without him?

Still seated at my desk, I reached for my Bible and mindlessly flipped it open. The pages opened directly to Jeremiah 29. I had previously underlined only one verse on the whole page. It captured my attention:

> *"For I know the plans I have for you," declares the Lord, "plans to prosper you and not to harm you, plans to give you hope and a future."* —Jeremiah 29:11 (NIV)

I pressed my lips together in stubborn agreement and, as quickly as I had opened it, I closed the book again. Feeling immeasurable frustration, I had to admit that verse was the reminder I needed. Though I sometimes wrestled with God, I knew He would guide my steps. And I knew, in His timing, healing and answers would come.

Pens for Progress

Robin Meade was still chewing on our Pens for Progress story. After learning about Larry's death, she wondered if she should still run it. The division public affairs officer called and, with an abundance of respect, asked me what I wanted to do.

"Run the story," I said without hesitation. "That story is about our children collecting pens for the children in Afghanistan. Run it. It's what Larry would want us to do."

Robin Meade and her team came to Fort Bragg for the Memorial Day broadcast of *Robin & Company*. The girls and I watched from home. During her show, Robin presented several good news stories highlighting military families, showing our nation how truly resilient we are. Toward the end of her morning show, Robin rolled the Pens for Progress story.

In a rare moment of pure bliss, Ryann and Ellie giggled and pointed as they saw themselves on TV. The story was fabulous and truly blessed us with a chance to escape the sadness of the previous two weeks. It was nice to go back in time to the month before, when we collected the pens and prepared to send them to Larry. The kids in the video were so cute, so innocent, and so happy to be a part of this little mission to help other kids.

The producers caught me off guard at the very end of the story when a picture of Larry appeared on the screen. My heart stopped when I saw his face on TV. Robin's voice-over told her audience that Larry was killed in action three days after we taped the story. It was incredibly respectful but still hard to see. I didn't know it at the time, but things like that would continue to happen for years and years. We would have those special moments of joy only to have our grief pop up in our faces like targets on a firing range. How do you balance joy and grief? How do you allow yourself to be happy during happy moments when there is so much to be sad about? The emotional roller coaster of early widowhood never stopped.

An hour or so after her show wrapped, Robin Meade came to our house for a personal visit. Our house lit up with excitement the moment she walked in. She wore a navy blue, white, and yellow outfit with the coolest navy and white striped wedges. Ellie could not take her eyes off those shoes. Smiling at her, Robin took them off and let her try them on. My sweet baby girl clunked around the house in Robin's shoes during her entire visit. I didn't think she would ever take them off.

Robin was very playful and gracious with both girls. Ryann proudly showed her our butterfly pavilion. We had ordered caterpillars, took care of them, and watched them turn into butterflies. Robin said she was very impressed. Next, Ellie showed Robin her fish, a Beta named Ben.

Not to be outdone by her sister, Ryann showed off her Beta fish, too.

"His name is Sushi. Get it? A fish named Sushi," she giggled.

She always giggled when she said his name. Everybody laughed.

At one point in her visit, Robin asked how I was doing and waited with compassion to hear my answer. Of course, I said I was fine, completely masking how I really felt. She read my face, saw through my answer, and offered me a hug. She commented on my strength but noticed that I had lost weight since we first met.

"Grief does strange things to a body," I said.

"Take care of yourself. You need energy to keep up with these girls."

She was right, and I told her I would try.

Toward the end of our visit, Robin let us take a few pictures with her. Ellie was still wearing Robin's shoes. A little disappointed when she had to return them, Ellie did eventually give them back. I thanked Robin for coming and told her how much her visit meant to us. She was positively lovely. We watched as she crossed the street, got in her car, and drove away. As I type these words nearly ten years later, we remain thankful to Robin for visiting us on that first Memorial Day, and Ellie still talks about those shoes.

Walter Reed Trip

Before Larry's death, I had thought about taking Ryann and Ellie on a summer trip to Washington, DC. Our nation was at war, and it seemed like a meaningful time to introduce them to our patriotic roots. After Larry's death, I was even more steadfast in my desire to take the girls up there. Our family may have been sucker-punched, but we were still wildly patriotic. I wanted the girls to remain proud of our country.

My aspiration to visit DC was coupled with a new desire to visit our wounded paratroopers at Walter Reed. My first step was to call First Sergeant John Condliffe, one of the 4th Brigade rear-detachment leaders, and ask him for guidance. Offering his full support, he gave me the number to the 82nd Airborne Division liaison office at Walter Reed and gave me permission to coordinate with them directly. Nervously, I placed the call to Staff Sergeant James Babin, one of the two 82nd liaisons. After a quick but meaningful conversation, we made plans to meet on Friday, July 27, 2007.

As my visit approached, I placed another call to First Sergeant Condliffe.

"First Sergeant, I don't want to show up empty-handed. What should I take up there with me?" I asked.

Without hesitation, he responded by saying, "Anything with an 82nd patch. And, ma'am, you can't go wrong with chocolate!"

Two items from my family readiness group bag of tricks came to mind. The girls and I ran to town to get the supplies we needed. Visiting a local craft store, we bought royal blue and red card stock, ink pads, rubber stamps, cellophane bags, and red and blue ribbon. On our way home, we stopped at the commissary to pick up eight bags of Hershey's Nuggets. The girls giggled in delight when they saw how much chocolate we were buying. I think they thought it was all for them.

We went straight to work when we got home. I set up one craft station full of paper, ink pads, and stamps for the girls to play with and a similar station for me. Once the girls were happily stamping away, I pulled out two of my own ink stamps. One of them had an 82nd patch on it, and the other had "Thank You" written in a beautiful script. I stamped red 82nd patches and blue "Thank You" messages all over white printer paper, creating a beautiful and patriotic page. Repeating the process, I made ten pages. Cutting the paper into one-inch strips, I wrapped each little strip around a Hershey's Nugget and taped it at the end. Then, I placed the chocolates in little cellophane bags and tied them with a piece of ribbon. After nearly two hours of tedious work, I had twenty bags of chocolates. I hoped it was enough.

Working with the card stock, I made layered paper magnets. I printed out a bunch of 82nd patches on white paper and cut them into two-inch by three-inch pieces. Then, I cut the royal blue and red paper consecutively bigger to frame the patch and stuck them all together with scrapbooking tape. I glued little magnets on the back and finished the product by using a stamp that said, "Sending you a little prayer ... that God will keep you in His care."[1]

I stamped the saying on the back in blue ink and then signed it. I guess it sounds silly now, but I loved those little 82nd magnets.

I hoped the troopers would accept them as a small gesture of my appreciation.

The girls, my mom, and I took our trip to DC in late July. Enjoying the walk around our nation's capital, the girls were most impressed by the Washington Monument. Making themselves dizzy, they looked all the way up to the top and giggled as they watched the clouds move over the extraordinary tower. They also enjoyed the Museum of Natural History. They loved seeing the animals, especially the flying squirrels. But their favorite place in all of DC was a cookie shop in the Pentagon City Mall called Larry's Cookies. Seeing their daddy's name above a cookie shop was the epitome of cool.

Washington, DC is a special place. Being there that summer filled me with an interesting blend of patriotism and heartache. Walking along the mall and breathing the historic air filled me with pride. But I was still so heartbroken that my chest physically hurt.

On the last day of our DC trip, I made my very first visit to Walter Reed Army Medical Center. My mom and the girls were still sleeping when I left our hotel room. While I was waiting for the Walter Reed shuttle bus, I decided to inventory the two large canvas bags one more time. Paper magnets and little bags of chocolate just didn't seem like enough, so before we left home, I had gone to the Clothing Sales store on Fort Bragg to pick up several 82nd T-shirt and hat bundles and 82nd car magnets. Ginny Rodriguez, our division commander's wife and my dear friend, had given me several comfort items to bring up, as well. We hoped the items would bring our paratroopers a little comfort from home.

Staff Sergeant Babin was waiting for me in the second-floor lobby when I arrived at Walter Reed. He was tall and handsome, with a rugged edge. As we shook hands, I immediately noticed his combat medic badge. The fact that he was a medic who had served in a combat zone endeared him to me instantly. As we spoke, he shifted his weight from one foot to the other and took a step back, revealing a cane propped against the chair behind him. Noticing a limp as he reached for it, I would soon discover that Staff Sergeant Babin was not only a medic but also a wounded paratrooper. Serving at Walter Reed as a division liaison, he was caring for his Airborne brothers while he was healing from his own battle wounds. Refusing to let my emotions get the best of me, I swallowed hard and fought to withhold my tears. After only a few seconds of small talk, we began our walk through the halls to find our first wounded trooper.

Staff Sergeant Babin and I talked a little more as we stepped through the halls of Walter Reed. In advance of my visit, one of our division's ladies had told him about Larry. With sincerity and kindness, he said he was sorry for our loss. I thanked him but asked him not to tell the wounded troopers that I was an 82nd widow. I was there for them, not for me. They didn't need to know. He understood.

At every patient room, Staff Sergeant Babin entered first and asked the paratrooper if I could come in. Every one of them said yes. With his approving nod, I walked in slowly, respectfully. A shy but warm smile spread across my face as I neared each hospital bed. I started each conversation with a rather weak and humble, "Hi." Introducing myself as Wesley, I told them I was visiting from Fort Bragg.

I tried so hard not to ask, "How are you?" because I knew how stupid that question would sound. People had asked me that question in my early days of widowhood. The most natural, yet unspoken, response was, "How do you think I am?" I knew better than to back myself into that corner. Instead, I asked them where they were from and asked about their unit. Some of the troopers felt like talking while others did not, but every one of them was completely respectful. And even confined to hospital beds, those 82nd Airborne Division Paratroopers were mightily impressive. I knew I was in the presence of greatness.

We visited nine paratroopers on the patient wards that late-July morning. During each visit, I gave the troopers the bags of chocolates and magnets, which were remarkably well received. (I guess you can't go wrong with 82nd patches and chocolate.) I gave the car magnets and T-shirt bundles to the parents and spouses I met. Before I left their rooms, I asked each paratrooper if they needed anything from Fort Bragg. They were all so humble. Not one of them asked for a single thing. I was incredibly blessed by every visit but left feeling like I needed to do much more.

After visiting with the paratroopers on the patient wards, Staff Sergeant Babin took me to the intensive care unit (ICU) to see a trooper who had arrived just the night before. When we got there, he was sleeping, but we were able to visit with his mom. Her face revealed the worry she so clearly had for her son. She was living a parent's worst nightmare. But in that very dark moment, she focused on the light. She was so thankful for Staff Sergeant Babin, the 82nd liaison office, and the medical team at Walter Reed. She told me they were receiving exceptional care, and she had faith that her son would recover. I was so thankful to hear her story and see how much she appreciated the 82nd liaisons during that very scary time. Once we finished our quiet conversation, I hugged her good-bye and went back out into the hallway.

I looked apprehensively around the ICU. A quiet busyness consumed the space. My eyes traveled the length of one of the walls and prayerfully read each name on the placards outside the ICU rooms. One name, at the very end, took my breath away.

Dudek.

I knew a Dudek at Appalachian. I took a few steps toward the room but stopped to ask a nurse if she could tell me his first name.

"His first name is Daniel," she quickly replied.

Danny Dudek? It couldn't be, I thought. *Please don't be him,* I prayed.

I asked the busy nurse if I could go in to see him, and she gave me a permissive nod. Nervously peeking into the ICU room, I saw a sleeping man. My heart was beating so fast that it made my legs tremble. The sleeping man didn't look like Danny at all. That made me feel a little better, but I still couldn't take my eyes off him. Just as I told myself to stop staring, the man opened his eyes.

He smiled one of his big Danny Dudek smiles and said, "Wesley Bauguess, what in the world are you doing here?"

"What am I doing here? What are *you* doing here?"

Danny Dudek had the best attitude of any cadet I had known at Appalachian. He always had a smile on his face. The man was always happy. Two years ahead of me and a year ahead of Larry, he had provided a great example for us to follow. As a tabbed Commando long before we were, he could have smoked us at any moment, but Danny encouraged us instead. In the worst moments of Commando training, he would give us knowing nods and that Dudek grin that somehow told us we were going to be okay.

Danny and Larry competed on the Appalachian Ranger Challenge team. Ranger Challenge teams practice army skills such as building and crossing one-rope bridges, land navigation, road marching, marksmanship, and weapons assembly. Other universities also had Ranger Challenge teams, and once a year they would all come together for a huge competition. The Appalachian team was a squared-away, tightly knit band of brothers. Remembering Danny as a super strong member of the Ranger Challenge team and as a Commando brother, it was hard to see him in that hospital bed.

Danny told me he had been on patrol in Iraq when his vehicle hit an improvised explosive device (IED). I could tell he was badly injured, but he dismissed it, saying, "It's no big deal. I just can't feel my feet."

Always positive, classic Danny, he shifted the focus to me. Having already heard about Larry's death, he told me how sorry he was and then asked how the girls were doing. Fully knowing I could talk about Ryann and Ellie for hours, I kept my report brief and told him we were fine.

I'll never forget Danny Dudek's smile at school or in that ICU room. He was still Danny. Full of life and as positive as the day is long, he knew he would get through it. He told me he was thankful to be alive. I was thankful, too. We talked a while longer, and then I asked him if he needed anything.

Of course, he said no.

I kissed his forehead, promised to visit him again, and stepped back out of his room.

By the end of my Walter Reed visit, I was physically, mentally, and emotionally spent. I thanked Staff Sergeant Babin for guiding me through the wards and allowing me to tag along. He thanked me for coming and told me again he was sorry for my loss. Turning and stepping away from Staff Sergeant Babin, I felt incredible sadness. I was sad because our troopers were badly injured and their lives were forever changed. I was sad for their families. I was sad because I felt useless. I felt like I should do more for them. I wondered if I had helped them at all.

Follow-up WRAMC Visit

I returned to Walter Reed a few weeks later, mostly to check on Danny. No longer in the ICU, I found him in a new room on a new floor. He was still smiling as he updated me on his injuries. There wasn't much progress with his legs, but his spirits were still high.

We talked about Larry. Neither of us could believe he was gone. Danny shared with me that he had lost a soldier in the IED blast. Trying to decide if he should talk with the fallen soldier's mother, he asked my opinion. I told him how meaningful it had been for me to receive the phone call from Lieutenant Colonel Baker. It was so good for me to hear his voice. I encouraged Danny to reach out to her.

I hope those words helped Danny and inspired him to meet with his soldier's mother. At the end of our visit, I hugged him gently and kissed his forehead just like I had done before. I asked him if he needed anything.

Predictably, he smiled and said no.

I promised to keep in touch and slowly stepped out of his room. Danny is still in the Army. In January 2015, he was promoted to full-bird colonel. He is a champion and an advocate for fellow wounded soldiers. I was lucky to meet Danny in college and truly blessed to know him now.

Meaningful Steps

That first summer without Larry was emotional, to say the least. It began with a visit from a sweet news anchor. I found comfort in knowing that someone outside of our army community recognized the significance of Larry's loss. Ellie found comfort when she stepped into her shoes. My experience at Walter Reed revealed a meaningful connection to others affected by this horrible war and laid a foundation for future service. Finding Danny Dudek in the ICU filled me with sadness at first. But seeing him smiling through it gave me hope. His positivity was a tremendous boost. All those opportunities were unexpected, but they were all connected. I know God led me to and through each one of them. I suspect Larry had a hand in them, too.

Chapter 15

Somewhere I Belong

Go back to the basics. Focus on what you know.
—*Albion Robert Burton*

Whenever my golf swing gets out of whack, I hear my grandfather's voice: "Wesley Ann, focus on what you know. Slow it down, three-quarter swing, picture finish." I close my eyes, lean on my instincts, and rely on muscle memory. In life, I do that, too. When things get out of hand or out of control, when my life is in danger of running off the rails, I try to focus on what I know. Slow down. Be still. Listen to the whisper of God.

Sometimes, we can grip too tightly to the worldly things we know. By so doing, we lose our focus on God's picture. In Luke 22:42 (NIV), Jesus prays, "Father, if you are willing, take this cup from me; yet not my will, but yours be done." Not my will, but Your will. Not my will—God's will. I lost sight of that completely in the fall of 2007 as I struggled to hold on to what I knew.

Holding On

During the summer of 2007, the girls and I nursed our broken hearts and began the process of mending our broken family. All summer long, in the midst of our grief, I tried to focus on what I knew. I knew how to be a good mommy to Ryann and Ellie. I knew how to be a good daughter. I knew how to be a friend. And I knew the Army. Having served as an officer and as an army spouse, I was intimately familiar with two shades of army green. I convinced myself I could still exist in the army world. I had to. I didn't want to let it go.

As summer turned to fall, my mom and I prepared the girls for a brand-new school year. They would return to McNair Elementary School, and we would remain residents of Virginia Place until May 2008. I was so thankful to keep at least that part of our life consistent. Staying in our home for one more school year, we could focus on what we knew and settle back into a familiar routine. As the girls geared up for the new school year, I prepared for the new family readiness group year.

Family readiness groups typically hit the pause button for the summer and don't hold meetings in June, July, or August. We stay in touch with our unit family members the best we can, but all the summer traveling makes it difficult to host meetings and plan events. By the end of August, I was eager to see my unit friends and continue serving our 82nd families.

Division

The division command and staff spouses group met once a month inside Gavin Hall, an administration building located next to division headquarters. I could hear the room buzzing with activity as I made my nervous approach. I wondered if they would still accept me as their peer. Did I still belong there? Would I still have a place at the table?

I had spoken with Shanna several times over the summer and expressed my desire to continue leading the family readiness group. She and Lieutenant Colonel Baker supported my decision completely. Other division ladies did, too. But when that moment arrived, I froze in the hallway. Could I really do it?

Ginny Rodriguez welcomed me at the door with a warm embrace and answered every one of my questions with a resounding, "Yes!"

The hugs and smiles I received from the division ladies validated my desire to continue serving the All-American Division. Receiving well wishes along the way, I crossed the room to the 4th Brigade table and found an open seat next to Shanna.

To kick off the beginning of the family readiness group year, we were treated to a performance from the 82nd Airborne Division All-American Chorus. They are magnificent! Paratroopers in the chorus represent different units within the 82nd and different branches within the Army, to include infantry, artillery, service support, and the cavalry. They are handsome young men, active-duty paratroopers, and they sure can sing.

As they always do, the chorus marched into the meeting room, calling cadence and forming two semicircles in front of the division ladies. Hearing their cadence filled me with pride and brought me back to my army days. They began the show with "My Girl" by the Temptations, a favorite among the division ladies. The lead singer serenaded Ginny, making her blush. It was lighthearted and sweet. Their second song was "It's All Right," an upbeat and catchy little number made famous by Huey Lewis and the News. The chorus's rendition was fabulous. It was hard to sit still when they sang that song. Looking around the room, I could see that everyone was enjoying their performance. I did, too, until I actually listened to the words they were singing.

> It's all right. Everybody knows that it's all right. Oh, it's all right. (Peter Hans and Robert Rans [Huey Lewis and the News], "It's All Right")

The little voice in my head woke up and said, *Wait a minute. No, it isn't! It's not all right. How can it be all right? I'm not all right. Larry's not all right. Ryann and Ellie aren't all right.*

Then, I heard, "Eve-ry-bo-dy clap your hands. Boop-um-mow-mow."

And I thought, *What in the world? How can they be singing this song? How can they be all joyful and happy? Do they not know what we've been through? Our country is at war! This entire division is deployed right now! We suffered tremendous losses over the summer. Walter Reed is full of wounded soldiers. And these dudes are singing about everything being all right? They're not over there fighting for their lives. They're here singing for a bunch of ladies! It's not all right! Larry's not all right! Danny's not all right! I'm ... not ... all ... right!*

I tried very hard to squelch my impending doom. I tried to swallow my tears and sniff away my runny nose before anyone saw me or noticed my change in mood. I tried so hard to keep my cool, but such an attempt proved to be futile. Shanna noticed and handed me a tissue. I just shook my head, sunk deep into my chair, and tried to hide my toxic concoction of sorrow and rage.

I pulled myself together by the end of the song and politely clapped in response to their performance, but I began to seriously doubt my own judgment. I was caught up in a vortex of emotions. I wanted to be there. I wanted to continue to serve, but how could I do that without betraying my own feelings? How could I suppress my sorrow? How would I control my newfound anger? Lord knows I tried.

The next song was Toby Keith's "American Soldier." Fully recognizing what was about to happen, I took a few more tissues and braced myself. I knew what was coming. All I could do was sit there and wait for the words to come.

> I don't want to die for you, but if dyin's asking me, I'll bear that cross with honor 'cause freedom don't come free. (Toby Keith and Chuck Cannon [Toby Keith], "American Soldier")

Call in the dogs and put out the fire—I was done. The floodgates could hold no more. Any attempt to stifle my emotions at that point would have been useless. I didn't even try to hide my sobs. Luckily, the compassion in that room was abundant. Everyone understood and probably expected it. The 4th Brigade ladies provided loving comfort, and my distraction was forgiven.

Believe it or not, the rest of the meeting went off without a hitch. Once we got down to business, I was fine. I just needed something tangible to focus on. I enjoyed hearing about all the upcoming events, and I was happy to have the opportunity to plug in. It was nice to see the division ladies again. It actually felt really good to be back in there.

Brigade

Later in the week, I attended the brigade meeting. The ladies of our brigade were delightful, every one of them a hard worker. It was our turn to host the division's annual silent auction fundraiser. One of the family readiness group leaders in our brigade volunteered to take the lead. She had been planning for the October event since early spring.

That sweet lady had called me one day early in the deployment, before Larry was killed. Her unit had just lost a soldier, and she was troubled. She didn't think we should even do the silent auction when our boys were at war. I understood her concern. Outsiders would probably agree. It was just a silly auction. But I told her Larry's great quote: "We are living the history that our children will study." I told her that we honor the men who are fighting for us by driving on. They would want us to. The silent auction raises money for good causes. We could host the event in an honorable manner, with style and class. By doing so, we would carry on a thirty-year tradition.

The entire brigade meeting that September was dedicated to silent auction planning. The theme would be "All-American Silent Auction." The brigade ladies wanted to celebrate and honor all generations of paratroopers, past and present. I thought it was perfect, and I was thankful for the opportunity to help.

Battalion

A few days later, Shanna and I hosted our battalion meeting. We met in the battalion conference room about ten minutes before our company family readiness group leaders arrived. Shanna placed all the meeting materials on the table while I prepared some refreshments. Our company ladies arrived one by one, each of them offering me a hug and a welcoming smile.

Shanna began the meeting and shared the information we had received from the division and brigade meetings. We covered all the current business and discussed future events. We were approaching the halfway mark for the deployment and, individually, our soldiers would begin rotating home for their two-week mid-deployment leave. Several ladies made comments about their husband's upcoming rest and relaxation (R&R). They were understandably giddy that their loved ones were coming home for a much-needed break. They shared vacation ideas and family plans. One of the ladies even talked about the romantic rendezvous she had planned for her husband. I played along at first, grinning, nodding, and smiling. But soon enough, I could feel my skin temperature rise, especially around my neck. I tried to hide it. I tried to talk myself down, but the vortex of emotions threatened to overtake me once again.

I felt like an idiot. I had put myself in that position. I was the one trying to hold on to my place in the family readiness group. Those ladies had every right to be excited about their husbands' homecoming. They should be able to freely express that excitement with their peers. They were allowed to be happy. I just didn't need to hear it. I didn't need the reminder that Larry and I would never have another romantic rendezvous. We would never have another family vacation. Right then and there, I realized I couldn't do that to myself. The revelation hit me like a ton of bricks and stole the breath from my chest. I couldn't do it. I could no longer be an effective leader within this family readiness group. I couldn't take away their joy and hope, but I didn't need to subject myself to it. I sat back in my chair, fully defeated. I endured the remainder of the meeting in silence and went home dazed and confused.

Now what? I thought. *I just spent the entire summer convincing myself that I could do this, but I can't. I hate this! What do I do now? Where do I belong?*

After dinner, Shanna called to check on me. She knew something had happened to me during the meeting. I plopped down on the couch and told her I couldn't do it. She understood, and we cried on the phone for nearly two hours as we realized transition was the only answer. I didn't want to abandon her. I didn't want to quit, but I couldn't keep putting myself in that situation. I was different. My "normal" had changed, and I couldn't pretend that it hadn't.

Eventually, we created a new plan. Shanna would be the "front man," and I would help from the shadows. She agreed to keep me in the loop, and I agreed to help her plan events. I'd participate as much as I could. It was important for me to stay connected and see them through the deployment, but I had to do it with self-imposed limits.

Darkness

At one point over the summer, Keli Lowman had told me she would be watching me. She was afraid that, while battling my grief, I would submit to the dark side. In September 2007, I went there for a visit.

One day, while the girls were at school, I went out to the garage and opened one of Larry's footlockers. I hadn't touched any of his gear since my casualty assistance officer and I had inventoried it in June. I wasn't looking for anything in particular. I just needed to busy my hands with something. Sifting through Larry's uniforms and t-shirts, I mindlessly moved them from one side of the box to the other. Frustrated by the sheer number of brown army t-shirts, I pulled all of them out to see if there was anything else in the box. Two CD cases at the very bottom caught my eye: Metallica and Linkin Park.

I thought about Larry and his younger brother, Terry. Looking at the clean-cut siblings, you would never guess that they were die-hard Metallica fans. The two of them had the time of their lives at the Summer Sanitarium concert in Atlanta, Georgia, in July 2003. Larry came back with Linkin Park and Limp Bizkit CDs to add to his collection of heavy metal and classic rock albums. Much to their mother's dismay, Larry and Terry grew up listening to KISS, AC/

DC, and Metallica. I think they did a pretty good job balancing their strong Christian upbringing and their love for this genre of music.

Holding the two CD cases, I remembered how Larry would make me crazy on long car rides. He would wait until Ryann and Ellie fell asleep in their car seats and then cue a Metallica CD.

"Good sleeping music," he'd say, with a crooked little smile. "Don't worry. The girls are too young to understand the lyrics."

I'd just roll my eyes, shake my head, and smile back at him. The truth is that I liked that music, too, though I never really admitted it to him.

Larry liked to quiz me when we were in the car listening to classic rock. A song would come on the radio, and he would say, "Who sings this song?" Sometimes, I would surprise him and actually answer correctly. I had a brother who listened to KISS and AC/DC, too.

I opened the garage door and climbed into my car, which was parked on the driveway. Sitting in our SUV with the windows down, I played disk two of Metallica's *S&M* (Symphony and Metallica) CD. I pushed the seat back, closed my eyes, and lost myself in Larry's music. The first song was "Nothing Else Matters." I smiled at the appropriateness of the title and the lyrics. I played it twice. Then, I skipped around a little and listened to "For Whom the Bell Tolls" and "Wherever I May Roam."

I glanced outside to the left and right. Virginia Place was especially quiet that day. No one was outside. That was probably good since I was sitting in my car, in the driveway, listening to Metallica.

After nearly an hour, I switched CDs. Larry's Linkin Park CD was a live recording of a concert they played in Texas. The album, *Live in Texas*, became my widow soundtrack. I hadn't listened to it nearly as much as Larry had, but I recognized some of the songs. I knew that one of his favorites was "In the End." I remembered it right away. I love the piano solos at the beginning and end of the song. I took a deep breath as I reflected on their lyrics.

> I tried so hard and got so far, but in the end it doesn't
> even matter. (Brad Delson, Chester Charles Bennington,
> Joseph Hahn, Mike Shinoda and Robert G. Bourdon
> [Linkin Park], "In the End")

That's how I felt! I tried so hard—and got so far. Larry and I had a beautiful marriage. It was the real deal. He was the love of my life. We were going to make it. We were going to grow old together. We were a perfect army family. I totally supported him. We were an awesome command team. I poured everything I had into taking care of our family and our unit families. I spent four years in the Army ROTC, five years on active duty, and eight years serving as an army wife and volunteer. Seventeen years! I lived my entire adult life in and around the Army. And in the blink of an eye, it disappeared. Like a paratrooper avoiding an obstacle on the ground, my army life slipped away. Did any of it even matter?

I thought about that very question as I played the song again and again. Finally, I let the CD advance and listened to another Linkin Park song, "Somewhere I Belong." It was as if the band had written the song for me. With my mouth open in disbelief, sitting in the car in my driveway by myself, I played it six times. The words expressed exactly how I felt.

> I wanna heal, I wanna feel like I'm close to something real.
> I wanna find something I wanted all along. Somewhere
> I belong. (Brad Delson, Chester Charles Bennington,
> Joseph Hahn, Mike Shinoda, and Robert G. Bourdon
> [Linkin Park], "Somewhere I Belong")

I wanted to heal. I wanted to feel something other than hurt and loss. I knew how to be Larry's wife and best friend. I knew the Army, and I knew how to run a family readiness group. He was the man I loved. That was the life I loved. It was all gone, and it had thrown me into a tailspin. I didn't belong anywhere. For years, I played that song every time I got into the car alone. I played it repeatedly. That song let me scream about my loss. It was a great outlet for those toxic emotions.

195

Over time, I did realize I needed to lean on someone stronger. I needed to find my footing. I needed to be still and pray for guidance and listen to a wiser voice. Eventually, I realized I needed to return to God. Eventually, I admitted that I needed to spend a lot more time with Jesus and a little less time in fellowship with Linkin Park.

Part 4

Making a Difference

One person can make a difference
and every person should try.
—*John F. Kennedy*

Ellie's elementary school principal told "The Starfish Story" during her fifth-grade graduation ceremony in June 2013. The principal's intent was to send the students off to middle school with an encouraging anecdote, but that story had a profound impact on me.

Her version was an adaptation of a short story written by Loren Eiseley, which is presented in his book, *The Star Thrower*, published in 1978.[1] In "The Starfish Story," we find a young boy standing on a sandy shore among a wide swath of abandoned starfish. Methodically, the boy attempts to save as many as he can by throwing them back into the ocean. A passerby notes the vast number of starfish and questions his effort, saying that he isn't making a difference. The boy picks up another starfish, returns it to the water, and replies, "I made a difference for that one."[2] What a profound statement!

Make a difference.

In the weeks, months and years after Larry's death, all I wanted to do was make a difference.

In addition to my grief and sorrow, I had survivor's guilt. Larry was gone. He gave his life so that others could live. Friends of ours have given life, limb, and eyesight to preserve our freedom. How do you repay that?

You can't.

How do you come out of it unchanged?

You don't.

I couldn't contain the overwhelming urge to do something with my hands, to raise my voice and to somehow earn Larry's sacrifice. I had to make a difference, even if it was for only one starfish at a time.

Chapter 16

82nd Airborne Division Wounded Warrior Committee

Faith, by itself, if it is not accompanied by action,
is dead.
—*James 2:17 (NIV)*

In recent years, I've come to know Major Dan Rooney, an F-16 fighter pilot and a Professional Golfers' Association (PGA) member. Dan created the Folds of Honor Foundation, a national military charity that provides educational scholarships to the children of fallen and wounded service members. (I'll write about that in chapter 22, but I want to quote him here). In his book *A Patriot's Calling: Living Life between Fear and Faith*, Dan writes about the word *synchronicity* and defines it as the moment when chance and purpose come together.

He writes, "Synchronicity—*chance with a purpose*—is all around us; those instances in our life when we are at an exact place at just the right moment."[1]

I agree with Dan, and I would take it a step further. I believe that God oversees those moments. I believe He has a plan for all of us. I don't believe in coincidence. I believe we are at the right place at the right time because it is God's plan for us to be there. He has set it up that way. The problem is — we also have free will. We may not always choose to do the right thing. We may not always recognize those moments of synchronicity.

During his speech at the 2013 National Rifle Association convention, Dan said, "That moment when chance and purpose come together is meaningless unless you have the courage and the faith to take action." God may lead us to those moments of synchronicity, but we must act upon them.

***

Whatever your hand finds to do, do it with all your might, for in the grave, where you are going, there is neither working nor planning nor knowledge nor wisdom.
(Ecclesiastes 9:10 NIV)

***

A New Mission

In chapter 15, I told you how lost I felt and how I longed for somewhere to belong. I had just lost my husband, my status in the army community, and my sense of purpose. Looking back now, I can see that God was preparing me for future service. He was shaping me, molding me, grooming me to help others.

In late September 2007, a sweet friend called with an incredible opportunity. Tara Farris—whose husband, Colonel Billy Don Farris, was the commander of the 2nd Brigade, 82nd Airborne Division—called to talk about the casualties that the division had suffered during the Taliban's Spring and Summer Offensive. She knew that I had visited Walter Reed over the summer, so she thought I might be interested in a new idea. A donation had been sent to division headquarters to be used specifically in support of our wounded paratroopers. Army units are not allowed to accept money from American citizens, so they were trying to find a way to honor the generosity of the donor and keep the division out of trouble.

While the division leadership was conducting the required legal reviews, the division ladies took the ball and ran with it. They wanted to build a committee of volunteers to visit our wounded and provide comfort items. They just needed someone to take the lead. Tara and I had served together within the ranks of the division spouses group, so she knew I loved our paratroopers. She also knew that I was struggling to find my place. Thinking I would be perfect, she asked me if I would consider leading the effort.

Without hesitation, I said, "Yes. Absolutely! I will do it!"

She cautioned me and asked if I wanted to think about it, but I didn't need to. It was exactly what I needed. I told her about the division, brigade, and battalion steering committee meetings and my realization that I could no longer serve in that capacity. I wanted to hold on to something. I needed to keep my hands busy. I still wanted to serve the division and the paratroopers I so loved.

Delighted by the chance to continue serving, I looked at Tara's offer as a gift from God. It was my moment of synchronicity. Using Tara Farris and a generous donation, God gave me a new purpose and helped me find my way out of the darkness.

"When can I start?"

Top Eight List from 82nd Liaisons

Tara had already communicated with the 82nd liaisons at Walter Reed to find out their immediate needs. Staff Sergeant Babin sent her a "top eight list" of items:

1. 82nd notebook with compartment for business cards (for family-member caregivers)
2. Breakaway pants (like basketball player warm-ups)
3. Fleece top (full-zip jacket)
4. "Proud Mom, Dad, Spouse of a Paratrooper" T-shirts
5. 82nd Sweatshirts
6. 82nd Pens
7. 82nd Flags
8. 82nd T-shirts

Right away, I called Staff Sergeant Babin to talk about the list and schedule my next visit. Over the phone, I told him about the donation and our fledgling committee. He sounded surprised but equally grateful and said anything we could do for the guys at

Walter Reed would be greatly appreciated. We arranged a visit for the following Friday.

Just as we were getting ready to end our conversation, an item on the list caught my eye. I asked Staff Sergeant Babin about the breakaway pants. He told me that the 101st soldiers already had them and our guys really wanted them. Their pants were black with snaps down the sides and a Screaming Eagle embroidered on the left upper thigh. Highly functional, especially for soldiers with lower body injuries, the breakaway pants allowed the doctors to tend to the patients' wounds without making them disrobe. The pants were discreet, and they were cool.

As I mentioned in chapter 11, there has always been a healthy competition between military branches and between army divisions. At Walter Reed, the competition was raised to an entirely new level. The liaisons saturated their patients' rooms with unit pride. Unit symbols were on posters, signs, and all kinds of trinkets and gadgets. Wounded soldiers, still craving attachment to their beloved units, put patches and symbols on their walls and on their wheelchairs. They even put unit stickers on their prosthetic legs. This kind of competition and unit pride is undeniably healthy. It keeps the fire burning and keeps the soldiers' spirits up, even during incredible trials. The 101st had cool breakaway pants, so I told Staff Sergeant Babin that our guys would have them soon.

Even though I still have an abundance of love for the Screaming Eagles, I told Staff Sergeant Babin, "We will not be outdone by another division, not on my watch."

Within a few days, Staff Sergeant Babin found out where the 101st got their pants and provided me with the supplier's contact information. Immediately, I called them and ordered a navy-blue set with an 82nd patch as a sample. The pants arrived the day before I left for my fall Walter Reed visit.

Fall Walter Reed Visit

Just as he had done during my summer visit, Staff Sergeant Babin met me in the second-floor lobby. And just as I had done during the summer visit, I arrived with 82nd magnets and little patriotic bags of chocolate. Staff Sergeant Babin had told me that the chocolate was a hit last time. Why re-create the wheel?

We visited seven paratroopers at Walter Reed that morning. Every one of them was amazingly resilient. Every one of them remains a national hero. Knowing I was in the presence of greatness, I humbly offered them each a bag of chocolates and a magnet. I offered a few car magnets and 82nd t-shirts to parent caregivers and asked them if they needed anything from Fort Bragg. Once again, none of them asked for a thing, but they all appreciated the visit.

After our time at Walter Reed, Staff Sergeant Babin and I traveled to Bethesda Naval Hospital to visit two inpatient paratroopers. After telling me that they both had significant head injuries, he cautioned me, so I knew it would be difficult. One of the troopers was in surgery, but I got to see the other one. He was a member of one of the cavalry units.

Because of a sizable dent in his skull and a multitude of stitches, his head injury was difficult to witness. As I stepped into his room, my heart instantly ached for him. With every step, I questioned my very presence in his hospital room, knowing I could do so little to comfort him. Defiant of my own apprehension, I stepped toward his bed and smiled at him. To my surprise, he was in great spirits. His bright smile welcomed me. He was friendly and more than willing to talk with me. His positive outlook was captivating.

Delighted that I had come up all the way from Fort Bragg to see him, he thanked me for stopping by. He was truly grateful, and I was incredibly humbled. It became clear to me that visitors from Fort Bragg were greatly welcomed. The visit had a positive impact on him, but the honor was mine.

During the ride back to Walter Reed, I asked Staff Sergeant Babin about the items on the "top eight list."

"The guys really like the set of breakaway pants you brought up," he said.

"I like them, too. Our start up-donation is five thousand dollars. I'll get as many as I can. The fleece jackets will be next."

I didn't know how much the breakaway pants would cost, but

I would stretch our funds as far as I could. When we returned to Walter Reed, I thanked Staff Sergeant Babin for the visit and for all he did on a daily basis for our paratroopers. After hugging him good-bye, I walked away heavy-hearted.

As I drove out through the Walter Reed gate, I could feel the tears building in my eyes. A visit like that is powerful, emotional, and physically draining. But I left even more determined to create something significant to help them. I started to think about how to build this committee and who I would recruit to help me.

***

And my God will meet all your needs
according to the riches of his glory in Christ Jesus.
—Philippians 4:19 (NIV)

***

82WWC

Upon my return home, I typed an e-mail introducing the 82nd Airborne Division Wounded Warrior Committee (82WWC) and sent it to nineteen of my closest Fort Bragg friends. In the e-mail, I announced the time and location of our first meeting and offered a quick synopsis of our mission. The first meeting was a success. I was so impressed by the turnout and the compassion of the Fort Bragg ladies who attended. We talked about the breakaway pants. As a committee, we decided to order them right away from a local supplier, The Trophy House, Inc., in Fayetteville. Fully acknowledging that the pants would consume our funding, we spent the rest of the meeting brainstorming about fund-raising options and plotting the way forward.

I ran the 82WWC for three years. We started with a simple meeting at a local sandwich shop. From those nineteen close friends, we eventually built the committee to over forty members. We conducted meetings every month and visited our paratroopers at Walter Reed and Bethesda at least once a month. We flew to San Antonio, Texas, twice a year to visit our wounded troopers at Brooke Army Medical Center. We also welcomed and visited troopers who arrived at Womack Army Medical Center at Fort Bragg. Every visit was emotional, spiritual, and meaningful. I never got tired of seeing our paratroopers. They are amazing.

We began our gifting with the breakaway pants. Our paratroopers loved them! We then offered fleece full-zip jackets, which provided comfort and warmth. The next spring, we presented our troopers with super cool t-shirts and athletic shorts. We eventually expanded our gifts to include umbrellas, rain jackets, mouse pads, water bottles, and key chains and offered a backpack to hold everything. We also provided a spouse/caregiver bag with girlie things like fuzzy slippers, soaps, lotions, pink 82nd t-shirts, and gift cards to local restaurants. Every item we provided had an 82nd patch on it. That little symbol reminded them that they were still members of the All-American Division.

We could do all of this with God's blessing and guidance. We couldn't have done any of it without Him. As good stewards of the committee's finances, we watched every penny and thoroughly analyzed every purchase. When our funds ran low, we prayed.

I often said to our committee members, "God will provide. I believe in this mission, and I believe that, if we're on the right path, we will be given what we need. When the funds run completely out, we'll know it's time to stop."

God is so good. Our funds never ran out. He provided what we needed exactly when we needed it.

I wish I could write about every visit, every lady who served on the committee, every item we created, and every encounter we had with our wounded superheroes, but there just isn't enough time or space. Instead, for the rest of this chapter and in chapter 18, I will highlight the most meaningful stories.

Breakaway Pants and Fleece Jackets

On November 12, 2007, I received a call from the awesome team at The Trophy House. Our breakaway pants had arrived. They came in just in time for my next Walter Reed trip. Without delay, I rushed down to check them out.

Made of a silky polyester material, the pants had snaps all the way down the sides and had a drawstring at the waist. The embroidery of the 82nd patch and master-parachutist wings on the left upper thigh was flawless. I was so impressed and thankful that they looked as good as they did. I loaded the boxes and thanked the staff for their great work. Once I got home, I laid out all the pants and separated them by size. Unable to resist, I tried on a pair. They were so cool; I started jumping up and down. I was so happy to finally have something other than magnets and chocolates to give to our wounded troopers at Walter Reed.

I began the tedious and frustrating task of folding the breakaway pants into a cute little package. It wasn't easy. The fabric was so slippery; it wouldn't cooperate at all. I wanted to roll them neatly and tie them with a patriotic ribbon, but that was easier said than done. Every time I rolled them up, part of them would slip out the side. I'd correct one side and they would slip out the other side. It was crazy! Finally, I found a way to neatly fold them without having them fall apart. It took me the rest of the day and part of the night to wrap all fifty pairs of breakaway pants.

Once I was done with the pants, I finished preparing the get-well cards. As a committee, we began a new function called Crafty Day and agreed to host one each month. During Crafty Day, we made the troopers get-well and "thinking of you" cards. We also made cards for upcoming holidays, like Thanksgiving, Christmas, and Easter. All the cards were hand-made, each of them unique. My favorite get-well card had red and royal blue card stock layered on top of a tan card. The front had an 82nd patch stamped on it. On the inside left, we stamped a Ralph Waldo Emerson quote: "What lies before us and what lies behind us are tiny compared to what lies within us."

Then Tara Farris, who has the most beautiful penmanship I have ever seen, wrote on the inside right, "You have blessed us with your service. May God bless you as you continue to heal. Love, the 82nd ABN DIV WWC."

They were beautiful cards! Once I was satisfied, I put the

neatly wrapped breakaway pants, several dozen bags of chocolates (because we couldn't stop giving those out), and the get-well cards in two canvas bags. I placed the bags by the front door and then went upstairs to play with Ryann and Ellie.

The next day, after a five-hour car ride, I met Staff Sergeant Babin in the second-floor lobby. Feeling like a little kid on Christmas morning, I couldn't wait to show him the breakaway pants. Looking ridiculous as I walked up with two bulging canvas bags, one on each shoulder, he shook his head and laughed when he saw me coming.

In the short time I had known him, Staff Sergeant Babin had endeared himself to me. He walked the line as a combat medic, saving lives on the battlefield until he became a patient himself. And then, he walked the wards at Walter Reed, tending to his Airborne brothers and taking care of their families. He was one of them, still recovering from his own wounds but taking care of others. He did it with a smile on his face and a sense of humor as dry as Larry's.

I showed him the breakaway pants and waited nervously for his approval. He laughed at the ribbon and the tag.

"It's a girl thing," I explained.

Untying the ribbon, he looked them over and smiled.

"They're gonna love 'em," he said. "The 101st won't have anything on us now!"

Staff Sergeant Babin escorted me to the patient rooms. One by one, we visited with our recovering paratroopers. I offered them each a card, a bag of chocolates, and a breakaway bundle. Most of them had seen the 101st soldiers wearing their breakaways, so they loved having a pair of their own. I was so happy to offer them.

After visiting all the troopers on the wards, I sat down with Staff Sergeant Babin, and we talked about the other items on the wish list. I told him the fleece jackets would be the next big purchase, once we raised the funds to order them. Jotting down his thoughts about colors and styles, he recommended a full-zip jacket as opposed to a half-zip pullover.

"Troopers with upper-body injuries wouldn't be able to manage a pullover very well."

Before I left Staff Sergeant Babin that day, we decided on gray jackets. They would look nice with the navy breakaway pants. I really wanted to order the jackets for our guys; I just didn't have the first clue where we would get the money.

In late November, we received three unexpected donations. God is so good! The 1-73 Cavalry family readiness group donated $150, and two private individuals each donated $1,000. It was exactly what we needed to pay for the fleece jackets. I went down to The Trophy House right away to order the charcoal gray, full-zip fleece jackets. We asked for an 82nd patch and master-parachutist wings to be embroidered on the left side, just like the breakaway pants.

The fleece jackets came in on December 14, and they were awesome. I wrapped fifty jackets into rolls and tied them with ribbons to give to the troopers who already received a set of breakaways. Then, I found a way to wrap the jackets and the rest of the breakaway pants together in one bundle to give to new patients. The bundles were perfect, ribbons and all.

During a Christmastime visit to Walter Reed, I met with Staff Sergeant Babin and showed him the jackets. Once again, I was relieved when he gave his approval, never wanting to disappoint him. We weren't able to visit many troopers that time. Those who could travel home had already left. I did see a few, though, and they liked the jackets. I handed each of them the bundle, a bag of chocolates, and a thank-you note and then wished them a merry Christmas. As always, I enjoyed talking with them and with their family members.

Just after the New Year arrived, I received an e-mail from one of the wounded paratroopers we had visited in December, a young private first class at Walter Reed. The e-mail said,

> Thank you for the work you do to help us soldiers returning from downrange. You make me feel proud to be part of my 82nd family. God bless you and thank you once again. I love the fleece and the breakaway pants as well.

Notes like that warmed my heart and inspired me to do more.

Chapter 17

Return to Golf

A faithful friend is a strong defense; and he
that hath found him hath found a treasure.
—*Louisa May Alcott*

Golf is a faithful friend. No matter how much time passes between
encounters, it is always easy for us to pick up right where we left
off. During golf season in high school and college, I practiced nearly
every day. Good swings became muscle memory. Good habits were
tattooed on my soul. Once I left my college golf days behind, rounds
with my beloved friend became rare treats. Early army life didn't
offer us much time to play, but Larry and I did find creative ways
to reunite with this wonderful game.

Call-for-Fire Missions

Larry grew up a baseball player, but once we were married, he
developed a fondness for golf and could parlay his baseball swing
into a decent golf swing. A talented athlete, Larry had good hand-eye
coordination, and he was strong. He could really crush his drives.
His approach shots were pretty good, too. As a married couple, it
was so nice to share a common sport. I was always thankful that
he took up the game.

As lieutenants in the 101st at Fort Campbell, we lived in a tiny duplex on a corner lot across the street from a wide-open field. When we were actually together and had time to play, Larry and I would grab our golf clubs, head over to Cole Park Golf Course, and play a few holes. Sometimes, when we worked late and didn't have time to play, we'd grab a few irons and a dozen golf balls and head out into the backyard to practice our short games.

As my best friend, my confidant, and my most-trusted advisor, Larry taught me everything I knew about being a soldier and a leader. Even though I was serving in the Medical Service Corps, Larry made sure I kept my infantry skills sharp. One skill that was easily lost if not practiced was calling for artillery fire.

Standing in our backyard, Larry would look across the street and pick out a target, keeping the location a secret. I would set up a makeshift tee box and drop a dozen golf balls, ready to serve as the artillery battery.

Holding his hands up to his eyes as if they were binoculars, Larry would say, "You, this is me. Enemy tank, in the open, at grid AB12345678. Looks like a seven-iron."

I would address the ball with my trusty seven-iron and launch the shot over the road, above the telephone wires, and out toward the open field.

When the ball was in the air, holding my finish, I'd say, "Shot over."

"Shot out," Larry would reply.

As the ball landed, I'd say, "Splash over."

"Splash out," he'd reply. Looking through his "binos" once again, he'd say, "Adjust fire. Add ten meters. Left fifteen meters."

I would club up to my six-iron for a little more distance and aim a little more to the left.

"Shot over."

"Shot out."

"Splash over."

"Splash out."

Larry would call the location changes and I would "walk the rounds" onto the target.

Eventually, he'd say, "Direct hit. Fire for effect!"

Then, in rapid fire, I'd hit the rest of the golf balls and try to land them on target. If I did well enough, he'd send a new message.

"Target destroyed. Nice work."

Then, we would trade places.

Keeping our golf and call-for-fire skills sharp, we played our little game as often as we could. We always enjoyed it, except for the time the military police sergeant caught us hitting golf balls over the road. I'm pretty sure MPs love nothing more than catching young officers doing something wrong. Luckily for us, the young sergeant was a golfer. After we explained our game, he laughed and let us off with a warning.

Larry and I continued to play golf, as time would allow, throughout our army careers. Fortunate to have commanders who loved the game, each of our army units hosted annual golf tournaments. That guaranteed at least two rounds a year. Larry loved it when his unit hosted one.

Leading up to a tournament, if his foursome lacked a player, he would say, "Well, I guess I could ask my wife to play."

"Ugh, sir. Really?" was the usual response from the soldiers who had never met me.

Larry would grin and withhold my golf history until we got to the first tee. After the first hole, they would change their tune and thoroughly welcome me into their group.

In late 2000, following sweet Ryann's arrival, my golf game fell by the wayside. I really had no choice but to leave my old friend behind. I loved everything about being a wife and mother and poured all I had to give into Larry, Ryann, and a little later our sweet Ellie. Motherhood was all consuming and wonderful. Golf retreated and became the furthest thing from my mind.

Public Affairs

The 82nd Airborne Division public affairs officer had a strong presence but a gentle side. Major Tom Earnhardt protected our family from the media so beautifully in our early days of loss. He knew Larry as he had served with him in Korea. I had met Major Earnhardt before the deployment during a division spouses meeting when he gave a public affairs briefing about handling the media in a time of loss. I paid particular attention when he said the media might call or visit the service member's home in search of information and ask for a comment. In my role as a family readiness group leader, I had a feeling that subject matter would come up again.

Larry and I had spoken with the media a time or two while serving with the 82nd. In December 2006, we participated in an article with the Associated Press about preparing for a combat deployment. When the reporter asked me how we prepared the kids for a yearlong deployment, I told him, "We tried to explain to them that Daddy would be gone for every holiday, one time." That helped our four- and six-year-old daughters put his absence into perspective.

The day after Larry was killed, I recalled the media briefing the public affairs officer had given us. I also thought about the nature of Larry's death. He was in Pakistan at a peace meeting. Assuming the horrific turn of events would be newsworthy, I wanted to get ahead of it by issuing a statement, but I had no idea what to say. Unable to put my thoughts together, I reached out to Major Earnhardt for help. Over the phone, with perfect compassion, he told me to find a quiet and comfortable place.

Then, he said, "Tell me about Larry."

Curled up on our living room couch, I began to tell him our life story. I told him that we had met in ROTC at Appalachian. I told him about serving together as lieutenants and captains. I told him about the girls and what an amazing daddy Larry was. I emphasized how happy he was to be serving in the 82nd and how much I supported him in everything he did. I said that I remained committed to the unit, the mission, and our country, and I told him that Larry would expect us to drive on.

After our long, highly therapeutic conversation, Major Earnhardt said, "Give me an hour. I'll send you something you can work with. Feel free to change it in any way, but it will give you a head start."

We bounced e-mails back and forth for the rest of the afternoon. Our final product was beautiful.

Bauguess Family Statement

Larry and I have publicly shared our family's perspective on life in the Army and life within the 82nd Airborne Division. We did this in the hopes that people could understand and grasp the mutual commitment we both feel toward our great Nation. Larry's untimely death has left a void in our family that will never be filled, nor should we expect it to be. We are left with many joyous and happy memories, and we are left with a lot of sadness of unfulfilled dreams. Over time, I expect the happy and joyous memories to outweigh the sadness. However, we are very sad and hurt now.

My family is now faced with life without Larry in our immediate presence, and this will require time to adjust to and cope with. I would like to ask that members of the media respect our privacy while we come to grips with the tragic changes our lives have so recently endured. I expect and anticipate there will be a time when I will again feel comfortable speaking publicly about our family and our lives, but now is not that time.

Larry and I shared a strong commitment to our Nation and its defense. It was our individual commitment to the Country that led us together. Now, he has given his life in defense of freedom, and I remain committed to everything we stood for before his sacrifice. Larry expects us to carry on and remain committed, and that's what we're going to do.

Larry would want to be remembered as a father, a husband, a son and a Paratrooper. He loved his family unconditionally, and he loved his work with his Soldiers just as much. He was a positive influence on all who knew him. He was passionate about his life.

Larry was in his element here at Fort Bragg and in the 82nd Airborne Division. He beamed with pride before leaving for work and when he came home. He just loved his Paratroopers. He had a special appreciation for his NCO's. Many of them privately told me how deep a bond they had with him. He loved them and they loved him.

Larry went to Appalachian State University, where we met, to play baseball. When baseball didn't work out, he was walking across campus one day and noticed a group of ROTC cadets rappelling off the side of the gym. He always said, at that moment, he knew what he wanted to do from then forward. He joined the ROTC program and never looked back. We met as fellow cadets in the ROTC program.

Larry was a man of great personal faith. He was raised in his church in Moravian Falls, NC, and he grew up in a loving Christian home. It was this faith, which became the bedrock of our relationship. He was able to express his faith in God to me so clearly, and it became a bond that sustained our family. We truly believe that, now, he'll watch over us as our own personal angel.

As a father and husband, Larry was amazing. He managed to achieve a remarkable balance in his life. He made sure our daughters understood the importance of everything that was happening within our family. He saw it as his duty to maintain a very strong connection with the girls. When he talked to them, he wouldn't do it standing above them. He would physically get down on their level. He was so good at talking to them and playing with them. He enjoyed letting everything else go and focusing on them.

In his Mother's Day email to me, he said, "Thank you, Wesley ... thank you for allowing me to be a Paratrooper in the US Army ... I am very proud of you and all that you do for me, our children and all of the troopers of this battalion ... I miss you but love you so much more." He never ended a phone call or email without personally acknowledging each of us and telling each of us, "I love you."

The Patriot Foundation

In early October 2007, seated at a table in the public affairs building on Ardennes Road, Major Earnhardt and I were plotting the direction of the 82WWC. In addition to all his other duties, such as protecting families of the fallen and speaking on behalf of the entire deployed division, he had been providing top cover for our fledgling Wounded Warrior Committee. Acting as our liaison to the 82nd Airborne Division, his guidance and protection was invaluable. I couldn't have led the 82WWC without him.

That day, we discussed upcoming events, hospital visits, and fund-raising opportunities. At the end of our meeting, almost as an afterthought, he told me about a rising charity in Pinehurst.

Well-known Pinehurst businessman Spike Smith founded the Patriot Foundation[1] in 2003. Retired navy captain Chuck Deleot was an original member. In 2007, Chuck became the Patriot Foundation president and chairman of the board of directors, positions he still holds today. The mission of this fantastic organization is to provide support for the families of fallen, wounded, injured, and ill Airborne and special operations soldiers through educational and child-care grants.

Patriot Foundation members recognize the importance of educating the children of our fallen and wounded service members. Those resilient and exceptional children represent the future of our country. At their core, they are military children who know what service means; they know what discipline is; they know how sacrifice feels. Children of our fallen heroes drive on after they lose a military parent. They want to make them proud. Children of our wounded, injured, and seriously ill service members press on, living with the wounds of their military parents, which is a daily reminder that freedom isn't free.

The Patriot Foundation also recognizes that the spouses left behind need help, too. Spouses of our wounded service members often have to go back to work or back to school for a degree or other training to provide for the financial stability of their families. The Patriot Foundation provides grants for child care to help those nonmilitary parents prepare for a return to the workplace. The grants provided by the Patriot Foundation are changing lives.

Of course, back in October 2007, I didn't know all of that. Major Earnhardt just told me that they host an annual golf tournament and a formal dinner to raise money for families of the fallen. This was the first I had heard of such a group. I was humbled and interested in their mission right from the start. As Major Earnhardt told me about the foundation and their upcoming event, I could see his wheels spinning.

"Do you have any interest in going to the dinner? It would be good for them to actually meet one of the widows they are hoping to help," he said.

I thought about it for a second. It did make sense. As compassionate and generous souls, they are raising money for people they don't even know. I thought it would be beneficial for them to actually meet one of us.

Out of nowhere, I conjured my golf-ego-from-high-school-past and said, "I'll go to the dinner if I can play in the tournament."

Stunned, he replied, "You play golf?"

"I do. Well, I did," I backpedaled. "I played in college. I haven't played in years, but I'd like to play again."

"I'll call Mr. Deleot. He may just love this."

Mr. Deleot, indeed, loved the idea, and I had less than two weeks to live up to my ego.

Return to Golf

The event took place at National Golf Club in Pinehurst, currently known as Pinehurst Number Nine. It was a two-day pro-am tournament (Saturday and Sunday), a three-player best ball (two amateurs and one golf pro). I drove to Pinehurst on Friday for the practice round and a sponsor dinner.

In the two weeks between the public affairs meeting and my practice round, I only had time to dust off my clubs and swing them in the backyard. As I drove through the sea of pine trees along

Midland Road, I began to panic. I hadn't hit a golf ball in years. Since motherhood had begun, I had barely touched my golf clubs.

What was I thinking? I thought as I pulled up to the gate. *I should have just agreed to go to the dinner.*

By the grace of God, my golf swing came back to me like a true old friend. Standing on the driving range at National, I stared at the little white ball sitting on the perfectly manicured grass. In that moment, I felt my grandfather's presence. My trusty seven-iron in my grip, I drew the club back, stopped at a three-quarter swing, followed through, and held my picture finish. The ball flew through the air, soaring toward my target. Golf is good. Thank you, Grandpa!

My confidence returned with every purely hit shot.

Satisfied with my warm-up on the driving range, I headed to the first tee. It felt so good to be out on the golf course again. The beauty of the course, the crispness of the autumn air, and the undeniable gift of returning to the sport of my youth wrapped me in strength and replenished my soul. My loyal companion had returned.

Satisfied with my game, I stopped after nine holes and spent the rest of the afternoon on the putting green. I practiced short putts and long ones, continuing to build my confidence. As I was nearing the end of my putting session, I saw Major Earnhardt and a few others walking toward me. After a warm greeting, he introduced me to Mr. Chuck Deleot, the Patriot Foundation president. As I shook his hand, I thanked him for including me in the tournament. He told me he was happy I was there but very sorry for my loss. We chatted for a moment, and then they went inside as I continued putting.

An hour later, in the security of the empty locker room, I began to question my own judgment. I scrambled to get ready and did my best to look presentable, but when it was time to make my appearance, I froze in the door like the girl in the "Yellow Polka Dot Bikini." The significance of that evening was not lost on me. It was my first formal appearance as an army widow and my first time representing other widows. Someone else may have looked at it as just a dinner, but it meant more than that to me. I couldn't explain it. I just felt like that dinner was the beginning of something bigger.

Standing in the locker room, completely abandoned by my golf ego and the confidence I had built on the golf course just an hour earlier, I turned to prayer. I knew God had led me to that moment. I asked Him to lead me out the door. I just needed a push.

At that moment, a lady entered the locker room to powder her nose, and we struck up a conversation. She and her husband, a Special Forces sergeant major, were invited guests of an event sponsor. Sharing the comfort of the locker room, she told me that she didn't know anyone in the Patriot Foundation, so she was thankful she had found me. *She* was thankful she had found *me*! God is so good! Together, we summoned the courage to leave the locker room and join the others.

The cocktail hour had already begun by the time we reached the immaculate bar room. The tavern lights were dim, the ambience was lovely, and the magnificent bar, constructed of a dark wood with brass embellishments, was perfectly polished. Not fond of alcohol, I ordered a Coke and tried to relax. Within a few moments of my arrival, Major Earnhardt found me and introduced me to several Patriot members and sponsors. My apprehension subsided when I realized how welcoming and compassionate they all were. As the social hour progressed, I was pleased to see a few military leaders from Fort Bragg. As I met more people, mingling became much easier.

At dinnertime, Mr. Deleot led us to our tables. I joined a circle table set for six. Lieutenant Colonel Dave Bair, who was representing the 82nd at the dinner, and his wife, Colleen, were seated to my right. To my left sat the wife of one of the primary sponsors of the Patriot golf tournament. Her husband was seated to her left. Major Earnhardt was seated directly across from me. We all introduced ourselves to one another and prepared for an amazing meal.

Just before dinner was served, Mr. Deleot rose to offer a few opening remarks. He thanked all the sponsors for attending and for supporting the Patriot Foundation. He spoke of their mission and relayed how important it was to continue raising educational funds for the families of Fort Bragg's fallen. Just as I had settled into the event and begun to relax, Mr. Deleot said that they were honored to have a "Gold Star mother" with them for the evening and directed their attention to me. I smiled and gave a shy little wave.

With innocent delight, the sweet lady to my left said, "Gold Star mother? How wonderful for you! How do I get a Gold Star?"

I'm sure she meant no harm, but she completely caught me off guard. I didn't know what to say. I glanced across the table at Major Earnhardt and felt heat radiating from Lieutenant Colonel Bair. Gathering my thoughts and recalling my best etiquette, I turned to face her. She was still looking at me, smiling with delight and eagerly expecting an answer.

As politely as I could, I finally said, "Ma'am, you don't want to be one. A Gold Star family member is someone who has lost a soldier in combat. My husband was killed in action in Pakistan in May. A Gold Star wife and a Gold Star mother isn't something you'd ever want to be."

She swallowed hard and sincerely apologized. Then she took a sip of her wine and sat deeper in her chair. It was an awkward moment, but we recovered rather nicely. The dinner was fantastic. I was very impressed by the club and by the Patriot Foundation. At the end of the night, I thanked Mr. Deleot once again. I told him I was honored by the dinner and really looking forward to the golf tournament.

Back on the Links

National was buzzing with excitement when I arrived the next morning. Volunteers were eagerly helping at the registration table, and players were competing for practice space on the driving range and putting green. Four of the golf pros entertained the crowd with a golf clinic and trick-shot show. High above the country club, an airplane circled, waiting for perfect winds and perfect timing.

After the golf clinic and before the shotgun start, the Golden Knights treated us to a demonstration. The super star paratroopers of the US Army Parachute Team jumped right onto the driving range, each of them carrying a meaningful flag. One jumper had an 82nd flag; another had the flag of a special operations unit. The final jumper delivered our national colors. After he arrived, we sang the national anthem with lumps in our throats and tears in our eyes. Moments later, the head pro at National explained the rules of the tournament and sent us off to our starting holes. Major Earnhardt and I were on the same team, and our golf professional was Chris Tucker. Since there is no rank on the golf course, I'll call them Tom and Chris for the remainder of this chapter.

I had been fighting with my nerves the entire morning. Excited to play and hopeful that I wouldn't embarrass myself, I said a silent prayer as we approached our first hole. The first drive on the first hole is always the most fearful shot for me, especially when I am playing with someone new. After the men teed off, I walked to the ladies' tee.

"Swing easy. Don't hit the big ball first. Picture finish," I said to myself.

I produced a good swing and a solid hit. Praise God! I was so happy when the first shot was over.

We had a great day and got along very well as a team. Having played National several times before, Tom and Chris gave me excellent guidance. I enjoyed the luxury of their help and actually played pretty well. As we approached our final holes, we started thinking that we might have a good score to post. After the round, we turned in our scorecard and found out that we were in the hunt.

Measures of Devotion

I put my clubs in the car and grabbed my backpack, just like I had the day before. When I entered the clubhouse, I heard lots of chatter coming from the floor above me. Cocktail hour had already begun. I hurried into the ladies' locker room. With no time to shower or even change my clothes, I did the best I could. I removed my hat, adjusted my ponytail, put on a little powder and lined my eyes. Calling it "good enough," I headed out the door. I was really late.

When I reached the top of the elegant staircase, my apprehension from the night before returned. The grief I had outrun all day finally caught up with me. Hitting me in the back like a sack of bricks, I felt terribly alone even in that very crowded room. I stood there silently, looking at all the couples socializing and enjoying happy hour. The husbands and the wives were so happy.

Fighting the urge to run back downstairs and hide in the locker room, I told myself, "Be strong. Just breathe in and out."

Just as God had sent that sweet lady into the locker room the evening before, He blessed me with two more of His angels. Colonel Paul Bricker and his beautiful wife, Katie, spotted me standing alone and welcomed me with a loving embrace. They remained by my side all evening. A lady after God's own heart, Katie is the kindest and wisest person I know. Colonel Bricker is a ball of fire, an impeccable leader whose energy is limitless. Serving as the 82nd Airborne Division rear detachment commander, he showed incredible compassion for his paratroopers and every member of the All-American family. He especially had a heart for families of the fallen and wounded. When I first met him earlier in 2007, Colonel Bricker told me he had served with Larry in the XVIII Airborne Corps during the Iraq deployment in 2005. He said his job back then was incredibly stressful, but Larry and his fellow majors kept him in stiches and broke the tension almost every day. I was happy to know that Larry and his peers provided comic relief. Colonel Bricker spoke very highly of Larry and, since 2007, he and Katie have been the truest friends.

After the social hour, we made our way into the dining room. Floor-to-ceiling windows surrounded the dining space and provided a stunning view of the golf course. Tables decorated in red, white, and blue heightened the patriotic theme. The members of the Patriot Foundation are unapologetic about their American pride. I loved the atmosphere and being surrounded by people who love our country as much as I do. That night, I was very pleased to be seated next to the Bricker's.

Just as we finished another amazing dinner, the 82nd's All-American Chorus appeared in the doorway. A chill raced up my

221

spine as they marched into the dining room. Flashing back to my emotional response when I had last seen them, I wondered what they would sing and braced for the impact. Showing her tender support, Katie took my hand. The chorus was flawless and wildly patriotic as they performed Lee Greenwood's "Proud to Be an American" and Toby Keith's "American Soldier." Surprisingly, I made it through those songs without shedding a tear.

Just as I started to think I could get through an entire performance without crying, the chorus sang a song that turned me inside out. "Last Full Measure of Devotion," written by Robert Jager,[2] is a beautiful song but an emotional nightmare for someone who has lost a loved one at the hands of the enemy. As the chorus sang that song, I became undone.

The song's roots are in President Abraham Lincoln's Gettysburg Address.[3] In it, President Lincoln spoke of the Union soldiers' last full measure of devotion and the importance of honoring those who gave their lives. Robert Jager took President Lincoln's words and crafted them beautifully into song.

> The last full measure of devotion, beyond the call of duty
> were their deeds,
> The last full measure of devotion, they gave themselves
> to serve the greater need
> (Robert Jager, "Last Full Measure of Devotion")

The All-American Chorus took that song and transformed all of us into puddles of mush. There wasn't a dry eye in the room. The impact was huge. By the end of the night, I was mentally, physically, and emotionally exhausted.

Final Round

The next day started early with a 9:00 a.m. shotgun start. As a team, we continued to play very well. I enjoyed playing with Tom and Chris. They were both great players, and I held my own pretty well. At the end of the round, after turning in our scorecard, Chris and I went upstairs for lunch. Tom stayed downstairs to keep an eye on the scoreboard. When he finally joined us, he met us with good news—we had come in second! During the awards ceremony, Mr. Deleot gave each of us a beautifully embroidered Patriot Foundation crest, matted and framed. It is a personal treasure, hanging in a special place in our home. I was so honored and proud of my team. What an amazing return to golf that was!

Before I headed home, I thanked Mr. Deleot and the other Patriot members. I thanked him for the tournament and the dinners but, more importantly, for all they are doing for the children of fallen soldiers in the Fort Bragg area. Chuck Deleot is a great American who has surrounded himself with exceptional leaders. He and his team volunteer their time to run the Patriot Foundation. Their sole mission is to make a difference in the lives of children whose military parents have given that last full measure of devotion. Daily, they choose the hard right over the easy wrong. They honor our fallen heroes, and they remember those left behind. By providing educational grants, they are changing lives. They are making the world a better place by their example. And they are doing all of that through the game of golf.

Golf is a game that continues to give back—a faithful friend and a treasure, indeed!

Chapter 18

Tattoos and T-shirts

Yeah, he's yelling about my tattoos. We
all live with the scars we choose.
—*Jeffrey Cohen, Kristian Bush, and
Jennifer Nettles (Sugarland),
"Take Me as I Am"*

Larry had six tattoos. Six! You'd never know it by looking at him. He was as clean-cut as they come, a good Christian man. But he loved his tattoos. All six of them were on his upper back.

I remember when he got his first one. He was at Fort Benning, Georgia, for an army school. I was finishing up my lieutenant time at Fort Campbell, Kentucky. As always, in times of separation, we visited each other as often as we could. On this visit, I flew to him. He met me in the tiny Columbus airport with a look in his eye that told me something was not quite right.

"I have something to tell you," he said after a much-needed kiss and hug.

"What is it?"

"I got a tattoo! Don't tell my mom and dad."

"Get out of here!"

"It's true!"

Then, he showed me the Ranger tab he had inked on his upper right shoulder. Completing Ranger School was a very big deal. It was the hardest thing he had ever done at that time in his life. Proud of his tab, Larry wanted it to always be a part of him.

"Did it hurt?"

"Not really."

"You're crazy!"

"About you," he said with a sideways grin.

Larry's second tattoo followed his first rather quickly. On his next trip to Fort Benning, he added a Japanese torii directly below the Ranger tab to symbolize his time with the Rakkasans at Fort Campbell. He was very proud to have served in a unit of such distinction, and he was proud of his torii.

Larry's third tattoo came along after he and his "Geronimos" got out of the slammer at Fort Knox. He and his men came home from that adventure with a great story and cool Opposing Forces Airborne wing tattoos. Larry had his inked on his left shoulder blade, opposite his tab and torii.

Larry's fourth, fifth, and sixth tattoos were all done at the same time. We were finally stationed at Fort Bragg, and Larry's wheels were spinning. I often caught him doodling after dinner. Trying to come up with the perfect tattoo, he knew he wanted it to cover his whole back, and he wanted it to include the girls and me.

"Family is the most important thing. Your family has your back," he'd always say.

One day, he came home for lunch flashing that classic Larry grin.

"I got it!" he said. "Where's the camera? Get the girls. I have to take your pictures."

He only wanted pictures of our eyes and wouldn't say anything else about it. Once he finished the whole roll of film (yes, film), he kissed us all and left again. Hours later, he came home with three sketches. Once the girls and I were seated, he revealed them to us one by one. They were black and white sketches of the eye areas of our faces, the parts that would be covered by a masquerade mask. My eyes were green, and Ryann's and Ellie's were blue. The sketches were amazing! They looked just like us. Larry asked if he could get the artwork tattooed on his back.

"Family always has your back. Will you let me put you on mine?"

The girls squealed and said, "Yes!"

I agreed.

The tattoos were designed and inked by "Big Al" at the Smokin Guns Tattoo shop on Yadkin Road, just outside of Fort Bragg. Taking several weeks to complete, the final product was beautiful, though it was odd to see ourselves when Larry had his shirt off. Many nights, I awoke with a start when Larry was facing away from me and I was staring at myself.

Tattoos and T-shirts

As I said good-bye to a heartbreaking and life-changing 2007, I set my sights and hopes upon a brighter 2008 and continued my quest to keep my hands busy. In early January, I skipped down to the bottom of the original 82WWC top eight list and began searching for cool t-shirt ideas. One day, as I was brainstorming about possible designs, my mind traveled back to a conversation I had with one of our Virginia Place neighbors. Eric Saulsbury, an artillery officer and a dear friend of ours, told me about a meeting he had once had with Big Al.

Eric met with Big Al to begin the dialogue for a new tattoo. Big Al asked Eric if anyone had referred him to the shop. He told him that his buddy Larry Bauguess had gotten a tattoo there, and he thought he'd check them out. Big Al didn't recognize Larry's name, so he asked Eric if he knew what the work looked like.

As Eric described the eyes on Larry's back, Big Al said, "Oh, the major! How is he doing?"

Eric froze in place and then realized he had no choice but to tell Big Al what had happened. Completely shocked, Big Al had to sit down. That was the first time he'd ever heard someone he had inked had been lost. Big Al asked about the girls and about me. Eric told him that we were his neighbors and were doing well.

Then, Big Al told Eric to tell me to stop by anytime and he'd give me a tattoo "on the house." I had to laugh at that. Larry had wanted me to get a tattoo for years.

A smile crossed my face as I recalled Larry's tattoos and Eric's conversation with Big Al. I wondered if Big Al, being the amazing artist that he was, would help us with a t-shirt design in lieu of the complimentary tattoo.

Sonny with the Chance

By the grace of God, no customers were in the shop when I arrived. The only soul in sight was a tattooed guy with a thick beard seated behind the desk. Smiling at him as I nervously approached the elevated counter, I told him my name and asked if I could see Big Al. Much to my disappointment, the bearded man told me that Big Al didn't work there anymore. He had moved to Wilmington.

Great. Now what do I do? I thought.

The gentleman behind the desk must have seen my dismay because he offered me a consolation prize.

"We have lots of talent here. Someone else can help you with your tattoo."

"Oh, I'm not here for a tattoo!" I replied.

He looked at me like I had lobsters crawling out of my ears. So I realized I had some explaining to do. I told him about the tattoo that Big Al had done for Larry. Then, I told him that Larry had been killed in action and that Big Al had offered me a free tattoo as a bereavement gift. I wanted to ask Big Al if he would help us with a T-shirt design instead of the tattoo. Then, I told him all about the 82WWC. The poor guy got more of a story than he expected because, clearly, I am incapable of making a long story short.

"I'll talk to my boss and see if any of the guys would consider helping you. Do you want to leave your number?"

I gave him my business card and backed away from the counter.

He picked up the card and said, with correct pronunciation, "Bauguess."

His eyes narrowed, and he wrinkled his brow.

"Major Bauguess?" he asked.

"Yes. That's my husband."

Then, it was his turn to talk. He told me he had served in the 82nd, in 2-508 when Larry was the executive officer. Tattoo dude had been a medic in the headquarters company. He actually knew Larry pretty well. He had served with him during the summer training mission at West Point. He said Larry was a good guy. I knew that, of course, but it was nice to hear it from one of his men. Tattoo dude told me his name was Sonny. He wasn't in the Army anymore, which explained the full beard.

Moved by our story, he took a renewed interest in the project. Without any further discussion, he told me he would do it. He said he'd start working on a design and call me when he had something. I was so excited. I wanted to hug him but thought I should stay cool. I thanked him half a dozen times and walked out of the shop, grinning from ear to ear.

At the end of January, I got a call from Sonny at Smokin Guns. He was done with the first draft of a t-shirt design. I drove to the tattoo parlor right away. Sadly, his sketch wasn't exactly what I had in mind. It was beautiful artwork but a bit too violent and a little too graphic. I respectfully hid my initial opinion and told him that I would show it to the liaisons at Walter Reed during my next visit. I thanked him for his work and told him I'd let him know what came next.

For the next two weeks, I prayed about our t-shirt design and asked God to send me something great. One day, the image of our class t-shirt from my officer basic course at Fort Sam Houston popped into my head. One of my classmates had designed a t-shirt that had the letters "AMEDD" on the front. Inside each letter was a picture. One letter had the face of a soldier; another had a medevac helicopter, and so on.

Could we do something like that? I wondered.

I went over to my computer and opened the PowerPoint program.

I made two slides. On the first one, I made a number eight as big as the page would allow. On the second slide, I typed a big number two. The numbers were big and thick, like bubble letters. Next, I went to the 82nd Airborne Division website and found some awesome pictures. Copying the pictures, I embedded them into my PowerPoint slides.

In the upper circle of the eight, I placed a picture of a paratrooper leaning against a rock wall and looking through the sights of an automatic rifle. In the lower circle of the eight, I placed a picture of two paratroopers kneeling. One was a leader talking on the radio, and the other was a communications soldier. In the middle of the eight, I placed a picture of a medevac helicopter and a litter team carrying a patient on a stretcher toward the aircraft.

On the next slide, I placed three more pictures. In the top curve of the number two, I placed a picture of an airplane flying high and dropping paratroopers out into the breeze. There were six parachutes exposed and one trooper exiting the aircraft. In the slant of the two, I placed an awesome picture of two troopers looking through the sights of their weapons. At the bottom, I placed a picture of four soldiers who looked like they were about to enter and clear a building.

Once I had all the pictures in place, I printed the slides. Hoping Sonny could do something with them, I went back to Smokin Guns to present my idea. From behind the desk, he asked how the guys at Walter Reed liked his design. Politely, I told Sonny we had a new idea.

I pulled out the two PowerPoint slides and asked him, "Can you draw this?"

He took a good long look at it and said, "Yeah. I can draw that. Give me two weeks."

I had been eagerly anticipating Sonny's sketch for our 82WWC t-shirts. So when he called and told me he was done with the first draft, I couldn't wait to see it.

My heart was in full flutter when he came down from behind the desk with papers in his hand. Cautiously, he laid them out on a pool table and waited for my reaction. The moment I saw his artwork, I wanted to jump up and down. It was awesome! I couldn't believe how good it was.

His sketches looked just like the pictures, but he had added toughness to them. They definitely had the flair of a tattoo artist. It was exactly what I was hoping for.

"It's just the first draft. I can clean them up a bit," he said humbly.

"No way. They're perfect. I can't wait to show this to my team."

This time, I did hug Sonny. After telling him I really loved his work, I asked him what I owed him.

"Just bring me a shirt when they're done."

That's it. That's all he wanted. I promised him I would.

Leaving the tattoo shop while staring at the artwork, I was so entranced that I almost walked into the door.

I visited Sonny several more times throughout my tenure as the 82WWC leader. Every time we used his design on a new item, I brought him one. He is a great American. I am thankful that our paths crossed when they did.

Striking Gold

We had an awesome t-shirt design, but we lacked the funds to create them. So, again, I began to have little conversations with God. I prayed for guidance. I prayed for funding. I had felt God's presence in everything we had done so far, and I knew He was leading us. I continued to believe that if we were on the right path, God would provide.

A short while later, after a support group meeting, I was chatting with a dear friend and fellow widow about the committee. Casey Rodger's husband, Josh, was a CH-47 "Chinook" pilot in the 82nd Combat Aviation Brigade. She lost him on May 30, 2007, two weeks after Larry was killed. Casey and I met during my first support group meeting and had developed a beautiful friendship during the months that followed. One of the most generous and compassionate people I know, Casey asked me a few more questions about the committee and wanted to become involved.

I was delighted to tell her about all our comfort items and

hospital visits. I told her about the t-shirt idea and our small account balance. Before I knew what she was doing, Casey handed me a check for $1,500. At first, I refused. I couldn't take that from her. But she was adamant. She wanted to do something for our wounded paratroopers, and she made me take the check.

The next day, we received a letter and a check from a company in Oregon. The letter stated that the check was a donation to the 82WWC—in the amount of $2,370. I couldn't believe it. Within two days, we had received two checks totaling $3,870. That was more than enough for the first round of t-shirts. God is so good!

It took four months of prayer and creative thought, but we finally had a t-shirt design and the funding to place the order. We just needed a cool saying. Staff Sergeant Albert Comfort, the other superhero 82nd liaison at Walter Reed, provided the perfect quote:

"Americans can sleep peacefully … knowing there are Paratroopers willing to do harm on their behalf."

It is a paraphrase from the old George Orwell quote, "People sleep peaceably in their beds at night only because rough men stand ready to do violence on their behalf."

The committee ladies and the paratroopers loved it. It was just tough enough. Most importantly, it was *true*. It was a reminder, maybe even a poke in the eye, to those in our nation who have never served yet enjoy sleeping under the blanket of freedom our military provides. It was meant especially for those who question Department of Defense funding and those who want to draw down our military. I think some people need a reminder that a strong nation needs a strong military or the freedom they enjoy won't last.

Our liaisons asked us to include an 82nd patch with master parachutist wings and list the "Warrior Ethos" on the front of the shirt. The Warrior Ethos is an unwavering promise:

> I will never accept defeat. I will never leave a fallen comrade. I will never quit. I will always place the mission first.[1]

Paratroopers live and die according to the Warrior Ethos. Everyone should. It was a perfect addition to the t-shirt.

We ordered the t-shirts from Moore Exposure, a Fayetteville company specializing in promotional products. Their graphic designers took Sonny's sketch and turned it into a digital product. It was perfect! By the end of April 2008, the T-shirts were done and ready to make their debut at Walter Reed. The ladies of the 82WWC gathered for a springtime Crafty Day to make tags and cards and to wrap up the t-shirts. Neatly folded and tied with a patriotic ribbon, our very best gift was finally ready to go.

I accompanied Colonel Billy Don Farris during his April visit to Walter Reed. He was the 2nd Brigade commander, but he went up to see all the 82nd Airborne Division Paratroopers. Those who could leave their hospital rooms all gathered in the dining room at the Mologne House. A compassionate leader, Colonel Farris spoke to all of them collectively and then took the time to speak to each of them individually to find out how they were doing and if they needed help with anything. When the time seemed appropriate, I kneeled next to each trooper and offered a t-shirt.

Holding the t-shirt bundle in their hands, most of the troopers smirked at the red, white, and blue ribbon. Just as I had said to Staff Sergeant Babin, I told them it was a girl thing. They untied the t-shirts and took a good look at them, approving the front image immediately. Then, they looked at the back. To a man, they all grinned and nodded, knowing that shirt said it all. Beaming with pride, I thought about Sonny. I wished he could have seen their expressions. They really liked them.

A familiar paratrooper arrived just at the end of our meeting time. Though I had seen him several times before, he had never spoken to me or even let our eyes meet. A double above-the-knee amputee, he was understandably angry. Seated in a wheelchair, he rolled himself into the room, keeping his distance from the crowd. Colonel Farris sat in a chair right next to him and spoke with him for several minutes. He was quiet but respectful to his brigade commander. When I got my chance, I walked over to him. I knelt and told him I had a t-shirt for him. He didn't respond or even lift his head.

Showing him the t-shirt all wrapped up in the ribbon, I told him it was really cool and I hoped he liked it. In his absence of motion, I untied the t-shirt myself and held it so he could see the design on the back. In slow motion, he raised his head and took it all in. When he read the quote, he grinned.

Then, he looked me right in the eye and, through a half-smile, said, "Thanks."

My heart raced! My arms and head started tingling. I'm sure I was blushing. I was so happy to see him smile. He looked at me! He spoke to me! I was so happy. I wanted to hug him but thought I had better not. Instead, I put my hand on his and gently squeezed it.

I replied, "You are so welcome. Do you want another one?"

I would have given that kid anything he wanted. I was so happy to finally connect with him.

We had a wonderful visit that day. Everyone got at least one t-shirt, a pair of navy blue shorts, and a book donated by author Vince Flynn. I gave what was left to our superhero liaisons and promised to bring up more next time. I was positively beaming when I left Walter Reed that day. I loved those T-shirts, and the troopers loved them, too. It was a great day!

When I got home late that night, there was an e-mail waiting for me from Staff Sergeant Babin. It read, "Thanks Ma'am. I have already seen some guys wearing their new gear around. I think you struck gold. I will see you soon. Thanks again."

I'm pretty sure Larry got a kick out of the whole thing. He probably would have loved for me to get a tattoo, but the supremely awesome 82WWC t-shirt was the next best thing.

Chapter 19

W

This book has been brought to you by
the letter W and the number 3.
(Adapted from Sesame Street)

Sesame Street influenced my preschool life greatly. I watched it every day. That show taught me how to count to twelve in English and Spanish. I learned that everybody eats and everybody sleeps. I learned about manners and perseverance, and I learned how to deal with a grouch. Super Grover was my hero, and I dreamed about ladybug picnics. Most importantly, that television show taught me to look for the threads in our lives that tie everything together.

"This episode of *Sesame Street* is brought to you by the letter L and the number 7."

Every time, I'd review the entire episode in my mind.

Oh, yeah, I'd think. *They did have the letter L and the number 7 in there a bunch of times.*

As I reflect upon the tapestry of my life, I can see those threads, but I see the letter W and the number 3.

Grandma Burton always believed things happen in threes. I do, too. There are three golf balls in a sleeve; three outs in baseball. I played three years of collegiate golf. During our army careers, Larry and I served in three high-speed divisions (101st, 2ID, and 82nd). Larry had three deployments to three different countries (Saudi

Arabia, Iraq and Afghanistan). Having served as an army officer, an army spouse, and in my new role as an army widow, I am intimately familiar with three shades of army green.

Growing up as a girl named Wesley, it shouldn't come as a big surprise that my favorite letter is W. I love it. It's different. Every other letter in the English alphabet has a single syllable. W has three! (You just checked, didn't you?) W is unique. It represents the road less traveled.

Grandpa Burton played football at Wagner College on Staten Island, New York. My grandmother kept every one of his college letters. As a child, I loved to hold those green and gold W's in my little hands, rubbing the felt with my fingers. One day, Grandma Burton pinned one to my shirt.

"You can wear this one, Wesley Ann," she said. "It can be your letter until you get one of your own from your school."

I wore it proudly.

Larry grew up in Wilkes County. He went to Wilkes Central High School in Wilkesboro, North Carolina. A standout baseball player on the varsity team, his letterman jacket proudly displayed the letter W, and his high school colors were—wait for it—green and gold!

W

By May 2008, we had made it through our "year of firsts." We had survived everyone's birthday. December was especially hard. Larry's birthday, our wedding anniversary, and Christmas were brutal without him. Larry's unit returned home in April, and I went to Green Ramp to welcome them home. It was important to me to stand for Larry and welcome his troopers home. It was painful, but I'm glad I went.

One evening in May, the girls and I had just finished dinner when the phone rang. Amy Petrenko, the wife of our division chief of staff, was on the line. She was calling with very good news.

The commander in chief was coming to Fort Bragg to attend

the division review during All-American Week at the end of May. The division leaders were identifying a "welcome party" for the president. In addition to the highest commanders, they wanted to include a wounded paratrooper and a surviving family member for the official welcome. Amy called to ask me if I wanted to participate.

"You can think about it. We just need to know soon, so they can start the background checks," she said.

"Oh, my goodness! Yes. Of course, I'll do it," I eagerly replied.

All-American Week is a homecoming event for the paratroopers of the mighty 82nd Airborne Division. Paratroopers, past and present, travel to Fort Bragg from all over the country to attend. Seeing all the troopers in a mass formation on the green grass of Pike Field is magnificent! North Carolina pines line the back end of the field, and a giant 82nd patch stands proudly as a backdrop for the intrepid display. An 82nd Airborne Division formation is something every proud American should get the chance to witness at least once in his or her life.

On the morning of the division review, Pike Field was electric with anticipation. The commander in chief was coming. More importantly, this particular commander in chief was truly respected because he deeply cared for his troops.

Upon my arrival, the Secret Service agents ushered me into the welcome tent. It was dark, hot, and humid inside the windowless cave. I could barely see the other members of the welcome party. We stood in that tent for quite a while. Finally, the sound of crunching gravel and the entrance of a plume of dust told us the president had arrived. A flash of light nearly blinded us as the tent doors opened. I heard feet clopping and shuffling into the tent. When my vision returned and the dust cleared, I saw President George W. Bush standing at the end of the line shaking hands immediately. He spent several moments with each member of the welcome party.

On my right stood Captain Ivan Castro, a personal hero of mine. Ivan, a Special Forces officer and former 82nd Paratrooper, gave his sight for our country while fighting in Iraq back in 2006. Thriving despite his battle wounds, Ivan fought to remain on active duty until retirement. He has run in dozens of marathons, climbed mountains, and cycled across the United States, as chronicled his in memoir *Fighting Blind: A Green Beret's Story of Extraordinary Courage*.[1] That day, at Pike Field, his wife Evelyn accompanied him.

As President Bush approached, Evelyn guided Ivan's hand to meet him.

When their hands touched, Ivan said, "Who is this?"

With a twinkle in his eye, President Bush replied, "This is George W. Bush, el Presidente!"

Without skipping a beat, Ivan said, "Oh, sorry, sir! I didn't see you!"

I couldn't help but laugh at that. It was a wonderful tension breaker.

The president spoke with Ivan for several moments. I think he appreciated Ivan's sense of humor, and he definitely appreciated his commitment to our nation. When they were through, it was my turn.

I was still so tickled by what Ivan had said and so stunned that President Bush was standing in front of me, I couldn't even remember my name. Major General David Rodriguez, the 82nd Airborne Division Commander, was escorting the president that day. Coming to my rescue, General Rodriguez told him about Larry and spoke very kindly about me. President Bush took my hand in his and told me he was very sorry for my loss.

Returning to my senses, sort of, I thanked the president and said, "Welcome to Fort Bragg, sir. Thank you for coming to see us."

Thank you for coming to see us? I had a chance to speak to President George W. Bush and all I could think to say was, "Welcome to Fort Bragg"? I felt like an idiot! I felt like that kid in *A Christmas Story* who wanted a Red Rider BB gun more than anything on the planet. He knew everything about it, had been asking for it all year. But when he had his chance to ask Santa, he totally blanked and agreed that he wanted a football. *A football?* Why did I not have something profound and memorable to say to our commander in chief?

I totally blew it.

Second Chances

The division memorial ceremony took place immediately after the division review. We traveled from Pike Field to the 82nd Airborne Division Museum. Four huge, white tents covered the parking lot, housing rows and rows of white folding chairs. Larry's parents had traveled to Bragg for the ceremony; my mom was there, too. Upon our arrival, paratroopers serving as ushers handed each of us a long-stemmed yellow rose. With roses in hand, we found our seats and prepared for the long and emotional ceremony.

To my surprise, President Bush was there. Delivering a heartfelt speech during the ceremony, he demonstrated that he truly felt our losses as his own.

After the formal portion of the division memorial, each family member was given the opportunity to lay his or her yellow rose at the 82nd Memorial obelisk. Seated in nearly the last row, it took what seemed like forever for us to get our turn. Normally, the rose-laying ceremony takes about ten minutes, but we were still seated, waiting for our turn, for more than thirty minutes. And it was getting really hot under that tent.

As my patience grew thin, I stood to see what was taking so long. All I could see was a line of fellow survivors serpentine through a multitude of white chairs. Movement was terribly slow. Finally, the ushers approached our row, signaling that it was our turn to stand and begin our movement to the obelisk. It took us at least fifteen more minutes to reach the front of the line.

When I finally realized what was taking so long, I blushed, ashamed of my own impatience.

President Bush was standing at the corner of the sidewalk talking to and hugging every individual family member. Seeing him genuinely engaged in discussion with each family, my respect for him grew even more. Asking God to forgive me for my impatience and thanking Him for being a God of second chances, I took advantage of those extra moments to pull my thoughts together.

After the family in front of us received their last hug and moved on to the obelisk, President Bush turned to me and said, "Oh, I get to see you again!"

He remembered me.

Stepping closer to him, I shook his hand and said, "Sir, my husband, Larry, was a proud man, and he was very proud to serve under you as commander in chief. I just want you to know that."

President Bush hugged me and kissed me on the cheek.

Then, he asked me, "When do I get to meet those girls of yours?"

How does he know I have girls? I thought. Later, I found out that General Rodriguez and Ms. Ginny had spoken to him about our family and told him our story.

"Actually, sir, we'll be at Walter Reed visiting our wounded paratroopers several times this summer," I replied.

President Bush lifted his hand and motioned to a young man off to my right, who came over immediately.

The young man gave me his card, and the president told me, "Call this number and let us know when you'll be in town. We'd love to have you visit us in the Oval Office."

"Yes, sir. I will. The girls would love that!"

He smiled, hugged me again, and sent me on my way. I was so dazed and confused that I didn't know where to go or what to do. I nearly forgot to lay my rose down at the obelisk.

The next day, I called the number on the card, totally prepared to explain why I was calling. *My name is Wesley Bauguess. I met the president yesterday at Fort Bragg. He gave me this card and told me to call. He invited us to the White House.*

But when I called, all I had to say was, "Hi. My name is Wesley Bau—"

"Oh, yes, Mrs. Bauguess. We've been expecting your call!"

We made plans for a visit in July.

Daddy's Boss

My heart was racing as we waited outside the Oval Office. The girls looked so beautiful in their black and white sundresses.

We were all very eager to meet with the president. We had made it through multiple layers of security and enjoyed looking at all the beautifully framed photos on the walls of the White House. We were given a tour and met Barney and Mrs. Beasley (the first dogs). Everyone we met was delightful. The "command climate" was very positive and welcoming; it felt like an amazing place to work.

In my hands, I held a wooden 82nd Airborne Christmas ornament and a white three-ring binder. Both items had to go through additional layers of security before they were given the green light to go into the Oval Office with us. The ornament was a gift for Mrs. Bush. I had heard that she loved decorating for Christmas, and I wanted her to have something from Fort Bragg. The notebook was a very special keepsake that I wanted to share with the president.

When the door opened, a very nice young man appeared and welcomed us to enter. We were met with a golden hue, bright and welcoming.

President Bush smiled and said, "There you are!" as he walked over to us.

He immediately kneeled so he could talk with Ryann and Ellie at their level, something Larry always did. I was impressed. He chatted with the girls for a moment and then welcomed my mother and me.

As we took individual and group photos, President Bush told the girls about the Oval Office. He showed them the Resolute desk and told them about the pictures on the wall. He told the girls that the very first decision he had to make as the president of the United States was which rug to choose for his office. We thought he had chosen well. The rug displayed several shades of light yellow and cream. It reminded me of sunshine.

After the official photos, we stepped outside and took a quick tour of the Rose Garden. Ryann immediately noticed the Secret Service agents on the roof and thought that was so cool!

Once we were through talking about the flowers and the beautiful weather, we returned to the office and found a seat on one of the two yellow couches. All five of us sat together on one couch; President Bush was seated in the middle.

Ellie gave him the Christmas ornament and said it was for Mrs. Bush. He studied it for a long moment and then thanked our sweet Ellie. Turning his attention to me, he focused on the binder I was holding.

"What do you have there?"

"This is the binder Larry made before his deployment to Iraq in 2005. He updated it before he left for Afghanistan in 2007. Before he deployed each time, I asked him to tell the girls where he was going and why. They were only two and four when he left for Iraq, and only four and six when he went to Afghanistan, so he made this binder to explain things on their level."

The cover of the binder said, "Daddy's Deployments." It had an American flag on it, colored by Ryann and Ellie. President Bush opened the binder and found his own picture on the first page.

"I have a little less gray in that picture," he joked.

"Larry told the girls that you are the commander in chief. The girls looked at him funny, so he regrouped and said, 'This is Daddy's boss.' In our house, you became known as 'Daddy's boss.'"

He chuckled as I explained Larry's logic, and then he continued to look through the binder. He saw Larry's stick figure drawing of himself in Iraq and us at home and smiled as I told him that story.

President Bush looked at the maps of North Carolina and Baghdad and the map of Afghanistan on the next page. He seemed to be impressed by Larry's thoughtfulness and his ability to explain his deployments to the girls. After President Bush looked at every page, he closed the book and hugged it.

"Is this for me?" he asked.

"No, sir," I respectfully responded. "I'm sorry. That's a family treasure. But ... would you sign your picture for us?"

He laughed and said, "Of course!"

Before we left, President Bush commented on my smile.

"It must be hard for you, but you're always smiling. How is that?"

I told him, "Sir, I just do. It's who I am. Honestly, if we sat here crumpled and defeated, Larry Bauguess would come down here and kick us square in the backside. He would say, 'Get up. Drive on. The best way to honor me is to get back out there and continue to live.' So we drive on and we keep smiling."

He nodded and smiled back at me.

With that, we said our good-byes and floated out of the White House.

That day, President Bush made us feel like we were the most important people in his world. He has such a heart for our military families and goes out of his way to make us feel special. A commander in chief who truly respects his people and who totally understands their sacrifice is priceless.

President George W. Bush will always be one of my favorite W's.

Chapter 20

The Story Unfolds

What difference, at this point, does it make?
—*Secretary of State Hillary Clinton*

In January 2013, I watched Secretary of State Hillary Clinton testify in front of Congress about the 2012 Benghazi incident.

My stomach soured when I heard her say, "With all due respect, the fact is, we had four dead Americans. Was it because of a protest, or was it because of guys out for a walk one night who decide they'd go kill some Americans? What difference, at this point, does it make?"[1]

What difference does it make? When your loved one is murdered, knowing how they died, who did it, and why is crucial to the healing process. It makes a huge difference. I'm thankful for Secretary Clinton's public service, but she must not know how it feels to lose a loved one overseas. If she knew how it felt to thirst for information, if she knew how hard it is to wait for details, she never would have said that. If she knew how it felt to tell your children they would live the rest of their lives without their daddy, she would have more compassion for those of us who had to do that very thing. She wouldn't have asked, "What difference ... does it make?"

Details matter. They matter a lot. Knowing the details of a loved one's last moments on earth makes a huge difference in the grief process for those of us left behind.

Media Intel

When I first learned about Larry's death on May 14, 2007, the casualty notification officer told me that he had been shot in the head while boarding a helicopter. I refused to believe it; Larry wouldn't go down like that. Later that night, in an emotional phone call, Lieutenant Colonel Baker advised me to meet the early reports with caution.

On May 15, 2007, Jason Straziuso from the Associated Press wrote, "Militants killed a U.S. soldier and a Pakistani on Monday after a meeting held in a Pakistani frontier town seeking to calm the worst clashes in years between Afghan and Pakistani troops policing a border crossed daily by Taliban and al-Qaida insurgents."[2] The article included a comment by Afghan Army Brigade Commander, General Akrem, who attended the meeting. General Akrem stated, "From three directions the gunmen opened fire—from the window of a classroom, from a building outside the school and from a hill."[3] According to the article, Pakistani Major General Waheed Arshad said the shooters were unidentified "miscreants," which is a word defined as "a person who behaves badly, often by breaking rules of conduct or the law."[4] The way the Pakistani general simply waved off the incident by blaming random "miscreants" bothered me.

On May 16, 2007, Kevin Maurer, a staff writer for the *Fayetteville Observer* wrote, "A U.S. military official in Washington said U.S. soldiers had gotten into a truck and were preparing to leave when a Pakistani militiaman walked up and opened fire."[5] In the article, Maurer also revealed that "Pakistan has ordered a high-level inquiry into the shooting" and Pakistani general Arshad "denied reports from the Afghan Defense Ministry spokesman that a Pakistani soldier was to blame."[6]

On May 17, 2007, we had a memorial ceremony for Larry at Lafayette Baptist Church in Fayetteville. At the end of the service, we formed a receiving line in the fellowship hall, which offered us an opportunity to thank our family and friends for their love and support. Hundreds of army friends attended the service, including several unit ladies whose husbands worked very closely with Larry.

One unit wife approached and, through tears, told me her husband was with him on that fatal day. She was so distraught that she could barely speak. She hugged me and continued to sob. I did my best to comfort her.

Finally, she spoke.

"My husband told me to tell you that if it wasn't for your husband, they would all be dead."

"What did Larry do?" I asked.

She didn't know. She just thanked me and turned away, sobbing.

On May 26, 2007, Kevin Maurer wrote another article in the *Fayetteville Observer* under the title, "Gunman Was in Security Detail." He began the article by writing, "The gunman who killed Army Maj. Larry Bauguess in Pakistan was a member of a Pakistani paramilitary unit that patrols the Federally Administered Tribal Areas along the border with Afghanistan, according to military officials."[7] The gunman was in the security detail; he wasn't an unidentified "miscreant." He was "wearing a Pakistan Frontier Corps uniform." He was a member of the unit that was supposed to provide security for our men.

In the same article, Maurer quoted Colonel Martin Schweitzer, Larry's brigade commander, as saying, "The gunman acted alone." Colonel Schweitzer went on to say, "This was not sanctioned at any level by the Pakistani military. They had some hoodlums inside their organization."[8] Also in the article, Daniel Markey, a senior fellow for the Council on Foreign Relations (an organization that focuses on American foreign policy), said, "The United States and Pakistan want to defuse the situation, but the incident does raise some red flags." Maurer explained why. "The U.S. is about to pour billions of dollars of aid into the paramilitary unit." Markey continued, "The hope is the Frontier Corps will be able to force the foreign fighters (the Taliban and al-Qaida) out of the tribal area." He went on to say that the incident on May 14 "is a sign we have to be careful of how we assist the Frontier Corps."[9]

Fury Six Letter

One week later, I received an envelope from Afghanistan. In it, I found a Non-Article 5 NATO medal and certificate, a DVD of Larry's Fallen Trooper ramp ceremony in Afghanistan, and a letter from Colonel Schweitzer. The letter, dated May 17, 2007, expressed his grief.

> We are all struggling to find the words to express the deep sorrow that we feel over the death of your husband. Larry touched the lives of every Trooper in 508th STB and the Brigade staff. Whether he was training cadets at West Point, preparing Troops for this deployment, or making the citizens of Afghanistan safer by facilitating their security, Larry was always mission focused with a smile on his face and an inspiration to all of us. I have served with thousands of Soldiers over the course of my career and I've never met a man who cared more for his family, being a Paratrooper or getting the mission accomplished.

I searched his letter for answers. He went on to say,

> On May 14th, 2007, Larry was performing his duty as a member of a leadership team dispatched to the Afghanistan and Pakistan border to ensure that stability prevails in the region. At the conclusion of this meeting the leadership came under fire. Larry was at the point of attack and shielded others allowing his team time to react and ensuring there was no further U.S. loss of life. I can think of no greater measure of devotion or love a Soldier can give to another team member.

Larry shielded his men. Those words confirmed what our unit wife had told me in the receiving line at the memorial ceremony. Colonel Schweitzer's letter gave no other details about the ambush, but I was grateful to learn about Larry's final actions. My quest for further information continued.

Toy Trucks

In June 2007, I was blessed with the opportunity to sit down with one of the men who was with Larry in Pakistan. He had been wounded in the ambush. I was anxious to see him, to hug him, and to ask him a few questions. During our visit, he confirmed what I already knew about the peace meeting. Then, using his child's toy trucks, he re-created the scene for me. He mentioned a metallic click, a possible misfire of a machine gun, and told me about the Pakistani soldier who opened fire. I had hoped he could tell me more about Larry but quickly realized that he had suffered injuries of his own. Shot during the barrage of fire, he went down hard. On the bed of the pickup truck, fighting for his own life, he didn't see what had happened to Larry. He was so brave to talk with me that day, but I still had so many unanswered questions.

Requests for Information

By July 2007, I had no new information. So with the help of several other Fort Bragg widows, I learned how to submit a Freedom of Information Act (FOIA) request to the US Army Human Resources Command to ask for the AR 15-6 investigation results. The article from May 26 mentioned that the Army's investigation into the ambush was almost complete. I thought that by July the results would be available, so I sent in the request and wondered if I would get anything back. I assumed that most of the information about Larry would be classified. He had been killed in Pakistan—that wasn't exactly normal. The details would be "sensitive." I knew they wouldn't violate operational security, and I wouldn't want them to do that. But I had to ask. I figured even a small piece of the puzzle would be helpful.

Shooter Identified

In August 2007, a friend of Larry's came home for a well-deserved R&R with his family. He was an officer in the 82nd; his wife had been taking care of the home front and of unit families as a family readiness group leader. She invited us over for dinner while her husband was home. While the kids played upstairs, we talked in the kitchen. Telling our friends that I had something I wanted them to see, I pulled out the mysterious camera. I told them I didn't think it was Larry's, but there were interesting pictures on the memory card.

Taking the card out of the camera, the officer plugged it into his computer. Flipping through the first few pictures, he confirmed that they had been taken during the border flag meeting on May 14. He clicked through the remaining pictures at a steady rate, not focusing on any one in particular. Then, on one picture, he stopped for a long look before he clicked to the next one.

"What did you see? Why did you stop on that picture?" I asked.

He hesitated. Then, he clicked back to the picture of interest but didn't say a word.

"Is the man who killed Larry in that picture?"

"Yes," he said sadly.

I had him pegged instantly. I knew exactly which one did it.

Pointing to a bearded man wearing khaki fatigues and a helmet, I asked, "Is that him?"

He nodded.

"And he's no longer breathing?"

He nodded again.

"Good," I said.

I understand that I should not be happy when someone dies, but I was overjoyed that that particular Pakistani was dead. Dressed in the uniform of a Pakistani Frontier Guardsman, he was among those who had been given the mission to protect our soldiers. Instead, he turned on our men and shot them at close range. He killed my Larry. Forgive me, Lord, but I am glad he is no longer breathing the air of his homeland.

Request for Information Responses

In early October 2007, I received a piece of certified mail from Afghanistan. The return address said, "FOIA Officer." I opened it immediately and found a twenty-seven-page document. The first page was a letter from the 82nd Airborne Division Chief of Staff acknowledging my Freedom of Information Act request. He enclosed a copy of the AR 15-6 investigation, though he included the obligatory comment, "In accordance with FOIA exemptions, certain information was withheld." As I suspected, when I thumbed through the remaining twenty-six pages, I found most of them to be completely useless.

Of those, two of them were identical copies of the same table of contents. There were two copies of the same three-page set of instructions for the investigating officer, which totaled six more pages of little use. There was a four-page copy of the investigating officer's report, but most of it was blank or redacted. I found two title pages, one legal review letter that said the 15-6 investigation was "legally sufficient," and one agenda page for what I assumed was the out-brief slide package. Nine more pages were blank except for a tiny message that said, "Pages removed for the following reason," followed by a series of letters and numbers. So, doing the math, of the twenty-six pages that followed the cover letter, twenty-five said absolutely nothing of use.

There was only one page that had any value at all. Formatted as a PowerPoint slide, it said "Findings/Recommendations" at the top. As the title suggests, this page listed the findings and the recommendations of the investigating officer.

Findings:[10]
- I find that MAJ Larry Bauguess was killed by a(n) individual wearing a Kurram militia uniform when he was shot a(t) close range with a volley of AK-47 automatic weapons fire. Prior to the shooting, there were no indications that the shooter was either out of place or not a member of the Pakistani Military. This individual (incident) appears to

have been a premeditated event on the part of the initial shooter. There is little evidence to support collaboration within the Pakistan militia or military. Based upon this finding there is little the coalition forces could have done to prevent the ambush and they reacted appropriately, with measured force, to protect themselves and the lives of their fellow soldiers after the shooting began.

• I find that the sporadic fire from Pakistani military forces from within the building following the death of the original shooter probably was in response to the suppressive fires coalition forces utilized to cover their withdrawal. The lack of coordinated fires by other Kurram or Pakistani soldiers or civilians indicates that this incident was limited to a few individuals.

Recommendation:[11]
• I recommend that the following measures be taken to mitigate risk at future BFMs (Border Flag Meetings): (Measures withheld by the author for operational security)

• CPT (Captain - name redacted) acted above and beyond the call of duty as the events unfolded to lead and protect coalition forces and move them to the HLZ for extraction. I recommend the command consider recognizing him for his valorous actions during this engagement. (*Parentheses added*)

I read through this slide several times. It was consistent with what I had been told so far. I believed the incident to be premeditated, as well, though I couldn't let go of the feeling that it had been a coordinated event. Before I put the papers away, I paused to give special consideration to the last bullet statement. I wanted to know more about the captain and his actions.

Diablo Six Visit

In October 2007, Lieutenant Colonel Baker came to see me while he was home for his mid-deployment R&R. When I found out he was coming home, I couldn't wait to see him, but when he pulled into the driveway, I suddenly became very nervous. After a long and slow breath, I opened the front door and greeted Larry's battalion commander. We exchanged knowing glances and half-smiles and hugged each other hello.

Seated at the circular table, we began a lighthearted chat. At first, we talked about little things. He told me about his leave, about how he and his wife got to play some golf. His kids were doing well. All of that was nice to hear. Once we were comfortable, we turned our conversation to Larry. It may have surprised him, but I took the lead. I guess I did that because I wanted to show him that I could talk about Larry without falling apart. I didn't want him to feel uncomfortable around me, and I didn't want him to hold anything back. I wanted him to feel free to give me any details he could.

I began to tell the story, as I knew it.

> They went into Pakistan for a border flag meeting. They arrived by helicopter and walked to the schoolhouse, where the meeting took place. Larry participated in the peace talks. By all accounts, the meeting was successful. After the meeting, the leaders shook hands, took pictures, and exchanged coins. The leadership got into SUVs and drove off very quickly, so quickly that it made our paratroopers take notice. Larry stayed behind to ride with the PSD. He and his men were still boarding the backside of a pickup truck when the SUVs took off. A similar pickup truck, with a machine gun above the cab, was positioned behind the truck our men were boarding. One of our paratroopers heard a metallic click, similar to the sound that a gun makes when the hammer falls and there is no round in the chamber. It could have been the machine gun behind them.
>
> After the sound of the metallic click, a man in a Pakistani military uniform started yelling. He opened

fire on our men. Larry was on his feet when he was hit. Colonel Schweitzer's letter says, "Larry was at the point of attack and shielded others, allowing his team time to react and ensuring there was no further U.S. loss of life." One of the ladies in our battalion told me at the memorial service that her husband said if it weren't for Larry, he wouldn't be alive today. At least one of our troopers was hit. I don't know what one of the captains did, but it was cited in the 15-6 investigation that he "acted above and beyond the call of duty as the events unfolded to lead and protect coalition forces and move them to the HLZ for extraction."

My military experience is limited, but I know if I were initiating an ambush, I would use my most casualty-producing weapon. In this case, it would have been a machine gun, mounted on the truck that was directly behind our men. Maybe the metallic click was the machine gun misfiring. When the gunner didn't open fire, the Pakistani gunman started yelling and initiated the ambush himself. If that's true, then this whole thing was planned. The same Pakistanis who were shaking hands and accepting coins knew what they were getting ready to do. And that's what I know ... or at least what I think I know.

Lieutenant Colonel Baker sat back in his chair, raised his eyebrows, and nodded in a way that led me to believe I had most of it right. Then, we continued to have a very meaningful conversation.

Forever Scarred

On June 13, 2008, a producer from *FOX News* called me and asked if I had a comment about what General Dan K. McNeill had said about Larry during a press conference at the Pentagon. After telling him I had no idea what he was talking about, the producer politely referred me to a website and encouraged me to watch the press conference footage. I knew General McNeill was the commander of the International Security Assistance Force in

Afghanistan, but I didn't know he was back home. I thanked the producer for his call.

Later that day, I watched General McNeill's opening statement online. Giving his assessment of the war in Afghanistan, he spoke about the Taliban and about Pakistan. During the question-and-answer portion, the general spoke about the Pakistani Frontier Corps. Those three words piqued my interest and prepared me for his next comment.

"If I live to be as old as Methuselah, I will be forever scarred by one event that occurred. And that was the assassination, and I don't have a better expression for it, of Major (Larry) Bauguess—a fine officer in the 82nd Airborne Division."[12]

Assassination. Initially, I was shocked by his use of that word, but then it sank in. Larry was assassinated, killed in cold blood at a peace meeting to make a statement. What happened to Larry and his fellow paratroopers was a very big deal. It was an international incident, a wicked sucker-punch. I appreciated General McNeill's comment, and I, too, am forever scarred.

The Captain

In August 2008, I was blessed with the opportunity to meet with the captain mentioned in the AR 15-6. In our conversation, he confirmed that our paratroopers traveled by foot to the meeting place, a schoolhouse in Teri Mengel, Pakistan. The leaders entered the school to conduct the peace talks. The captain and the personal security detachment stayed outside to help the Pakistani soldiers secure the perimeter.

He told me about his interactions with the Pakistani soldiers, which offered a completely new point of view and information I had not yet heard. The Pakistanis were friendly and treated our men as comrades. The US captain's counterpart was a Pakistani major who spoke fluent English and asked a lot of questions. He talked about politics and religion and made his dislike of Afghanistan abundantly clear. When the Major began asking personal questions, the captain thought about walking away from him, but he didn't want to be disrespectful. Instead, he answered the Pakistani major's questions with false information.

Before and during the meeting, the captain observed Pakistani soldiers taking pictures of the US and Afghanistan personnel with their cell phones. He told me that one of the Pakistani leaders asked him where Fury Six was. Fury Six was Colonel Schweitzer, the 4th Brigade Commander. They showed disappointment when they had learned that Fury Six wasn't with them.

The captain confirmed that after the meeting, the leaders came out of the schoolhouse, shook hands, exchanged coins, and posed for pictures. He told me the original plan was to walk to the helicopter landing zone, but the Pakistani leadership insisted that our paratroopers ride in their vehicles, saying it was for their own protection.

Lieutenant Colonel Baker and the Afghan governor were directed to a vehicle in the front of the formation. Larry chose to stay with the personal security detachment, who were told to get into the back of a pickup truck with a cage on it. The captain confirmed that Lieutenant Colonel Baker's vehicle sped away before the personal security detachment was fully seated. A moment later, a Pakistani soldier at the rear of their vehicle started yelling and opened fire with an AK-47. Within seconds, other gunmen were firing from the left and the right. They received fire from three sides.

I asked him if he saw what happened to Larry, and he confirmed that Larry was on his feet.

"Major Bauguess stood up in the path of the gunman's rage and shielded the rest of us from the hail of bullets," he said. "He conciously stood up in the path of the incoming rounds and saved our lives by using his body as a human shield."

I had to let that sink in.

A few moments later, the captain continued. He said he maneuvered around the vehicle and shot and killed the initial shooter. Another personal security detachment trooper began to lay down suppressive fire.

The captain and the trooper continued to fight for their lives and those of their 82nd brothers. At that point, the truck had no driver. One trooper attempted to start the truck but didn't know how to drive a stick shift. So the communications noncommissioned officer, who was wounded, maneuvered toward the vehicle and climbed into the driver's seat. The captain said he yelled, "If you are American, rally on me!" Then they began their hasty departure.

The American soldiers linked up with the remaining Afghan personnel and fought their way out of the schoolyard. They continued to fight all the way to the helicopter landing zone, especially against a position on a hill on their left flank. Imagine their relief when they saw two helicopters waiting for them. The paratroopers loaded the wounded onto the first helicopter. As the captain prepared to load the second bird, he realized that Lieutenant Colonel Baker wasn't there. Just as he turned to go back to look for his commander, he saw Lieutenant Colonel Baker and the Afghan governor running toward him. They boarded the second helicopter and flew to the combat support hospital at Forward Operating Base Salerno.

As the captain relayed his account to me, all I could do was listen in silence. The whole thing played in my head like an action movie. I was blown away by his ability to recall the firefight with such detail. But, then again, if I had lived through something like that, I wouldn't soon forget.

New York Times Article

From 2008 to 2011, I received no new information. When Osama bin Laden was found and subsequently killed in Pakistan in May 2011, I just shook my head and, honestly, wasn't at all surprised that he was living there.

On September 26, 2011, the *New York Times* published a front-page story titled, "Pakistanis Tied to 2007 Border Attack on Americans."[13] The article, written by Carlotta Gall, focused on the "duplicity of Pakistan" and stated that the May 14, 2007, incident "takes on new relevance given the worsening rupture in relations between Washington and Islamabad." Gall wrote that the ambush in Teri Mengel had been "kept quiet by Washington," implying that our government "seemed to play down or ignore signals that Pakistan would pursue its own interests or even sometimes behave as an enemy."

The article explained the events leading up to the border flag meeting and provided details of the ambush. Most of that information was consistent with what I already knew. However, Gall offered the point of view of two Afghan commanders. The commanders said that after the Pakistani soldier initiated the ambush, "several other Pakistanis opened fire from inside the classrooms, riddling the group with gunfire."

"I saw the American falling and the Americans taking positions and firing. We were not fired on from one side, but from two, probably three sides," said Brigadier General Muhammad Akrem.[14] This quote is consistent with his comments from the May 15, 2007, Associated Press article.

Colonel Sher Ahmed Kuchai, the Afghan border guard commander, concurred with his fellow commander and added that he saw "at least two Pakistanis firing from the open windows of the classrooms and another running across the veranda toward a machine gun mounted on a vehicle before he was brought down by American fire."[15] The article stated that both commanders believe the "rapid American reaction saved their lives."

The article includes an interesting recollection from Colonel Kuchai. He "remembers the way the senior Pakistani officers left the yard minutes before the shooting without saying goodbye, behavior that he now interprets as a sign that they knew what was coming."[16]

Gall also states that Colonel Kuchai believes that "at least some of the attackers were intelligence officers in plain clothes." As I read that statement in the article, I recalled my conversation with the captain. He said that the Pakistani major had asked a lot of questions and the Pakistanis took a lot of pictures of the American and Afghan personnel.

Rahmatullah Rahmat, the governor of Paktia province, was in the SUV with Lieutenant Colonel Baker when it sped away from the schoolhouse and drove past the helicopter landing zone. In the article, he stated that the driver, a Pakistani colonel, didn't stop until Lieutenant Colonel Baker "drew his pistol and demanded that the car halt." According to the article, "Mr. Rahmat remains incensed that back in Kabul an attack on a provincial governor by Pakistan was quietly smothered."[17] The article states that Afghanistan did not investigate the ambush.

Second FOIA request

Carlotta Gall's article resurrected some unresolved issues in me and apparently in others, as well. It prompted the US Central Command to release a declassified excerpt from the AR 15-6 investigation. The document, dated October 24, 2011, delivered a summary of the facts and findings and restated, "There is little evidence to support collaboration within the Pakistani militia or military."[18]

I need to take a moment here and state that I respect the 15-6 process and the officers who conducted the investigation. I just wanted to see it; I wanted to hold it in my hands.

On November 3, 2011, I filled out a DA Form 1559, Inspector General Action Request, and wrote an e-mail to Major General Jim Huggins, the 82nd Airborne Division Commander, who was deployed to Afghanistan at that time.

> Dear MG Huggins,
>
> I can only imagine how busy you must be and I hope this email finds you well.
>
> Sir, I wanted to give you advanced notice that tomorrow morning I intend to submit a letter to the Division IG's office requesting information about the Teri Mengel Border Flag Meeting AR 15-6 Investigation. I have attached the letter.
>
> I have several unanswered questions and will certainly keep my inquiries on a professional and appropriate level. My intent is not to add work for you or your staff, as I realize you are deployed in a combat

environment. However, I believe I have patiently waited long enough to receive the full story.

As you and your staff consider my request, I only ask that you consider your own expectations of your spouse if the roles were reversed. As a former soldier and leader, I know Larry would pursue the story if this had happened to me.

Thank you for your time and attention. I sincerely look forward to welcoming you and the Paratroopers home at the conclusion of your mission.

Respectfully,
Wesley

Within a few hours, he responded.

Wesley,

Thanks for bringing this up in the manner you have, you are an amazing woman and I have always been in awe of the way you handle yourself under a situation that I cannot imagine myself.

I appreciate you sending this to me first, you obviously did not have to do so, but again it just shows what kind of person you are. Please go forward as you have described and I will also sit and review with the SJA and IG tomorrow to determine how we can best proceed. I don't need to explain to you that I have to follow a process but this is deeply personal for me and obviously for many of our staff. It goes without saying that I will do all I can to assist with your request.

Hope all is well, the Division continues to amaze me as it always has and the mission we have here is served well by the most selfless and talented men and women in our Army ... paratroopers.

V/R,
Jim Huggins

Witness Statements

Several months later, with the help of follow-up e-mails and letters, I finally received a partially declassified copy of the Teri Mengel Border Flag Meeting investigation, dated February 21, 2012.[19] Seated in Major General Huggins's office with the division rear detachment commander, I read through the entire report.

The details listed in the "Sequence of Events" subsection were consistent with the stories I had already heard. In the "Facts" subsection, I learned that the gunman had yelled, "Move!" in his native language to the Pakistani driver who was initially in the driver's seat of the pickup truck. The shooter was only eight to ten feet away from the back of the pickup truck when he opened fire with his AK-47 and emptied his entire magazine, approximately thirty rounds. The investigation officer reported that the initial shooter caused all the casualties and caused the "sporadic" engagement between the Pakistani and American soldiers. In his "Findings," the investigation officer concluded that the fire from the Pakistani soldiers was uncoordinated and "limited to a few individuals."

After reading the official findings, I flipped to the witness statements. They were the most important documents to me, so I read every word. Even though the report was still heavily redacted and the names were withheld, they were relatively easy to follow. All the statements were beneficial, but the statements that carried the most weight for me were from two enlisted paratroopers and the communications noncommissioned officer. Their statements seemed honest and true. I could tell by their words that they simply wrote about what they saw and what they did.

The first statement of value was from one of the enlisted paratroopers. I suspect he was the paratrooper whose wife had found me during Larry's memorial ceremony. He had witnessed the "toy truck" paratrooper's gunshot wound at the very beginning of the ambush. The impact of the round(s) caused the "toy truck" trooper to fall forward into the bed of the truck. The enlisted trooper dove on top of him to protect him from further harm. He then saw "MAJ Bauguess" and wrote that Larry did not fall until the shooter ran out of ammo. He stated that Larry saved their lives and gave them time to get out of the truck. He witnessed the captain and the personal security detachment trooper kill the initial gunman and engage the other Pakistani shooters. Once they got to the helicopters, this enlisted trooper rendered combat life support to the "toy truck" paratrooper, treating his wounds and doing all he could to save his life. At the end of his statement, he confirmed that the captain and the personal security detachment trooper had put their own lives in danger to save everyone else. He said he would be dead if not for them.[20]

The next statement of value was from the personal security detachment trooper. He confirmed that the SUVs left the compound just before the ambush. He was sitting in the truck when the shooter opened fire. As quickly as he could, he jumped out of the truck and returned fire. While his fellow soldiers were trying to get a driver for their pickup truck, he observed three Pakistani "army guys" shooting at them. He began shooting to provide suppressive fire. After leaving the compound, they headed toward the helicopter landing zone, where he said they received fire from a hill to their left. He also wrote that there were Pakistani "army guys" behind them as they maneuvered to the helicopters. At the end of his statement, he wrote that Major Bauguess "shielded us from a massacre" and that the captain "took charge of the dismounts all the way to the HLZ."[21]

The third statement I found helpful was from the communications noncommissioned officer. He described the meeting place as a school that was completely closed in and added that the only way in or out was through one gate. He and the captain stayed outside of the building during the meeting, monitoring radio communications. Confirming the captain's account, the communications noncommissioned officer described the inquisitive Pakistani soldiers. One soldier asked him pointed questions about the leadership inside the schoolhouse and asked him which one was his commander. Practicing deception tactics and preserving operational security, the communications noncommissioned officer said he didn't know who the leaders were. Then, the Pakistani asked pointed questions about the Americans' weapon capabilities. Without answering, the noncommissioned officer asked the Pakistani what his job was. His reply was, "Intelligence." The noncommissioned officer, like the captain, continued his deception tactics and gave the Pakistani false answers, telling him that the range of his M4 rifle was four thousand meters, a remarkable exaggeration.

The communications noncommissioned officer's statement about the ambush was consistent with the other accounts I had heard or read, but he offered an additional detail about what had happened to Larry. He wrote that he was sitting on the bench seat in the back of the pickup truck. When Larry was about halfway on board, a "Pakistani soldier" standing behind the truck "raised his weapon and opened fire... He fired point blank at MAJ Bauguess." He sprayed the back of the pickup truck, completely emptying his magazine. The communications noncommissioned officer was wounded in the initial barrage, but he was able to grab "MAJ Bauguess by his IBA (individual body armor) and turn him over to get him down inside the bed of the truck." He checked for a pulse, but Larry was already gone. When the noncommissioned officer learned that the pickup truck needed a driver, he dismounted, maneuvered to the driver's seat, and prepared to drive the pickup truck away from the schoolhouse. His statement confirmed that the captain shot the initial gunman and, with the personal security detachment trooper, cleared their path all the way to the helicopter landing zone. When they got to the landing zone, they loaded Larry and the other wounded paratroopers onto the first helicopter and "took off."[22]

At the end of the meeting in General Huggins's office, I closed the investigation report and gave it back to the rear detachment commander. To my surprise, he told me I could have it.

Diablo Six

Over time, I learned more about Lieutenant Colonel Baker's experience on that fatal day in Pakistan. I am so thankful for his courage, his candor and his steadfast commitment to our family. His recollection of May 14, 2007 is another crucial piece of the puzzle.

The border flag meeting had lasted more than four hours. At times, the arguments between the Afghan and Pakistani leaders nearly became physical. Larry, in his job as the operations officer, provided over-watch for the meeting inside the schoolhouse, but he also oversaw radio communications and perimeter security. He kept an eye on all the moving parts.

They hadn't planned on taking vehicles up to meet the helicopters after the meeting. They intended to walk out, just as they had walked in. The Pakistani general insisted that they accept a ride in the SUVs. Lieutenant Colonel Baker politely refused at first. He refused several times, actually. His Pakistani counterpart said the security situation outside the school compound had changed and insisted that they accept a ride. Lieutenant Colonel Baker moved to the pickup truck that Larry would eventually board, but the Pakistani general again insisted that the senior officers ride in the SUVs.

The vehicles took off quickly, before the personal security detachment fully loaded the pickup truck. The vehicles left the compound and turned toward the helicopter landing zone. As soon as they made the turn, the shooting began. Lieutenant Colonel Baker could hear AK-47 fire, but because of the echo, he couldn't tell where the fire was coming from. Seconds later, he heard a squad automatic weapon, which told him our soldiers were returning fire. At that moment, he knew something was very wrong.

The driver of his SUV didn't go to the helicopter landing zone, instead he sped past the turn. Lieutenant Colonel Baker told the driver to stop, and when the driver ignored him, he realized they weren't just getting out of the kill zone; he believed that they were being taken somewhere else. He pulled out his pistol, pointed it at the driver's head, and ordered him, in colorful language, to stop the car.

Lieutenant Colonel Baker and the Afghan governor of the Paktia province, who was in the back seat, got out of the car. They linked up with another American officer and an Afghan border patrol general and ran several hundred meters toward the helicopter landing zone, jumping and falling along the way. Sporadic weapons fire continued as the leaders made their way toward the helicopters. Upon arrival at the landing zone, Lieutenant Colonel Baker found one of the captains and asked if he had accountability. The captain said he had everyone but told him that Larry was gone. Lieutenant Colonel Baker didn't understand what he meant by *gone*.

"Sir," he said again, "Major Bauguess is gone."

Christina Lamb

On February 23, 2015, I received an e-mail from Christina Lamb, the chief foreign correspondent for the *Sunday Times* and the author of *I Am Malala*. Having spent most of her career as a journalist in Pakistan and Afghanistan, she was writing a book called *Farewell Kabul* and wanted to include the May 14, 2007, incident.[23] I agreed to a telephone interview, and we spoke the next day.

In her book, Lamb penned the details of the border flag meeting in a chapter titled, "Whose Side Are You On?" After writing about early 2007 events, she wrote, "Then something shocking happened that, had it been made public at the time, would have provoked outrage in the US."[24] She chronicled the back-and-forth accounts of that fatal day. Pakistan blamed a "rouge troop." The men on the ground "reported seeing other Pakistani military personnel shooting at them from the building." Lamb added, "Pakistan later claimed they [the Pakistani soldiers] were firing at the gunman."

As she summed up the chapter, Lamb noted the account of an American colonel who had attended a meeting in Pakistan the day before the fatal border flag meeting. The colonel noted "odd signs" and "reported something was wrong." In the final paragraph, Lamb quoted Colonel John "Mick" Nicholson as he referred to the May 14, 2007 assault in Teri Mengel.

> "It wasn't a spontaneous thing, it was obviously planned," said Colonel Nicholson. "It could have been a lot worse— we believe the Pakistanis had planned to take hostages. But the Americans reacted well, fought back, and killed some of the Frontier Corps. Obviously it set things back a lot in terms of trust."[25]

Final Thoughts

Over the years, the story did unfold, but it still lacks a definitive ending. Every time I talk with a trooper who was on the ground with Larry, I am convinced that it was a coordinated assault. My suspicions line up with Colonel Nicholson's comments, but there really is no way for me to prove them. The official report says, "There is little evidence to support collaboration within the Pakistan militia or military."

I respect the Americans and the Afghan leaders who were on the ground that day, and I respect those leaders who conducted the investigation afterward. We'll never know for sure if the incident was planned by one or two or twelve. I don't know if big Pakistan knew about it or if it was limited to the Pakistani Frontier Corps. All I know is our guys were sucker-punched; paratroopers were wounded, and Larry is "gone."

But I will tell you this—details matter to the loved ones left behind. And details matter for the history books. As Larry said, "We are living the history that our children will study." If we don't document this incident correctly and learn from it, it will happen again.

***

What has been will be again, what has been done will be done again; there is nothing new under the sun.
—Ecclesiastes 1:9 (NIV)

Chapter 21

Finding Zero

You are the light of the world. Let your
light so shine that others may see your good
deeds and glorify the Father in Heaven.
—Pastor John Cook

In the Army, when an enlisted soldier approaches an officer outdoors, he or she renders a proper hand salute and offers a salute motto. A junior officer approaching a senior officer will do the same. When I graduated from Airborne School in 1992, my favorite salute motto became, "All the way, sir!" to which the senior officer would respond, "Airborne!"

John Cook, senior pastor at Snyder Memorial Baptist Church in Fayetteville, North Carolina, served in the Army as a field artillery officer. While John was on active duty, God called him into ministry. Once he graduated from seminary, John continued his army service as a chaplain and later retired as a colonel. During one of his Sunday sermons at Snyder, John told us about the salute motto he preferred. When a junior officer approached the army chaplain, he or she would say, "God is good, sir!" to which John replied, "All the time!"

God is good, all the time. In our deepest lows and our highest highs, He is there and He is good.

Larry's Legacy

Ryann and Ellie are the light of my world. God truly blessed me when He chose me to be their mother. They are the best part of my life, and they are their daddy's legacy. Those sweet girls have his eyes and his spirit. I am so thankful that they have his sense of humor. And they have his drive to succeed. Ryann had a bumpy start to life and got to ride in a helicopter when she was eleven hours old. Ellie came into the world fit to fight and ready to go. They are beautiful, and they are beyond resilient. Even though they are living in the absence of their daddy, I have no doubt that they make him proud every single day.

Ryann is funny with a quick wit, like her dad. She is driven and has a healthy dose of my stubbornness. When she was little, she couldn't pronounce her R's. I remember thinking, *Great job, Wes. You named her Ryann. She can't even pronounce her own name.* One of my most prized possessions is a picture of my sweet Ryann in a green camouflage picture frame. In the picture, which was taken when she was in kindergarten, she is holding a certificate that says, "The Greatest Dad on Earth." On the line where the dad's name was written, it says "Lawey." Her teacher must have asked her what her dad's name was. I can just hear her reply, "Lawey," because she couldn't pronounce those R's. The teacher wrote what she heard. That picture still makes me laugh out loud. Luckily, Ryann grew out of that and now pronounces her R's beautifully.

Ryann has always been my guardian and strong beyond her years. When her dad was killed and our door remained in perpetual motion, Ryann was always right next to me holding a box of tissues. It was her way of being helpful. She didn't talk about Larry much. Every time I asked her if she was all right and if she wanted to talk, she simply told me she was good. She sucked it up, just like her dad would have. She's stubborn and independent like me; she's quiet and strong like her daddy. She looks so much like him.

Ellie is thoughtful, so deliberate in her actions. She's my rules girl. She does as she's told, always striving to make me proud. People often say she's my "mini-me" and they are right, but she is so much like Larry, too. She may look like me, but she takes on challenges like he did. She doesn't give up. She will get frustrated, but she doesn't back down. She is driven. The more people tell her she can't do something, the more driven she is to do it. But Ellie is also my tender-heart. She feels pain, and she suffers. She sympathizes with her peers. She's sweet and affectionate.

When Ellie was a toddler, she would get so frustrated when she couldn't do something. When Ryann wouldn't share or play with her or if she couldn't get a puzzle piece to fit, she would cry great big tears. Once she got it out of her system, she would take a deep breath, wipe her eyes, and say, "I happy now." Then she would drive on to her next task as if nothing had ever happened. Her hurt never lingered. She never held on to that frustration, and it never resurfaced later. She simply got over it, just as quickly as she got under it—that is, until she lost her daddy.

Ellie was only four years old when Larry was killed. Ryann was six. A loss like that seemed impossible for them to process. How do you tell a four- and a six-year-old that their daddy isn't coming home? How and when do you tell them what actually happened to him?

Three-Year Plan

About six weeks after Larry's death, I had a meeting with the general who had presided over the funeral. He was the general officer who presented our family with Gold Star pins, all of Larry's awards, and a folded flag. The general was leaving his job in the

XVIII Airborne Corps and leaving Fort Bragg. Before he left, he wanted to check on me.

Comfortably seated in his nearly packed-up office, the general asked me how I was doing and how the Army was treating me. I told him I was doing well and that I had great support. Then, he asked me a question I had anticipated. I knew from my army days that senior leaders like to ask junior officers about their future plans. They usually expect to hear a one-year, five-year, and ten-year proposal.

"Have you made any plans for the future?"

I told him the best I could do was a three-year plan.

Year one was called Continuity. We would stay on Fort Bragg for one full year. We would try to keep everything the same. We would have the same school, same neighborhood, same friends, and same neighbors. I would strive to keep things simple and consistent for the girls.

Year two was called Stabilization. At the end of year one, we would have to move. The Army would only let us live on post for twelve months after Larry's death. We would have to find a new house, a new neighborhood, and a new school. We could keep the same friends, hopefully, but we would be starting over. During that year, I would focus on building a stable environment for the girls.

Year three was called Onward Movement. I assumed that after two years of grieving and rebuilding, I would be ready for the next chapter. Maybe I would go back to school and get another master's degree or even a doctorate. Maybe I would work, if the right job offer came along. I really wasn't sure what onward movement meant, but it briefed well.

The general smiled. He said my plan was well thought out, and told me I had a lot to offer the Army if I wanted to stay around. I appreciated that and walked away from our meeting a little taller. I crave feedback. It was a nice feeling to get a nod from a general officer. God is good.

Finding Zero

As army cadets and army officers, we sometimes spent entire days calibrating our weapons at the firing ranges. The most important thing we did was zero our rifles. We had to know, without a doubt, that our weapons were set up just for us as individual shooters. Before we fired the first shot, we set our rifles to "mechanical zero," which meant the rear sight (the left/right adjuster) was in the middle and the front sight (the elevation) was flush. Once we achieved "mechanical zero," we moved to our positions on the zero range.

With a paper target set up twenty-five meters away, we had to "battle-sight zero" our rifles using fewer than eighteen rounds. Lying in the prone position, we fired three times at the target, hoping to achieve a tight shot group (three rounds close together). After walking down range to look at our targets, we would take note of the center mass of the bullet holes and then go back to our weapons to make adjustments—right or left, up or down. For example, if my bullets hit the target in the upper right section, I would adjust my weapon so that my next rounds would hit further down and further left. We would fire three more rounds and repeat the process until we had five out of six rounds inside a four-centimeter circle. Once our weapons were calibrated, we could go to the big range to test our skills with pop-up targets.

The concept of zeroing my weapon was never lost on me. I got it. I totally understood the process and the meaning of the exercise. You start in the middle at "mechanical zero" and then adjust to find your true "battle-sight zero." You must be satisfied with the end product, and then you have to trust it. When the enemy closes in, you know that your weapon is zeroed and it's zeroed just for you.

The process of finding your zero translates nicely to golf. I have had the same golf swing since I first hit those mushrooms with Grandpa Burton. It may not be perfect, but I trust it. I've tried to tweak it. I've had lessons over the years to try to correct its imperfections, but I usually go back to what I know works for me. If my swing ever gets out of whack, I go back to the driving range and find my zero. I go back to the basics, recalibrate, and find my swing.

The same is true in my daily life. When life comes at me fast and temptations and complications are abundant, I do my level best to remember my zero. Just like the church's one foundation is Jesus Christ, so is mine. I lean on Jesus. When we lost Larry and our lives were flipped upside down, I did my best to remember what is important and who is important. I leaned on Jesus. I let the Holy Spirit guide me and did my best to maintain my zero.

***

A father to the fatherless, a defender of widows,
is God in His holy dwelling.
—Psalm 68:5 (NIV)
***

In May 2008, the girls and I moved off Fort Bragg and into Fayetteville. We were embarking on the second year of our three-year plan, the Stabilization year. We had a new house and a new school, and we were slowly making new friends. Looking back, that second year is a blur. I think I was on autopilot through most of it. I fixed my eyes on Jesus and focused on leading the 82WWC. Running that committee gave me purpose. It kept my hands busy. Ryann was in third grade. She had a very kind teacher and made a few new friends. Ellie's first-grade teacher, however, just wasn't the kind soul she needed, and she was slow to make friends. My little tender-heart spent most of that year snuggled up next to me. I didn't mind. I knew she was hurting.

In May 2009, we began year three, the Onward Movement year. I continued to run the 82WWC and continued to reap the benefits of a job well done. I traveled to our military hospitals at least once a month to check on our wounded troopers, but I also paid careful attention to the girls at home. They each suffered their fair share of separation anxiety, so I tended to them completely when I was home. We still had plenty of heartaches and "I miss Daddy" moments.

In the years after their daddy died, the girls often took turns sleeping with me. Some nights, they both slept with me. Some people say that time heals all wounds, but I'd challenge the word *all* in that statement. Healing certainly does happen, but not all wounds heal. The farther we travel down this road, the more we realize just how long forever is. Not all of our wounds have healed; we just got used to them. But, all in all, as we began that third year, it seemed like the girls were adjusting well. We had good times. We smiled and laughed, even with our heavy hearts.

One day in late August 2009, Ryann made a comment that stopped me in my tracks. It was the beginning of the school year, and her fourth-grade teacher sent home a get-to-know-you questionnaire. It had the typical icebreaker questions: "What is your name?" "What's your favorite color?" "What's your favorite subject in school?" "What's your favorite flavor of ice cream?" "Who is your hero?"

"Who's your hero?" That's a cool question, I thought.

Sitting with Ryann as she filled out the questionnaire, I noticed that she skipped the hero question and went on to the next one. I watched in silence as she completed the sheet and started to put it away, leaving the hero question blank.

"Aren't you going to answer that one?" I asked gently.

"No," she quietly replied.

"Baby, that's an easy one. Daddy's your hero, right?"

Under her breath, with a hint of anger, she said, "He's not my hero."

She walked away, leaving me in stunned silence. *How could he not be her hero?* I was completely numb. Slowly, I realized, *She doesn't know what he did.* I had never told them what happened the day their daddy gave his life. They only knew that he had left for war and never came back. They knew he was in heaven with Jesus, but I never told them what had actually happened that day. I kept thinking they were too young to know the details. But in August 2009, Ryann was almost nine and Ellie was seven. Were they old enough to know?

I struggled for the remainder of the week. I didn't know what to tell them or how to tell them. I prayed about it often. Then, I thought back to my college days. Whenever I was troubled, I would get in my car and take a drive on the Blue Ridge Parkway. There was one particular overlook not far from Boone that brought me peace and soothed my soul. The view was magnificent! I used to sit on the stone wall with my legs dangling over the side and stare at the mountains. I know God is always with us, no matter where we are, but I always felt especially close to Him in the mountains. With that mountain view fixed in my mind, I realized it was time for a road trip. We would find comfort in the mountains.

***

The mountains are calling and I must go.
—John Muir

***

My beloved Blue Ridge Parkway overlook was crowded that day, as well as windy and cold. I parked as close as I could to the stone wall, but we decided to stay inside. Leaving the van running so we could enjoy the heat, I unbuckled and spun around in my seat. Facing the girls on my knees, I hugged my seat back and put my chin on the headrest. Deep in thought, I stared at the girls. Their sweet little faces and big blue eyes stared back at me.

"Okay, girls, look out that window. What do you see?" I asked sweetly, gently.

"I see mountains," Ellie replied.

"Take a good long look and then tell me who made them."

"God made them," Ryann replied softly.

Ellie nodded in agreement.

"I will tell you, with all the love in my heart, that if God can make something that amazing, that breathtakingly beautiful, He can get us through this."

I paused for a long moment, trying to swallow the lump forming in my throat.

"Girls, we're doing okay, right? I mean, we're hurting, I know, but I think we're doing okay. Right?"

They shrugged their shoulders, sadly, in response.

"I need to tell you that, earlier this week, I was hurt when Ryann said that Daddy isn't her hero. But then I realized I haven't told you what happened to your daddy. I think you're old enough to know what happened. I just need to find the right words to tell you."

Ryann and Ellie shared a look of apprehension and innocence. I knew I was about to take a little bit of each away from them.

"You know that Daddy went into Pakistan for a peace meeting. And you know that he died that day. But what you don't know is what he did. After the meeting, Daddy's men were getting into the back of a pickup truck, like Papaw's, so they could begin their journey back to Afghanistan. Daddy let his men get seated first, and then he climbed into the truck."

I paused, trying to choose the right words. I spoke as softly, slowly, and tenderly as I could.

"A bad guy—a Pakistani soldier, actually—decided he wanted to hurt Daddy and our soldiers. So he fired his rifle. Daddy was standing in between the bad guy and our soldiers. Daddy protected them with his body ..."

I had to stop. I had to catch my breath and regroup. I wanted to put that moment in perspective for them.

"It's exactly what I would do if a bad guy tried to harm you girls. If we were in a bank or a store and a robber came in and had a gun, I would put myself between the bad guy and you girls every time. It's my job, as your mommy, to protect you."

The girls looked at me in perfect silence, their big blue eyes filling with tears but still fixed on mine.

"So, just like it's my job as your mommy to protect you, it was Daddy's job as a leader to protect his men. Daddy didn't want to leave us. He doesn't want to be away from us. But he didn't have time to do anything else. He protected his men, just like he would have protected us. Daddy's a hero. He's my hero, and I hope he's your hero, too."

Through her tears, I could see that Ryann finally understood. For more than two years, she had quietly resented her daddy. She was angry that he hadn't come home, but she concealed it well. I never saw it, and she never shared it with me. But after I explained what happened, she understood, and I think she forgave him for not coming home to her.

275

On that chilly fall day at my favorite Blue Ridge Parkway overlook, we found our zero. As a family, we recalibrated. In the warmth of the van, with a breathtaking view, we talked about Larry and shared our favorite stories. We talked to God and asked Him to stay with us and guide us through our grief. Ours was not an easy journey. Grief is not for the faint of heart. We would have plenty more bumps along the way that would knock us out of sync. In those moments of troubles and trials, we always remembered that God is good. We fixed our eyes on Jesus and took the time to find our zero.

Baptisms and Bin Laden

From that day forward, Ryann and Ellie carried themselves with an extra dose of resilience. I did my best to keep them zeroed and lead them as children of God. We attended Lafayette Baptist Church under the fine leadership of Brian Lee until it became too painful to worship there any longer. It was so hard to see the happy families and, especially, the happy daddies with their kids. The dads who were deployed at the same time as Larry came home, and their families moved on. It just became too painful to watch. We needed a change.

The girls had been taking music lessons at Snyder Memorial Baptist Church in downtown Fayetteville, so we thought we'd give the preacher a try. John Cook is an army veteran and a brilliant preacher. I loved the way he weaved his army experience into his sermons. I felt an instant camaraderie with him, an attachment I craved. He welcomed us with open arms.

Snyder Memorial is an old and historic church on a hill. It is a huge church, but there is a "sweet, sweet spirit" in that place.[1] We enjoyed worshipping there. We especially liked to sit in the balcony. The girls could see much better from up there. Through John Cook and through that sweet church, God was working on all of us. In April 2011, Ryann told me she was ready to be baptized. She was ready to live her life for Jesus. I was delighted. Ryann, Ellie, and I met with Pastor John, who shared our joy that she was ready.

On May 1, 2011, Ryann danced in the back hallway of the church. In her white robe, she twirled and jumped and laughed until it was time for the service. John always did the baptisms at the beginning of the service so he would have time to change before delivering his sermon. He called to us when it was time. Like an angel, Ryann tiptoed down the stairs into the warm water. Pastor John took her left hand into his and placed his right hand on her shoulder. In front of the entire congregation during the 11:00 a.m. service, he asked Ryann if she was ready to make her public profession of faith.

"Yes," she said.

Pastor John guided her under the water and raised her up anew. She lit a candle, held it with two hands in front of her, and looked at Pastor John.

"Ryann, you are the light of the world. Let your light so shine that others may see your good deeds and glorify the Father in heaven."

I watched the whole blessed event from backstage with tears in my eyes and an abundance of love in my heart. God is so good!

Twelve hours later, lying in my bed reflecting on the day, I thanked God for Ryann, and I talked to Larry. She did it. She gave her life to Jesus. I was so proud of her. Her life was renewed. What a tremendous blessing. I knew Larry had to be proud of her.

My blissful moment of prayer and thanksgiving was interrupted when my cell phone chimed. A text from my sister-in-law told me to turn on *FOX News*.

When the television came to life, I saw Geraldo Rivera at the anchor desk announcing that Osama bin Laden was dead. I couldn't believe it. Moments later, standing completely still in our pitch-dark living room, I watched President Obama deliver the official news. They got him. He was gone. Imagine the irony of that day. Ryann gave her life to Jesus. She rose from the water, born again. Osama bin Laden, our nation's number-one enemy—the man who started this treacherous war—was gone. The next day, he was put into water, never to rise again.

Following close behind her big sister, my sweet Ellie was baptized by John Cook at Snyder about six weeks later. Equally as meaningful, I was delighted to see her rise from the water. Holding her candle, she looked at Pastor John with admiration and affection as he repeated the challenge to "let her light so shine." A girl after God's own heart, Ellie has let her light shine every day since.

Seated in the congregation on Ellie's baptism day was a member of the team who found and killed Osama bin Laden. The incidence of fortuity was not lost on me. As a family, we were healing and growing. Both of our girls were new believers of Christ. Ryann was baptized on the same day that bin Laden met his maker. On Ellie's baptism day, we had the privilege of shaking the hand of one of the men who had helped facilitate the introduction. That didn't happen by accident. In that moment, we found our zero once again.

Chapter 22

Educate the Legacy

For we cannot help speaking about
what we have seen and heard.
—*Acts 4:20 (NIV)*

Major Dan Rooney is a good Christian man, an F-16 fighter pilot, and a member of the PGA of America. A perfect example of *God, Country, Golf,* I am proud to call him my friend and look up to him as a mentor. Having served three tours in Iraq as an F-16 fighter pilot, flying with the Oklahoma Air National Guard, Dan has seen his share of death and destruction in combat. But he will be the first to admit that his perspective of war is from high above it—that is, until Major Dan, as he is affectionately known, saw the other side of war while he was on a commercial flight between his second and third tours of duty.

In early June 2006, Major Dan was flying from Chicago, Illinois, to Grand Rapids, Michigan, to do some work at his family's golf club. Boarding the flight, he noticed an army corporal wearing a dress green uniform seated in first class. Thinking the airline had bumped the soldier up to first class to honor his service, Major Dan offered an approving grin and then walked on by to find his seat in coach.

After a short flight, the plane landed, and Dan set his sights on his work ahead. As the plane taxied to the gate, the pilot made an announcement.

"Ladies and gentlemen, we have an American hero on board with us tonight."

Dan immediately thought of the corporal seated in first class and wondered what he did.

The captain respectfully continued, "We are carrying the remains of Army Corporal Brock Bucklin. His twin brother, Corporal Brad Bucklin, has brought him home from Iraq."

Major Dan's heart sank when he heard the captain ask him and his fellow passengers to remain seated while the casket was honorably removed from the plane.

Obediently keeping his seat, Major Dan Rooney witnessed the sad reunion. Looking through the plane window, his eyes traveled from the flag-draped casket to a little boy who couldn't have been more than four years old. Standing completely still, the little boy was enveloped by the arms of a woman who appeared to be his grandmother. Dan realized that the little boy would never again be wrapped in his daddy's arms. His dad won't be there to play catch with him, teach him how to drive, or send him off to college. Dan's heart broke as he thought of his own children and how their lives would be forever changed if something had happened to him.

What if the tide of war turned on my family? What would their future be like without me? he thought.

Major Dan was so moved by what he saw and so lost in his own somber thoughts that he didn't notice what was happening around him on the airplane. When he was finally able to take his eyes off the tarmac and return to life inside the plane, his sadness turned into disgust as he focused on a half-empty plane. Dan chronicled his reaction in his book, *A Patriot's Calling: Living Life between Fear and Faith.*

> They had ignored the captain's request to remain seated as a sign of respect. There were no connecting flights, there was nowhere else to go ... except to crawl under the warm blanket of freedom we all sleep under each night as a result of sacrifices made by people such as Brock Bucklin and his family.

That night, on that commercial flight, Dan felt a new calling. Major Dan leaned on golf to help him in his quest to make a difference for a little boy named Jacob Bucklin. He knew that many golfers are patriotic. They love the game of golf, and they love the country in which they play. Dan hoped they would follow a call to action. In his book, Dan writes, "Golf has been a benevolent friend to our troops. Some of the greatest golfers in our nation, including Bobby Jones, Chick Evans, Walter Hagan, and Francis Quimet, donated their time and talents to raise money for our troops." Dan was determined to carry on that tradition, speak about his experience, and host a golf event to benefit the children of our fallen heroes.

The golf tournament fund-raiser took place at his family's club, Grand Haven Golf Club, in August 2006. Through Dan's efforts and the generosity of the patriotic golfers, the tournament raised over eight thousand dollars. Major Dan was thrilled, but more importantly, he tasted the "fulfillment that comes from giving" and realized that the Grand Haven golf event was only the beginning.

Dan truly believes that he was given a mission from God on that commercial flight. He was on that plane for a reason. It was his moment of synchronicity. He humbly accepted the call to serve and, with the help of an incredible team of patriots, he created the Folds of Honor Foundation, a military charity that provides educational scholarships. Since 2006, Dan Rooney has continued his mission and has made a difference in the lives of thousands of children and spouses of fallen and wounded service members. He is an iron major and an American hero.

A Speaker Is Born

I expect and anticipate there will be a time
when I will again feel comfortable speaking
publicly about our family and our lives ...
—Bauguess Family Statement, May 15, 2007

The above statement turned out to be an incredible predictor of where I am today. Over the years, I have been blessed with many opportunities to say Larry's name, to tell our story, and to lift my voice to raise awareness for the families of fallen service members.

Care Team Huddles

Back in 2007, I taught quite a few care team classes in preparation for the Afghanistan deployment. Through those classes, I taught our unit ladies how to serve a grieving family. Never would I have guessed, not even in my worst nightmare, that I was training those ladies to take care of me. A few weeks after Larry's death, I realized the significance of that situation. I understood, rather quickly, that I had a unique viewpoint. I had taught all those classes. I had served as a care team leader. And I had been a care team recipient. I could choose to keep all that experience to myself. Or I could speak about what I had been through. Recognizing the unprecedented opportunity and drawn toward the hard right, I just had to share what I learned.

Six weeks after Larry was killed, Shanna and I organized a "Care Team Huddle." The family readiness group leaders and rear detachment commanders of the 4th Brigade gathered in the brigade conference room to listen to my personal experience as an 82nd Airborne Division widow. I offered praise for the ladies who had served us in our home. They answered our phone and the front door. They accepted deliveries, prepared meals, and cleaned my kitchen. I shared with our brigade how helpful my care team truly had been. I encouraged them to continue the training and continue to offer care teams as needed.

The ladies and the officers of our brigade welcomed the information and provided wonderful feedback. Sadly, our brigade had suffered multiple losses that summer. Some of our rear detachment commanders had served as casualty assistance officers, and several of the family readiness group leaders served on care teams. During that Care Team Huddle, everyone got to share some of his or her own experience, though no one breached the necessary confidentiality. Our round table discussion was highly therapeutic and, in the end, made future care team missions more effective, though every bit as emotional. The entire meeting proved to me that my experience was worth sharing and my story was worth telling. By sharing my story, I could help others. By doing so, I was giving back some of the comfort I had received.

As the news of our brigade Care Team Huddle spread throughout the division, I was asked to lead a similar huddle for the division ladies. Following that meeting, I received invitations from battalion commanders division-wide to speak to their family readiness groups. By giving me the opportunity to speak about my personal loss in the open, those division leaders gave us all permission to talk about the losses we had collectively suffered. With the utmost respect, we turned a taboo subject into a priceless fellowship.

I spoke about my care team experience and taught care team classes to Fort Bragg units from 2007 until 2012. Each time I spoke, I encouraged them to offer the best support they could for the families of our fallen. With each class, my number-one goal was to make a difference.

The Patriot Foundation

Following my very first experience with the Patriot Foundation (the dinner and the golf tournament back in September 2007), Chuck Deleot offered me the chance to serve as a Patriot Foundation ambassador. (I knew that first dinner was the start of something special.) Speaking twice a year to their corporate sponsors since 2008, the Patriot Foundation has given me a beautiful opportunity to hone my public-speaking skills and give back to an organization that is investing in the education of the children of the Airborne and special operations community. The Patriot Foundation was the first military charity to reach out to us. I am so thankful to have met Chuck Deleot and his amazing team. I am delighted to lend my voice to them, help them raise funds, and play a small part as they strive to take care of those left behind.[1]

Challenge America

Because of my work leading the 82WWC, I was invited to attend a Wounded Warrior Symposium at Lipscomb University in Nashville,

Tennessee in March 2010. The event, "Operation Yellow Ribbon," provided an opportunity for the leaders of military charities to come together and share best practices. Challenge America,[2] a national military charity with the mission to "connect service members, veterans, and their families to resources in their local communities," hosted the event. My mom and the girls accompanied me for the trip.

Inspired by all the amazing work done to benefit our nation's wounded, I enjoyed learning about all the national military charities but wondered why I was there. The 82WWC was such a small endeavor. Visiting our paratroopers in the hospital and providing comfort items was a big deal for us at Fort Bragg, but I didn't think it was a big deal on the national level. Thankful to have a voice on a discussion panel during one of the sessions, I still wasn't sure I was helpful in the grand scheme of the event. Knowing that God often works in mysterious ways, I just had to wait and see. I had to believe we were there for a reason.

In the evening of the daylong symposium, we were treated to a concert at the Lipscomb University convocation center. We had heard that the event would be star-studded and beautifully patriotic. As country music fans, we were excited to see Amy Grant, Kix Brooks, and Charlie Daniels, the headliners for the event. The girls, my mom, and I walked into the Allen Arena with our eyes wide open, ready to enjoy the evening of music.

Standing in the lobby waiting for the concert doors to open, we were impressed by the military presence and the overall vibe of the Christian university. The anticipation for the event was electric. Just as we were about to enter the concert hall, we were stopped and introduced to an F-16 fighter pilot named Dan Rooney.

Dressed in his flight suit, Major Dan presented Ryann and Ellie with Folds of Honor pins and challenge coins. We enjoyed talking with him, and the girls loved the coins. An hour later, during the concert, Major Dan called us by name up to the convocation stage. In front of Amy Grant, Larry Gatling, and Army General Tommy Franks, Major Dan presented Ryann and Ellie with college scholarships from the Folds of Honor Foundation. Major Dan explained that their mission was to "honor the sacrifice of our fallen and wounded service members by educating their legacy."

We were blown away. God is so good!

The Folds of Honor Foundation

Two years after Major Dan presented the girls with their scholarships, I received a phone call from Marsha "Max" Maxwell, the director of scholarships for the Folds of Honor Foundation.[3] Their organization was growing, and they wanted to create a speaker's bureau to help spread the word about their incredible mission. Max was calling to see if I would like to join the team. Delighted to have the opportunity to tell Larry's story, I eagerly accepted her offer.

My first speaking engagements were local golf events in North and South Carolina. Soon after, they sent me farther out, expanding my travels from Florida to Texas, California to New York, and almost every state in between. As a speaker and a golfer, I was often requested by name to speak and play in golf tournament fund-raisers. The Folds of Honor Foundation offered me so many beautiful opportunities to say Larry's name, to tell our story, to thank an amazing group of people, and to return to golf.

Because of the Folds of Honor Foundation, I have played some of the most beautiful golf courses in America, to include Pebble Beach; Bandon Dunes; The Patriot Golf Club; and, most recently, Mountain Air Country Club in the gorgeous North Carolina mountains. I've played golf with Lee Trevino, Brian Kilmeade, Craig T. Nelson, Brandon Weeden, Brad Faxon, and Scott McCarron. In 2012, I attended the PGA Championship on Kiawah Island and spoke to the Folds of Honor board of directors. I have also been blessed to attend the PGA Merchandise show in Orlando, which is a golfer's dream event, and speak on stage at the House of Blues in Downtown Disney. In recent years, I have been blessed with the opportunity to speak to PGA Sections across our beautiful country. In every place, every event, every moment, I felt Larry with me. I have been so honored to say his name out loud for so many years.

Every golf professional, every club member, and every American I have met on my Folds of Honor journey has had a heart for our fallen and wounded service members and their families. The great Americans I have met are true believers in God, country, and golf. They are magnificent. They give me hope. The wildly patriotic events have boosted my spirit in troubled times. I draw strength from their patriotism. I'm so thankful for this experience and will continue to lift my voice for the Folds of Honor Foundation and their scholarship recipients for as long as they will have me.

Making a Difference

I want to end this chapter by sharing my Folds of Honor speech. I tailor each speech to fit the location and event, but my core message remains the same. Included here is the speech I gave on Labor Day weekend 2016 at Mountain Air Country Club.

I'm so thankful to the Folds of Honor Foundation. Their steadfast support of our fallen and wounded service members, their commitment to educate their legacy, and their loving encouragement to continue speaking about what I have seen and heard are tremendous gifts. Every time I speak, I feel close to Larry. I am incredibly blessed to say his name out loud. As you read this speech, you will find familiar themes. They are the threads that tie this book together and the threads that keep Larry close to my heart.

Good afternoon. My name is Wesley Bauguess, and I am delighted to be here at Mountain Air Country Club. This experience today is at the top of my list of truly magnificent golf rounds. Mountain Air is stunning! Thank you so much for having us.

I am always grateful to have the chance to speak about the Folds of Honor Foundation. It is an organization I love because they honor the sacrifice of our fallen and wounded service members by helping to educate their legacy.

My late husband, Major Larry Bauguess, is one of our nation's fallen heroes, and I see his legacy every time I look into the eyes of our daughters, Ryann and Ellie. These girls have his eyes, his spirit, his sense of humor, and his drive to succeed.

Larry was an amazing man, a beautiful blend of warrior and gentleman. He was an infantry officer, an Airborne Ranger. He loved nothing more than jumping out of airplanes and going to the field with his men. But Larry was also a strong Christian who wasn't afraid to share his faith. He was a kind-hearted daddy and a wonderful husband. He had the biggest blue eyes and the coolest Southern drawl.

Larry and I met in college as fellow cadets in the Army ROTC program at Appalachian State University in Boone, North Carolina. He was driven to be the best at everything he did. But Larry was also driven to share his knowledge, to invest in other people, and to make those around him better. More than anything, he wanted to make a difference.

Larry was a true leader. He led from the front. He never asked his men to do anything he wasn't willing to do himself. He taught me how to be that kind of leader. He taught me how to be the example for my soldiers and, eventually, for our children. We fell in love as cadets. We served in the Army together as lieutenants and captains. We were married for almost fourteen years.

Larry was serving with the 82nd Airborne Division and deployed with his unit to Afghanistan in the early part of 2007 in support of Operation Enduring Freedom. On May 14 of that year, Larry and his commander attended a peace meeting in a tribal region of Pakistan. They set out to attempt to negotiate peace along the unruly border.

The meeting, which included leadership from Afghanistan, Pakistan, and the US, was by all accounts successful. The participants reached an agreement. After the meeting, the leadership shook hands, exchanged coins, and even posed for pictures.

As our paratroopers prepared to move back to the helicopter landing zone, Larry probably could have ridden in the senior leader vehicles, but in true Larry fashion, he stayed behind with his men and boarded a pickup truck instead.

Once his men were settled, he began to climb into the back of the truck. Without warning, a uniformed Pakistani Frontier Guardsmen opened fire at close range.

Larry stood between the shooter and his men. On his feet, he shielded his men and took the brunt of the assault. Several of his men were wounded that day, and Larry gave his life.

Larry was taken from us far too early, and we miss him every day. It's hard to be here without him. It's hard to watch the girls grow up without their daddy. It's hard to see other kids with their dads at the pool, at the movies, at school, on the golf course.

Ryann is a junior in high school. She's played on the JV tennis team for two years and is now on the varsity team. She loves her broadcasting class. She was a main anchor for her school's news program last year. This year, she will serve as a student director. Ellie is a high school freshman. She's a straight A student and is beginning her second year on the varsity golf team. She's my golf girl! Ellie is also a small group leader for her class, where she leads devotions and serves as a mentor for her peers. They are amazing young ladies.

The girls were six and four when Larry died. They are sixteen and fourteen now. They have lived longer without their daddy than they had with him.

But I will tell you that if we sat here crumpled and defeated, Larry Bauguess would come down here and kick us square in the backside. He would say, "Get up. Drive on. Live your life. The best way to *honor* me is to get back out there and continue to live." I know he would say that to me, and I would say the exact same thing to him.

So, we drive on. We live the best life we can, and we live in a way that we hope brings honor to him.

When I was a young lieutenant serving in the 101st at Fort Campbell, Kentucky, my company commander taught me a valuable lesson. He'd say, "Lieutenant Bauguess, in life, you always have two choices. You can choose the easy wrong or the hard right."

When I speak in front of a room full of golfers, my best example is fixing ball marks on the green. The easy wrong would be to just walk away. The hard right, of course, would be to bend down and fix your ball mark. And while you're down there, fix a few more—the superintendent will love you.

When Major Dan Rooney was on that commercial flight back in 2006, he could have done the easy wrong. He could have gotten out of his seat, collected his things, and gone about his life. But he didn't. He respected a fallen service member and his family by staying in his seat and watching a very sad reunion.

Even after that, he could have gone about his life, but instead he raised the money and provided an educational scholarship to Corporal Brock Bucklin's son, Jacob. And then he went on and created the Folds of Honor Foundation. He and his team have now made a difference in the lives of thousands of kids—and their parents. He didn't have to do that. Major Dan chose the hard right.

The Folds of Honor Foundation stands up and raises their voices for children just like Jacob, Ryann and Ellie. By supporting the Folds of Honor Foundation, you are *investing* in the futures of some amazing kids. And, trust me, these kids are worth the investment.

The children who have been left behind on our fields of battle are exceptional. At their core, they are military kids who know what service means. They know what discipline is, and they know how sacrifice feels.

The children of fallen service members are amazingly resilient. They drive on with a special motivation after losing their military parent. They want to make them proud. They want to earn their sacrifice.

The children of our wounded are exceptional, too. They press on. They are living with the wounds of their military parent, which—believe me—is a daily reminder that freedom isn't free.

These kids are worth the investment. They represent the future of our country. They *stand* for the values that make our nation great. They are going to be something special.

By supporting the Folds of Honor Foundation, you are changing the lives of the children of our fallen and wounded service members one child at a time. But think of how many lives those kids will go on and touch. A donation to Folds of Honor will produce a ripple effect that could continue infinitely.

I'd like to leave you with a quote from a fallen Marine. This quote is written on a plaque that has a place of honor on a wall in the lobby at the Center for the Intrepid, which is a state-of-the-art rehabilitation center for our nation's wounded at Fort Sam Houston, Texas.[4]

The quote is from a letter written by Staff Sergeant Dan Clay, a fallen United States Marine. Staff Sergeant Clay gave his life in Fallujah, Iraq, on December 1, 2005. December 1 was Larry's birthday.

When I read this quote, I hear Larry's voice because he would say the same thing. So, God bless Staff Sergeant Clay for writing these words in a letter to his family before he died. They tell you just how special our service members truly are.

> I know what honor is.... It has been an honor to protect and serve all of you. I faced death with the secure knowledge that you would not have to.... Never falter! Don't hesitate to honor and support those of us who have the honor of protecting that which is worth protecting. [5]

Our country is worth protecting. The children of those brave men and women who gave the last full measure of devotion to our country are worth the investment. Thank you for choosing the hard right over the easy wrong. Thank you for supporting the Folds of Honor Foundation. Thank you for investing in our kids.

Chapter 23

God, Country, Golf

"For I know the plans I have for you," declares
the Lord, "plans to prosper you and not to harm
you, plans to give you hope and a future."
—*Jeremiah 29:11 (NIV)*

As an army cadet, we conducted countless patrols. Sometimes, we were actively looking to engage the "enemy." Sometimes, we were just conducting reconnaissance patrols to watch the enemy and collect intelligence. No matter what our mission was, every time we left the friendly area and traveled a few hundred meters into enemy territory, we conducted a listening halt.

Upon the order of our squad leader, we would stop movement and take a knee or lay in the prone position. Facing out and pulling security for our element, we took that time to familiarize ourselves with the sights and sounds of our environment. It was our chance to limit distractions, clear our heads of everything other than our mission, and listen to and focus on our surroundings.

Today, on our living room wall, we have a wooden sign with a Ralph Waldo Emerson quote that reads, "Let us be silent, that we may hear the whisper of God." That wooden sign is my listening halt reminder. It prompts me to pause, reflect upon my surroundings, and assess my life direction. That sign encourages me to be still, talk to God, and listen to His whispers.

Writing this book has been a labor of love for over six years. Six years! As I transitioned out of my leadership role with the 82WWC back in 2010, I conducted a listening halt and began to hear God's call to tell our story. I always knew that Larry's life was worth honoring and remembering, and I believe that what the girls and I have been through is worth sharing.

Over the years, I've have been burdened with doubt, often wondering if anyone would actually read this book. *It's just another book. Would I even make a difference?* In my strongest feelings of self-doubt, however, God would send someone to come alongside me to provide much-needed encouragement and motivation. I'm so thankful for those faithful servants. And I'm thankful that you, the reader, are still with me.

Feeling his presence as I type this final chapter, I'm reminded of Grandpa Burton and his "picture finish" lesson. Grandpa always told me to finish well. In keeping with that tradition, I will share my most recent return to golf.

Coach Wesley

The fall of 2014 found us in a new city and a new school. The opportunity for change had presented itself, and we were eager to spread our wings and begin again. So, after twelve years, we left the tight military community of Fort Bragg/Fayetteville to begin a new life in the civilian world.

Our new home had elevation changes, rolling hills, plush green grass, and stunning hardwood trees. The topography was so different from the sand hills of Fort Bragg. The girls, my mom, and I found a wonderful neighborhood, a golf course community, near a really great school. Loving our new home, Ryann and Ellie adjusted to the move very well. Their new school is an awesome Christian/college prep academy. The girls attend the school with the help of their Folds of Honor Foundation scholarships.

That fall, Ryann played on the junior varsity tennis team, and Ellie dove head first into her classes. Ryann loved playing tennis.

She had the most wonderful coaches who taught her a little about tennis and a lot about life. Sharing a Christian devotion every single day, they set beautiful examples of what right looks like. Rooting for Ryann and her teammates, Ellie and I enjoyed watching the practices and matches from the stands. Ryann grew so much that year as a tennis player and as a Christian.

On team picture day, Ellie and I watched Ryann's team pose on the tennis court under a brilliant blue sky. A crisp autumn breeze wrapped us in comfort as we continued to build trust in our new environment. After the shoot, as we began to leave, something caught my eye. Four girls in bright gold and blue argyle golf skirts posed for their team photo in a little area between the tennis courts and the concession stand. Their golf skirts were certainly memorable, but the image of them standing together with their drivers in hand, exuding camaraderie, reminded me of my high school golf team. Memories of golf practice and matches flooded in; what a fun time that was for me! Delighted to know that the school had a girls' golf team, I couldn't fight the urge to talk to the coach after their photo shoot ended.

Coach Robby serves as a physical education teacher and the assistant athletic director for the school. He also coaches the varsity girls' golf team and the middle school boys' basketball team. Once he dismissed his golfers that day, the busy coach turned to head back inside the school.

"Hi, Coach. Do you have a second?" I asked, extending my hand as he walked by.

"Of course."

After introducing myself and explaining that we were new to the school, I shared my golf history with him. His eyes lit up when I told him I had played in high school and at the collegiate level. I told him I might be interested in helping him someday, if that was possible.

"When can you start?" he eagerly replied.

I asked him to give me the school year to get my feet under me. A new home and a new school were enough for us to deal with. I told him I'd help him the following season, if he'd have me. He eagerly accepted my offer.

Another Return to Golf

Preseason practice for the 2015 varsity girls' golf team began in late July. We had six players. One of the original four decided not to play that season, but Coach Robby, an avid golfer himself, successfully recruited three new ones, including Ellie. Every time he saw her in the hallway or in gym class, he encouraged her to play. As her mom and a lifelong golfer, I never actually pushed Ellie into golf. The decision to play was her own, but I was delighted when she said she would give it a try.

I had prayed for the team all summer long and prayed that I would be helpful as a coach. Wanting to come up with a theme for the season and a preseason gift, I searched and searched for ideas. One day during a listening halt, I got the idea to connect the dots between army values, Christian values, and golf values. They are very similar, and all together they provide a solid foundation for life.

I made bag tags for the girls using a PowerPoint slide, card stock, and laminate sheets. On the slide, I typed out the army values: loyalty, duty, respect, selfless service, honor, integrity, and personal courage.[1] Then, I added a Scripture:

> Forgetting what is behind and straining toward what is ahead, I press on toward the goal to win the prize for which God has called me heavenward in Christ Jesus. (Philippians 3:13–14 NIV)

I recruited one of the tennis moms, who runs her own sports marketing business, to embroider our school symbol and each girl's name on a navy-blue golf towel. The final products were perfect. Just before the official start of our 2015 season, I presented a bag tag and a golf towel to each girl on the team. Explaining the army values listed on the tag, I told them that every week we would talk about one of them. The girls were thankful for the towels and thought the bag tags were cool, but I wasn't sure they were thrilled with the idea of "army value lectures" with Coach Wesley.

In mid-August 2015, the girls began a new school year, and I embarked upon my first season as an assistant golf coach. That first week, we began our value huddles. As expected, the girls weren't super thrilled about the talks. They were middle and high school kids who sat in class all day long. The last thing they wanted was a lecture at golf practice. But I thought it was important and Coach Robby supported me, so I drove on. After promising to keep the lectures short and on point, we began with loyalty.

- **Loyalty.** I told the girls on the golf team that, as Christians, we are loyal followers of Jesus. We support our church, and we stand in fellowship with one another. In the Army, loyalty is required of every soldier. Our soldiers take an oath to support and defend the Constitution of the United States. Soldiers are loyal to our country. They are loyal to their leaders and to one another. Without that loyalty, there is no trust. Likewise, as a team, we are loyal to our school, proudly displaying our gold and navy colors. We are loyal to one another, supporting and encouraging one another as teammates. As golfers, we are loyal to our sport and to its history, rules, etiquette, and traditions. Loyalty is important and must be there for us to be successful as a team.

- **Duty.** During week two of golf season, I told the girls that as Christians, it's our duty to read the Bible, trust in God, and obey His commandments. We are to "be strong in the Lord" and "let our light so shine that others may see our good deeds and glorify the Father in Heaven." In the Army, our soldiers are committed to do their duty. Soldiers are trained in common skills and in specific military occupational skills. Every soldier has a job to do. Individual soldiers are part of a collective team. They need to do their duty and work together to accomplish their mission. Golf is an individual game, but in high school golf the scores are combined for a team total. Every score, every shot, and every putt counts. I encouraged the girls to do their best, to focus on every shot, and to try to keep their focus for the whole round. High school golf is a team sport; every player must do her duty.

- **Respect.** During week three, as a team, we talked about the universal value of respect. As Christians, we respect and serve others, we respect the church, and we respect God. In the Army, our soldiers respect their leaders, their country, and their flag. Respect is given, and respect is earned. As golfers, we respect the game, our opponents, and our teammates. We also respect the golf course. We repair ball marks and divots. We walk on the green with angel feet and leave the golf course better than we found it.

- **Selfless Service**. In week four, we focused on service. As Christians, we are called to love and serve everyone. Jesus died for us. We are called to serve others in His name. Our soldiers live selfless lives. They volunteer to serve. Putting their lives on the line, they are the 1 percent who fight for our blanket of freedom. There is no greater gift than the precious freedom our soldiers provide. During that week of golf, I encouraged the girls to think about our service members and to go above and beyond their normal duties. And they did. I saw them make an extra effort to clean up the driving range and pick up all the practice balls in the short game area. That week, they were kinder to one another, too.

- **Honor.** To honor people is to treat them with respect and admiration. During week five, we talked about honoring our mothers and fathers, teachers, and coaches. And, of course, we talked about honoring God and one another as Christians. In the Army, honor is a soldier's touchstone.

They honor the oath of office, and they live and serve according to the army values. In golf, we honor traditions, customs, and courtesies. The golfer who scores the best on the previous hole has the honor of teeing off first on the next hole. I love golf for its etiquette and courtesies. I love how its lessons permeate into our daily lives.

- **Integrity.** If I had to choose one value that means the most to me, it would be integrity. I learned a long time ago that no one can take away your integrity. You are the only one who can give it away. To live with integrity means you do the right thing even if no one is watching. In week six, I told the girls that my integrity is my most prized possession. I want people to see me as honest and fair. When I was in the Army, my soldiers knew I was on their side. I didn't always know the answers to everything, but I was always honest and fair. They trusted me. They knew I would always choose the hard right. Golfers must live and play with integrity, too. The way the game is set up, golfers have the responsibility to call penalties on themselves when they do wrong. If a golfer swings and misses the ball, she needs to count that stroke, even if no one saw her do it. She must count and report her score honestly and accurately. Living with integrity means choosing the hard right even when the easy wrong is so tempting.

- **Personal Courage.** The final of the seven army values is personal courage. In my life, I believe, as it is stated in Philippians 4:13 (NKJV), "I can do all things through Christ who strengthens me." I can do anything knowing that Jesus is by my side. I can't imagine serving our country and fighting in these wars without leaning on Jesus. I can't imagine raising children and living life in these days of troubles and trials without leaning on Him. In week seven, I encouraged the golf girls to lean on Jesus in their daily lives and in their golf careers. I encouraged them to take chances.

It takes courage to hit a golf ball over the water onto a tiny green. For our newest players, I praised them and told them it took courage for them to try out for a varsity golf team in the first year they ever touched a golf club. For our more highly skilled players, I told them it takes courage to play in big tournaments and put themselves out on display for college recruiters. Most of the time, the reward is worth the risk, and when you press on with Jesus by your side, your courage multiplies.

Challenge Coins

In the interest of finishing the season well and closing the loop on the army values theme, I wanted to give the golf girls a meaningful gift. During a quiet moment of reflection, I recalled an old army tradition and decided to order challenge coins for each member of our golf team. The coins I selected were black and gold with the Army logo on the front and the Army values on the back. Military commanders instill unit pride and build esprit de corps by presenting challenge coins. Following their example, I thought the coins would be a cool reminder of our season.

The tradition of challenge coins dates back to World War I, when a wealthy aviation officer gave his pilots bronze medallions that displayed the unit's insignia. Placing the medallions in small leather pouches, the pilots often wore them around their necks for safekeeping. Shortly after receiving his medallion, one of the aviators was shot down behind enemy lines and captured by the Germans. His captors took everything away from him except the little leather pouch. Eventually, the pilot escaped and evaded to France, but the French army thought he was a spy and threatened to kill him. In a desperate attempt to prove his identity as an American pilot, he presented his bronze medallion. One of the French soldiers recognized the insignia, delayed his execution, and after confirming his identity, sent him back to his unit. The bronze medallion saved his life.[2]

Today, nearly every military commander carries on the tradition of presenting unit coins, to include the secretary of defense and the commander in chief. They are now called challenge coins because commanders expect their soldiers to always carry their coins. Challenge coins are unique representations of the values and emblems that the commanders hold dear. Coins are often presented with a handshake. Some people call it a secret handshake because the coin is initially hidden in the palm of the commander. After a firm handshake, possession of the coin changes to the receiver. It is a meaningful moment for both the commander and the person receiving the coin.

Picture Finish

I am very pleased to report that we had a wonderful golf season, and I thoroughly enjoyed coaching those sweet girls. In late fall, our team won the conference tournament and advanced to the state tournament. At the state tournament, we finished seventh out of eight teams, but the experience of playing at that level was priceless. We learned what we had to work on and began gearing up for the next season. As a young team, our oldest players were only sophomores, so I knew the next two years would be fun to watch. I have every faith and confidence that each year will be better than the last.

At the end-of-season awards ceremony, Coach Robby honored our players with their varsity letters and pins and other special awards. After his presentation, he turned the floor over to me. Addressing our players and their parents, I told the girls how much I enjoyed coaching them and told their parents about our army value huddles. I spoke of each value and then told the history of the military challenge coin, hiding a stack of them in my hand. I was delighted to share a beautiful military tradition with them.

Calling the girls up one by one, I prepared for the secret handshake. Each golf girl looked me in the eye and shook my hand with pride. Smiling, they walked back to their seats with an army coin in hand, which served as a tangible reminder of a fun and meaningful season.

God, Country, Golf

Looking back now, in another listening halt moment, I can only hope that those army value lectures made a difference in the lives of the members of the 2015 girls golf team. I can only hope that the girls took those army coins and put them in a place of honor or maybe in their golf bags so they could see them and remember what they represent.

I truly love those girls and will keep them close to my heart. I'm so thankful for them. During that golf season, those girls reminded me of my former self. That coaching experience reminded me of my youth and how spiritual golf can be. No matter what happens to those golf girls or to me in the future, that moment, standing in a Christian school and presenting army value coins to a girl's golf team, was a beautiful ending to a wonderful season. It was a picture finish, a make-a-difference moment. It was another beautiful return to the game of my youth and a perfect example of God, Country, Golf.

Acknowledgments

As I reflect upon this entire project and begin to craft my acknowledgments page, I realize it will read like a prayer of thanksgiving. I have so many reasons to be thankful.

First and foremost, thank you, Lord God, for inspiring me to write this book. Thank you, Lord Jesus, for sitting next to me as I typed every word. It has truly been an enlightening and therapeutic experience. Thank you, Lord God, for Larry. I'm so grateful I got to walk with him for as long as I did. You created such an amazing man. I'm so thankful for the example he set and the legacy that he has left behind. Thank you, Lord Jesus, for coming alongside me and leading me through Larry's loss. Thank you for giving me the strength and motivation to drive on.

Thank you, John and Martha Bauguess, for raising such a wonderful son, and thank you for welcoming me into your beautiful family. You have taught me so much about how to live and how to treat others. Thank you, Terry Bauguess, for being such a wonderful brother to Larry, such a good daddy to your kiddos, and such a fantastic coach. You, too, set an amazing example. Thank you, Laura Bauguess Collins, for your friendship, sisterly love, and brilliance. You are a proofreader and editor extraordinaire. I couldn't have finished this book without your love, acceptance, and guidance.

Ryann and Ellie, my darlings, you are the light of my world. I am incredibly thankful that God chose me to be your mother. I am thankful for every day I get to spend with you. You are your daddy's legacy and your mommy's greatest gift. You give me hope, you inspire me to be better, and you fill me with immeasurable joy. Thank you for supporting this book and enduring my long hours at the computer. I'll no longer have to say, "When my book is done ..." No more future promises. We can get back to Be Here Now and live for today. I love you so much!

Thank you to my wonderful mother, Jan. Mom, you have lovingly pushed me to write this book, and I'm so thankful you did. Thank you for helping me keep my eye on the ball and push through to the finish. Thank you for the years of support on the golf course. Thank you for supporting me through my college and army years. I'm so thankful that God delivered you to us when Larry deployed to Afghanistan. Your presence in our house at the time of Larry's loss brought us comfort, carried us through the worst of times, and provided much-needed comic relief.

Thank you to the leaders, coaches, and mentors I've had through the years. Thank you, Grandpa Burton, for teaching me how to play golf. Thank you, Bill Duffy, for introducing me to Mother Army. Thank you, Cindy Wallace, for teaching me to Be Here Now. Thank you, Brian Gray, for inspiring me to always choose the Hard Right. Thank you, Mike Linnington, Steve Baker, Paul Bricker, David Rodriguez, Dan K. McNeill and Jim Huggins, for showing us all what right looks like. Thank you, John Cook, for inspiring new believers in Christ and for baptizing Ryann and Ellie. Thank you, Chuck Deleot, for taking care of those of us left behind on our battlefields. Thank you, Dan Rooney, for honoring the sacrifice of our fallen and wounded service members. Thank you, Chet Nuttall and Jerri Greene, for coming alongside Ryann, Ellie, and me and investing in our futures. Thank you all for educating Larry's legacy.

Thank you to an entire platoon of proofreaders: James Babin, Colleen Bair, Steve Baker, Martha Bauguess, Rusty Bradley, Katie Bricker, Paul Bricker, Laura Bauguess Collins, John Cook, Chuck Deleot, Danny Dudek, Tara Farris, Brian Folino, Samuel Gotti, Brian Gray, Tara Green, Wayne Green, Neal Hatfield, Jan Hobbs, Skip Lewis, Mike Linnington, Kevin Maurer, Shon McAteer, Tim McAteer, Corey Morgan, Shanna Ratashak, Betsey Riester, Coach Robby, Dan Rooney, Dana Rucinski, Martin Schweitzer, Morgan Wood, and Allen Wronowski. Thank you to the Defense Office of Prepublication and Security Review for providing a thorough security review and blessing the release of this book. And thank you to the brilliant team at A Larry Ross Communications! I love you all!

And, once again, thank you, Lord God, for being a God of second chances. I always thought true love only happened once in a lifetime. I figured I was lucky to find true love with Larry. We had a beautiful life and a love that would sustain me until the end of time. I never expected to find true love again, but I did. In 2013, God led me to a good Christian man named Morgan. Two years later, we married and began a new life together. Living now as one girl shy of a Brady Bunch, I have a wonderful husband and three amazing stepsons. The girls and I are happy, incredibly busy, and loving our new family. Thank you, Morgan, Braden, Evan, and Caleb for welcoming us into your family, for loving us as we love you, and for honoring and remembering Larry daily. I thank God for all of you!

Finally, a huge thank you to you, the reader. Thank you for taking this journey with me. If you feel led, please reach out to me at godcountrygolf@gmail.com. I'd love to hear from you.

Glossary of Acronyms and Abbreviations

101st: 101st Airborne Division (Air Assault) Fort Campbell, Kentucky
2ID: 2nd Infantry Division, Republic of Korea
82nd: 82nd Airborne Division, Fort Bragg, North Carolina
82WWC: 82nd Airborne Division Wounded Warrior Committee
ABN: Airborne
AC/RC: Active Component/Reserve Component
AK-47: Automatic Kalashnikov 1947, Russian Automatic Rifle
AMEDD: Army Medical Department
AR 15-6: Army Regulation 15-6, Investigation Report
BLUFOR: Blue Force, Friendly Force
BSTB: Brigade Special Troops Battalion
CH-47: Cargo Helicopter, "Chinook"
CNO: Casualty Notification Officer
CPR: Cardiopulmonary Resuscitation
CPT: Captain
CQC: Commando Qualification Course
DA: Department of the Army
DISCOM: Division Support Command
DIV: Division
EFMB: Expert Field Medical Badge
EIB: Expert Infantryman Badge
FOIA: Freedom of Information Act
FRG: Family readiness group
HHC: Headquarters and Headquarters Company
HLZ: Helicopter Landing Zone

IBA: Individual Body Armor

ICU: Intensive Care Unit

IED: Improvised Explosive Device

IG: Inspector General

JRTC: Joint Readiness Training Center

LTC: Lieutenant Colonel

MAJ: Major

Medevac: Medical Evacuation

MILES: Multiple Integrated Laser Engagement System

MP: Military Police

NCO: Noncommissioned Officer

NICU: Neonatal Intensive Care Unit

NIV: New International Version

NKJV: New King James Version

OBC: Officer Basic Course

OC: Observer/Controller

OPFOR: Opposing Force, Enemy

PGA: Professional Golfers' Association

PSD: Personal Security Detachment

ROTC: Reserve Officers' Training Corps

R&R: Rest and Relaxation

S-1: Staff Officer, Personnel, Adjutant

S-3: Staff Officer, Operations

SJA: Staff Judge Advocate

STB: Special Troops Battalion

SUV: Sport Utility Vehicle

TF: Task Force

TOW: Tube-launched Optically-tracked Wire-guided (missile)

TTIS: Tactical Training for the Individual Soldier

USMC: United States Marine Corps

XO: Executive Officer

XVIII: 18

Endnotes

Chapter 2: The Cart Path Less Traveled

[1] "The Sea Cloud," Sea Cloud Cruises, http://www.seacloud.com/en/yachts/sea-cloud/

[2] Ram Dass, *Be Here Now* (San Cristobal, NM: Lama Foundation, 1978)

[3] "Nine Core Values," The First Tee, http://www.thefirsttee.org/impact/nine-core-values/

Chapter 3: Train a Child

[1] Neal Hatfield, Uplands Reach Conference Center, http://uplandsreach.org/about-us/our-staff

Chapter 4: Good-bye, Golf Girl; Hello, Commando

[1] "The Army Values," U.S. Army, https://www.army.mil/values/

Chapter 6: Rendezvous with Destiny

[1] Oriana Pawlyk, "Khobar Towers: Reflecting 20 Years After the Attack," Air Force Times, June 25, 1996, http://www.airforcetimes.com/story/military/2016/06/26/khobar-towers-reflecting-20-years-after-attack/86404332/

[2] "187th Infantry Regiment (United States)," *Revolvy*, http://broom03.revolvy.com/main/index.php?s=187th%20Infantry%20Regiment%20(United%20States)&item_type=topic

Chapter 10: Living the All-American Dream

[1] 82ⁿᵈ Airborne Division War Memorial Museum, http://www.82ndairbornedivisionmuseum.com/

[2] U.S. Army Care Team Handbook, Operation READY, https://www.myarmyonesource.com/cmsresources/Army%20OneSource/Media/PDFs/Family%20Programs%20and%20Services/Family%20Programs/Deployment%20Readiness/Operation%20READY/CARE_TEAM_HANDBOOK_EDT_3.pdf

[3] 3. "A Leader's Guide to Trauma in the Unit," Spouses' Project, Army War College, 2004, page 12, http://huachuca-www.army.mil/files/ACS A Leaders Guide to Trauma in the Unit.pdf

Chapter 13: Critical Decision Point

[1] "Staff Organization and Operations," Department of the Army, page 5-1, http://www.globalsecurity.org/military/library/policy/army/fm/101-5/f540.pdf

Chapter 14: Steps of Faith

[1] The stamp was by My Sentiments Exactly©, purchased at Hobby Lobby

Part 4: Making a Difference

[1] Loren Eiseley, *The Star Thrower* (New York: Times Books, 1979).

[2] "The Starfish Story," http://www.starfishproject.co.uk/starfish-story.html

Chapter 16: 82ⁿᵈ Airborne Division Wounded Warrior Committee

[1] Major Dan Rooney, *A Patriot's Calling: Living Life between Fear and Faith* (Canada: Yorkshire Publishing, 2012), page ix.

Chapter 17: Return to Golf

[1] Patriot Foundation, http://patriotfoundation.com/

[2] Abraham Lincoln, "The Gettysburg Address," Abraham Lincoln Online, http://www.abrahamlincolnonline.org/lincoln/speeches/gettysburg.htm

[3] Robert Jager, http://www.rjager.com/

Chapter 18: Tattoos and T-shirts

1 "Warrior Ethos," U.S. Army, https://www.army.mil/values/warrior.html

Chapter 19: W

1 Ivan Castro and Jim DeFelice, *Fighting Blind: A Green Beret's Story of Extraordinary Courage* (New York: St. Martin's Press, 2016).

Chapter 20: The Story Unfolds

1   Hillary Clinton, U.S. Secretary of State testimony on Benghazi, January 23, 2013, https://www.youtube.com/watch?v=Ka0_nz53CcM
2   Jason Straziuso, "Pakistan Border Battle Leaves U.S. Soldier Dead," *The Fayetteville Observer,* May 15, 2007, page 8A.
3   Ibid.
4   "Miscreant," The Free Dictionary, http://www.thefreedictionary.com/miscreant
5   Kevin Maurer, "Border Attack Kills Major," *The Fayetteville Observer,* May 16, 2007, page 5A.
6   Ibid.
7   Kevin Maurer, "Gunman Was in the Security Detail," *The Fayetteville Observer,* May 26, 2007, page 1A.
8   Ibid., 4A.
9   Ibid.
10 "AR 15-6 Investigation Officer's Findings," from a PowerPoint slide mailed to the author.
11 "AR 15-6 Investigation Officer's Recommendations," from a PowerPoint slide mailed to the author.
12 General Dan K. McNeill, Pentagon Briefing, http://www.c-span.org/video/?205968-1/operations-afghanistan, Minute 22:52.
13 Carlotta Gall, "Pakistanis Tied to 2007 Border Attack on Americans," *The New York Times,* September 26, 2011, http://www.nytimes.com/2011/09/27/world/asia/pakistanis-tied-to-2007-attack-on-americans.html?_r=0
14 Ibid.
15 Ibid.
16 Ibid.
17 Ibid.

18 Teri Mangel Summary of Facts and Findings, partially declassified by U.S. Central Command, dated October 24, 2011, Findings, page 2.

19 "FOIA Review of the AR 15-6 Investigation Report in the Death of MAJ Larry Bauguess," from Headquarters, Combined Joint Task Force (CJTF)-1, Bagram Airfield, Afghanistan, dated February 21, 2012.

20 "Informal AR 15-6 Investigation (Border Flag Meeting Incident, Teri Mangel, Parachinar, Pakistan)," from CJTF-1, Bagram Airfield, Afghanistan, dated May 18, 2007, witness statements

21 Ibid.

22 Ibid.

23 Christina Lamb, *Farewell Kabul: From Afghanistan to a More Dangerous World* (London: William Collins, 2015).

24 Ibid., 349.

25 Ibid., 351.

Chapter 21: Finding Zero

1 Doris Mae Akers, "Sweet, Sweet Spirit," hymn.

Chapter 22: Educate the Legacy

1 Patriot Foundation, http://patriotfoundation.com/

2 Challenge America, http://www.challengeamerica.com/

3 Folds of Honor Foundation, https://www.foldsofhonor.org/

4 Center for the Intrepid, https://www.bamc.amedd.army.mil/departments/rehabilitation-medicine/cfi/

5 "Letter from SSG Dan Clay, USMC," Flying the F-4 in Combat in the Vietnam War, http://www.keytlaw.com/f-4/ssgt-daniel-clays-letter-to-his-family/

Chapter 23: God, Country, Golf

1 "The Army Values," U.S. Army, https://www.army.mil/values/

2 Rob Lammle, "A Brief History of Challenge Coins," *Mental Floss,* http://mentalfloss.com/article/12630/brief-history-challenge-coins

Works Cited

Dass, Ram. *Be Here Now.* San Cristobal, NM: Lama Foundation, 1978.

Eiseley, Loren. *The Star Thrower.* New York: Times Books, 1979.

Gall, Carlotta. "Pakistanis Tied to 2007 Border Attack on Americans." *The New York Times.* September 26, 2011.

Lamb, Christina. *Farewell Kabul: From Afghanistan to a More Dangerous World.* London: Williams Collins, 2015.

Maurer, Kevin. "Border Attack Kills Major." *The Fayetteville Observer.* May 16, 2007.

Maurer, Kevin. "Gunman was in Security Detail." *The Fayetteville Observer.* May 26, 2007.

Rooney, Dan. *A Patriot's Calling: Living Life between Fear and Faith.* Canada: Yorkshire Publishing, 2012.

Straziuso, Jason. "Pakistan Border Battle Leaves U.S. Soldier Dead." *The Fayetteville Observer.* May 15, 2007.

Praise for
God, Country, Golf: Reflections of an Army Widow

"In a world where the lines between wrong and right have become blurred, we need Christians, patriots, and golfers to stand tall and show the world what right looks like. Wesley does exactly that in this book. *God, Country, Golf* is unapologetic in its Christian nature. God is a powerful force for good, and He should be praised. In this book, He is."
— **Major Dan Rooney**, U.S. Air Force, author of *A Patriot's Calling*, PGA member, Folds of Honor Founder

"Wesley Bauguess calls golf a 'faithful friend.' I agree completely. As the thirty-seventh president of the PGA of America, a member of the PGA Hall of Fame, and a lifelong golfer myself, I have thoroughly enjoyed golf's friendship. In her book, *God, Country, Golf: Reflections of an Army Widow*, Wesley beautifully articulates how captivating, loyal, and generous this game truly is—the very best traits of a faithful friend."
— **Allen Wronowski**, Past president of the PGA of America

"Wesley Bauguess gives us a beautiful, compelling story about how she and her young daughters found the strength to cope with the death of their soldier. This powerful, artfully crafted book should be required reading for anyone who wants to better understand the brave military families whose sacrifices keep the rest of us free and safe. We are all indebted to them."
— **Captain Chuck Deleot**, U.S. Navy (Retired), Patriot Foundation President

"Powerful writing that comes from the heart. This book is certain to touch the lives of everyone who reads it."
— **Colonel John Cook**, U.S. Army (Retired), Senior Pastor of Snyder Memorial Baptist Church

"Wesley lets her light shine through the pages of this book! She is honest, respectful, likable, and relatable. What a beautiful way to honor our family and Larry's memory."

— **Laura Bauguess Collins**, Sister of Major Larry Bauguess

"Few opportunities are given to look inside the life of an army family and expose the glue that binds them together. *God, Country, Golf: Reflections of an Army Widow* is a perfect example of the mettle spouses are made of and how the author, Wesley Bauguess, has come to terms with loss and redemption. Books are designed to tell a story, and this is one worthy of your time."

— **Major Jerry "Rusty" Bradley,** U.S. Army Special Forces (Retired), author of *Lions of Kandahar*